IN THE SHADOW OF THE MAGIC MOUNTAIN

IN THE SHADOW OF THE MAGIC MOUNTAIN

The Erika and Klaus Mann Story

ANDREA WEISS

The University of Chicago Press / Chicago and London

The University of Chicago Press, Chicago 60637
The University of Chicago Press, Ltd., London
© 2008 by The University of Chicago
Published 2008
Paperback edition 2025
Printed in the United States of America

34 33 32 31 30 29 28 27 26 25   1 2 3 4 5

ISBN-13: 978-0-226-88672-5 (cloth)
ISBN-13: 978-0-226-83679-9 (paper)
ISBN-13: 978-0-226-88674-9 (e-book)
DOI: https://doi.org/10.7208/chicago/9780226886749.001.0001

Library of Congress Cataloging-in-Publication Data

Weiss, Andrea.
   In the shadow of the magic mountain: the Erika and
Klaus Mann story / Andrea Weiss.
        p.   cm.
   Includes bibliographical references and index.
   ISBN-13: 978-0-226-88672-5 (cloth: alk. paper)
   ISBN-10: 0-226-88672-7 (cloth: alk. paper)
   1. Mann, Erika, 1905–1969. 2. Mann, Klaus, 1906–1949.
3. Mann family. 4. Authors, German—20th century—
Biography. 5. Women authors, German—20th century—
Biography. 6. Artists—Germany—Biography. 7. Expatriate
artists—Biography. I. Title.
   PT2625.A42Z95   2008
   838'.91209—dc22
   [B]
                                        2007021032

PHOTO CREDITS: All photos are from the Erika and
Klaus Mann Archive, Literaturarchiv Monacensia,
Munich, unless stated otherwise.

CONTENTS

PREFACE

ERIKA AND KLAUS MANN once claimed to be twins, an outright lie which betrays an emotional truth. They shared the easy intimacy and fierce loyalty of twins, empowering them to live lives that were unconventional, adventurous, and in many ways exemplary. They were vehemently anti-Nazi in a Europe swept away by fashionable Fascism. They were openly, even defiantly, gay in an age of secrecy and repression. And although they both joined the American army, they were intellectual pacifists when the entire world was at war.

These two rebellious, free-spirited children of the Nobel Prize–winning author Thomas Mann were creative artists in their own right. They were serious authors, performance artists (before the term was coined), and political visionaries whose searing essays and lectures still have relevance today. I consider them to be an extraordinary "couple," even more fascinating together than either would have been alone. Born perhaps fifty years too early, Erika and Klaus Mann were so modern in their outlook and style that they strike a familiar chord with us today.

I can no longer recall the first time I heard the names Erika and Klaus Mann. They have achieved a kind of cult status in Germany today: among the youth culture for their uncompromising anti-Nazi stance, and among the gay/lesbian community for their liberated views on sexuality. All of their books are now in print in Germany, including many that were unprintable during their lifetimes. Berlin, that German capital of contradictions, is a city I adore and often consider my second home. So I knew their names and something of their reputations for a long time, but it was with my close friend Wieland Speck, roughly a decade ago, that I first entered their world. Wieland and I, both filmmakers, both guests of the Jerusalem Film Festival in the summer of 1997, sat on the veranda of the Jerusalem Cinematheque late one night and over a bottle of wine cooked up a scheme to collaborate on a film about them. That seed of an idea eventually became *Escape to Life: The Erika and Klaus Mann Story,* a fiction/documentary hybrid we co-directed, and my partner Greta Schiller produced, which was released theatrically in Europe in 2001 and broadcast in many countries around the world.

Wieland Speck's long-term hospitality, the loan of his books for indefinite periods, his willingness to translate a confusing paragraph for me at any hour of the day or night—for these and more, I am grateful. While we developed the film that grew up alongside of this book, Erika and Klaus Mann managed to creep into every breakfast conversation, every late-night musing on the meaning of life. At each stage of the project our collaboration pushed me to have new insights into and a better understanding of the lives of Erika and Klaus Mann.

My erstwhile writing workshop colleagues, Adam Levy and Lili Cole, read this manuscript in bits and pieces many times over in different versions, and are due my deepest thanks for all their astute and helpful critiques. Along with them I must mention David Hajdu, master wordsmith, who taught me so much about nonfiction storytelling. Carolyn Dinshaw at New York University was more helpful than she'll ever know, and NYU's Bobst Library was the ideal place for me to disappear for many months while I mentally occupied a far-distant time and place.

Speaking of Bobst Library, deep in the stacks on its eighth floor there is a row of bookcases roughly fifteen feet long, floor to ceiling, devoted solely to books by and about Thomas, Heinrich, Erika, and Klaus Mann. This row, which seemed quite daunting to me when I first began to read my way through it, is a tribute to the enduring literary legacy of the Mann family. In all the time I spent in Bobst Library, however, I never saw another person enter this particular row. I never was asked to return one of the many books piled high in my carrel so another library user could look at it. The Mann family's popular readership today, at one large urban university at least, doesn't begin to compare with that same family's literary stature. I hope, for Erika and Klaus's sake, that this book will begin to change that.

But the library stacks yielded only a small slice of the story I wanted to learn. With Wieland I ambled through Berlin, revisiting where Erika and Klaus spent the wild years of the Roaring Twenties in Germany's Weimar Republic. We explored Munich, where they were born and grew up, and we stood on the spot where the grand Mann family villa once graced the banks of the Isar River before it was destroyed by Allied bombs. We spent enough time in Munich to see the city through their eyes and learn to love it. We visited their large country house in Bad Tölz, which the family sold for war bonds during World War I, and which is now a nunnery, and we walked down the path to the pond where they learned to swim. We wandered along the shores of Lake Starnberg, where Erika and Klaus strolled in 1927 when they decided to make their first crazy round-the-world trip. Our path took us past the castle of the Bavarian king Ludwig II, about whom Klaus wrote his sad, lovely tale "The Barred Window," a personal favorite of mine. We flew to Zurich, to Hirschenplatz, where the Hotel Hirschen once showcased Erika's anti-Nazi cabaret after she could no longer perform it in Germany. Back in New York City, Greta Schiller and I lunched at the Hotel Bedford on East Fortieth Street, where so many of their romantic dramas were enacted and where they were "at home" for the first time since going into exile. From all these places, the ghosts of Erika and Klaus Mann called out to me, beckoned me further, teased me and taunted me before they would initiate me into their secret world.

In Paris I visited "Tomski"—the esteemed, aging drama critic Thomas Quinn Curtiss—who was the great love of Klaus's life. He had already begun to be confused and muddled in his mind, and I had to unravel his comments about Klaus to glean any meaning from them, but just to be in his presence and in his period-piece apartment on the Seine brought me closer to Klaus himself. I interviewed Elisabeth Mann Borgese, the younger sister of Erika and Klaus, who had only the kindest words for her brother and tried to temper her harsh words for her sister.* I met

---

* My interview with Elisabeth Mann Borgese took place in a forest outside of The Hague, though her home was in Halifax, Nova Scotia. She had just arrived in The Hague to give a speech to Holland's Queen Beatrix about the need for global protection of the oceans, a subject she had made her life's work. Via e-mail, she had proposed our meeting in the Netherlands to save me a transatlantic flight. She was a very youthful eighty-three at the time. I was very sad to hear three years later that she had passed away.

with friends of the siblings—the great, under-recognized author Sybille Bedford, the photographer Marianne Breslauer, the actor Igor Pahlen, all of whom have since died—to try and understand Erika and Klaus from the perspective of their close-knit circle of friends. Robert Lawrence, who worked with Klaus in Rome after the end of World War II, gave me new insights into the difficulties and disappointments Klaus faced in his final years. My heartfelt gratitude goes to these people, witnesses to a long-gone era, who shared their precious memories with me.

This book came out in an earlier, shorter version in Germany, under the same title as my film, *Escape to Life*, and timed to coincide with the film's release. I was fortunate and honored to have as my German editor Dr. Uwe Naumann of Rowohlt Verlag, a leading expert on the life and writings of Klaus Mann. His expertise saved me from sloppy mistakes and misunderstandings, yet he was careful never to impose his own interpretations. My literary agents, Faith Evans of London and Anoukh Foerg of Munich, were both excited and encouraging about this project in its initial stages, and it may well have never gotten off the ground without them.

Rowohlt Verlag in Hamburg, responsible for Erika and Klaus Mann's literary estate, has granted me carte blanche permission to quote from their published and unpublished writings. Frido Mann, nephew to the siblings, has graciously allowed me to reproduce their photographs. Ursula Hummel and Gabriele Weber of the Erika and Klaus Mann Archive in Munich went way beyond their job descriptions to locate materials for me and facilitate my many disruptions to their smooth-running archive. Anne Siegel helped with the seemingly endless research and organized procuring all the photographs. Dana Frank read an early version of the manuscript with enormous care and rushed her comments to me even though she was in the middle of a demanding cross-country launch of her own book. Her scrawls all over the margins saved my book from numerous contradictions and unclear formulations. My friends Katharina Oguntoye, Carolyn Gammon, and Jörg Fockele came through with translation help when I got lost in Erika Mann's somewhat impenetrable and cryptic correspondence.

With the great gift of an Independent Scholar Fellowship from the National Endowment for the Humanities, I was able to devote an uninterrupted year to completing the manuscript after working on it in fits and starts for way too long. It was a chance meeting with William Germano that directed my itinerant manuscript to its rightful home, the University of Chicago Press, where Executive Editor Douglas Mitchell immediately confirmed my own feeling of a perfect fit. Thanks to editorial associate Tim McGovern, production editor Leslie Keros, and copy editor Russell Harper for magically transforming the manuscript into a book.

Greta Schiller and Ilana Schiller-Weiss had to live with Erika and Klaus for too many years than was really fair to ask of them. My deepest gratitude goes to them for so many things, but most of all their relentless faith in me.

CHAPTER 1

KINDERTHEATER

ERIKA: Should the way be this long?
KLAUS: Oh, every way is long. The death-watch in our chest ticks
slowly, and every drop of blood measures its time. Life—
a lingering fever. For tired feet every way is too far . . .
ERIKA: And for tired ears every word too much.

In a large meadow behind an old villa, Erika and Klaus Mann enacted this scene from Georg Büchner's play *Leonce und Lena.* Erika, ever dramatic, wore a long white nightgown with a black wool cape thrown over her shoulder, while Klaus pranced about in a black vest, black silk suspender stockings, and short purple bloomers. There was no audience to be found, not even their adoring younger siblings Golo and Monika, although Erika in particular always craved an audience. They reveled in theatricality for its own sake, and did not need to prove their brilliance to anyone. It was the summer of 1922. Klaus and Erika were fifteen and sixteen years old.

"We were six children, and we came in three couples, always one boy and one girl," is how Elisabeth Mann, their youngest sister, recalled the family constellation. The eldest couple, Erika and Klaus, shared an exclusive make-believe world in which they created a secret language and role-played a variety of bizarre characters. They had little apparent need for their parents, younger siblings, governesses, or teachers, all of whom found them enchanting but were baffled by their enigmatic speech, their private jokes and sudden outbursts of laughter.

Erika and Klaus would wander aimlessly for hours around their Herzog Park neighborhood in Munich, or through the woods and meadows of Bad Tölz, a rural Bavarian village where they spent the long lazy summers of their childhood. During these walks they cooked up everything from ambitious theatrical productions to audacious pranks they could try out on the household servants. Often they came across curious strangers, who, mistaking the tomboy Erika for a "little fellow," would ask them casually about their father, hoping to glean some little piece of gossip about the famous author from his unsuspecting children. The children of Thomas Mann were far too clever to fall for such tricks. Klaus recalled these encounters with righteous indignation:

> Why was that stupid old lady so interested in our father? Why did she call him "dad" without even knowing his name? And what on earth made her say that we were "different" and "cute"? . . . Was it conceivable that people, in their colossal dumbness, found anything to object to in Erika and myself? . . . We did not need the outside world of the ribald strangers. What could it offer us? It was specious and dreary. In our own realm we found everything we could wish for. We had our own laws and taboos, games and superstitions; our songs and slogans, our arbitrary animosities and predilections. We were self-sufficient.

They were a striking, complementary pair: Erika, tall and imposing with her dark, unruly hair, defiant expression, and scraped knees; Klaus, androgynously beautiful with his shoulder-length blond curls, faraway eyes, and gentle manner. They didn't particularly look like twins, but they "acted twin-like in an almost provocative way," according to Klaus. He was fascinated by their mother Katia's close relationship with her twin brother (who was also named Klaus), and sought to replicate that closeness with Erika. He could have been describing himself and his sister when he imagined this idyllic portrait of his mother and uncle as children:

> Hand in hand with her twin brother, Klaus, a young musician, she [Katia] roved through the streets of Munich. Everybody was

struck by their peculiar charm. . . . From their aimless escapades they returned to the familiar palace, their home. There they hid from the vulgar world protected by their wealth and wit, watched and spoiled by servants and instructors. Two bewitched infants who knew and loved each other exclusively. . . .

Just how much Katia and Klaus Pringsheim loved each other was the subject of public gossip and private distress, especially when Thomas Mann, married to Katia for only a few months, used his wife's relationship with her brother as the basis for one of his novellas. *Blood of the Walsungs* centers on a twin brother and sister who share such an intense incestuous bond that even the sister's fiancé is shut out. The *Neue Rundschau*, which was to feature the story in its January 1906 issue, had already gone to print when Katia's father learned of it and demanded the story be withdrawn—although whether he, as a Jew whose family converted to Christianity during his childhood, was more disturbed by its explicit incest theme or its virulent anti-Semitism is anyone's guess.

In acquiescence to his father-in-law, Thomas insisted the printed copies be shredded—his clout as an author was already such that the *Neue Rundschau* complied—and the story was suppressed for another fifteen years. But the suggestion of incest continued to attach itself to the Mann family. The theme resurfaces in Thomas Mann's novella *Disorder and Early Sorrow* (1925) and his novel *The Holy Sinner* (1951), and it had also appeared in his brother Heinrich Mann's novel *The Hunt for Love* (1903), which hints at Heinrich's fixation on their younger sister Carla. The title characters in Klaus's play *The Siblings* (1930), a reworking of Cocteau's *Les enfants terribles,* happen to be lovers. Erika and Klaus themselves were dogged intermittently throughout their lives by the accusation that they were "more than siblings." Although their relationship had an emotionally incestuous dimension, it seems never to have crossed over into the physical realm. Whether that was also true for their mother, Katia, and her brother Klaus remains an unanswered question.

Born into a rich, highly cultured family at the center of Munich's artistic and intellectual circles, Katia and Klaus Pringsheim were the youngest of five children. Their father, Alfred Pringsheim, was a temperamental yet highly respected mathematics professor at the University of Munich. He inherited his wealth from his father, a railroad entrepreneur who converted his Jewish family to Protestantism when Alfred was still a child. Their mother, Hedwig Dohm, was a beautiful and successful actress who gave up the stage when she married the professor and took on the role of prominent society hostess. The Dohm family too had converted from Judaism to Protestantism in the nineteenth century; it was common practice in a country that historically alternated between venerating and despising its Jewish compatriots.

A well-read, intelligent young woman, Katia Pringsheim was afforded an education rare for women in her day. Because girls were not allowed to study at the Gymnasium, a college preparatory high school, she had private tutoring until she was able to pass her *Abitur,* the qualifying exam for study at university, in 1903. The first female student to enroll in the University of Munich, Katia Pringsheim was also one of the first women in the entire country to pursue a university education. Within the all-male academic community, she delved into the demanding fields of mathematics and experimental physics. After a few semesters, however, her university education and hopes for a professional career were cut short.

Katia Pringsheim was part tomboy and part scholar—not the usual qualities sought in a wife of that era, but qualities which attracted Thomas Mann. He first noticed her getting off a streetcar, math books in hand. Indeed, the entire streetcar noticed her, and not only because she was twenty years old, had sparkling black eyes, an elegant and self-confident style, and strikingly handsome features. The conductor demanded to see her ticket, and to his surprise she refused to comply. She insisted it was not necessary to produce it; she intended to get off at the next stop anyway. With all eyes on her, she called out, "Just leave me alone!" and jumped off in defiance. The conductor was not amused, although Thomas was. He determined then and there to meet her.

Thomas hailed from the northern harbor town of Lübeck, where the Mann family had a long and respectable history. He was the second son of a Brazilian actress and a wealthy German senator, who fully expected him to take over the family trading and transport business. Although this position had been held by eldest sons for three generations, it fell to Thomas because his elder brother Heinrich had no intentions of following in their father's footsteps. Heinrich left Lübeck immediately upon his graduation from school—to pursue his literary ambitions, as well as to get away from what he considered the "stink of prosperity" which permeated his patrician family. Thomas did not endorse this outright rejection of all their father stood for, but he too had doubts about whether he was suited to assume the role of Lübeck's leading merchant. Hurt deeply by his two errant sons and by the possibility that his glamorous Latin wife was unfaithful, the senator succumbed either to a cancer growing in his bladder (the local doctor operated on him unsuccessfully in the ballroom of the family mansion) or to a poison he took himself; no one ever knew which. The flags in Lübeck were flown at half-mast and the contents of his will became the subject of local gossip.

Still a schoolboy when the senator died, Thomas learned that his upright father had a vindictive streak. Executors were instructed to liquidate the company, sell the house and his ship, and give his wife and children no control over the capital. Forced out of the family home, humiliated by the town's most esteemed citizen, denounced as decadent by the local vicar, the forty-year-old Julia da Silva Bruhns Mann—never fully accepted into provincial Lübeck society on account of her "exoticism" anyway—packed up her three youngest children, Carla, Julia, and Viktor, and moved to an apartment in Munich. Thomas, who had never bothered applying his exceptionally sharp intellect to his studies, left school without completing his *Abitur*, and joined the family there soon afterward.

In 1901, when he was twenty-six years old, Thomas published his first novel, *Buddenbrooks*, a thinly veiled fictional account of the Mann family history. His initial impetus was his own personal dilemma; he wanted to tell the relatively short story of how he (just barely) managed to summon up the courage to break with duty and tradition by defying his father's expectations of him. To do that he first had to establish the family heritage, what he called the "pre-history." Over a thousand pages later, the book ends before his own particular dilemma ever presents itself. Ironically, the novel endorses continuity rather than dissent: it emphasizes the responsibility of carrying on a family legacy, of being a link in a long chain rather than breaking free.

Buddenbrooks drew so heavily on Thomas's close observations of real life that it angered the townspeople of Lübeck. Poorly received in its first year, the book had a sudden reversal of fortune when one critic in the *Berliner Tageblatt* championed it, saying that its reputation will "grow with the years." Sure enough, decades later the esteemed Swedish Academy singled out *Buddenbrooks* from the author's great body of work:

> Thomas Mann, recipient of the Nobel Prize for Literature for the year 1929, especially on account of his great novel *Buddenbrooks*, which in the course of the years has found increasingly secure recognition as a contemporary classic.

Katia Pringsheim read *Buddenbrooks* two years before she met and three years before she married its author. On February 11, 1905, almost exactly one year after he observed her on the streetcar, Thomas Mann and Katia Pringsheim were married at the register's office on Marienplatz. A small, formal wedding reception followed, held in Katia's family home, which was one of the finest mansions in Munich. Thomas was eight years older than Katia and dubbed by her four brothers "a liverish cavalry officer" owing to his pale complexion, his dark mustache, and his overly correct bearing.

The only daughter in the family, Katia was escorted to concerts and parties by her four protective brothers with closed ranks—a custom which did not stop once she was married. Perhaps it was the absence of a feminine influence among the siblings, or perhaps it was her feminist grandmother who insisted on equal treatment for her one and only granddaughter, but Katia was fiercely independent, and was merely amused by her brothers' attempts at chivalry. The streetcar incident and her determination to go to university in an age when virtually no women did reveal a spirited, self-confident, forceful personality, which is how Katia is often described by people who knew her much later in her life. Yet at the age of twenty-one, she capitulated to convention when she gave up her studies to marry Thomas Mann, support his career, and bear his many children. At ninety-one Katia looked back on her past and insisted, "I just wanted to say, I have never in my life been able to do what I would have liked to do."

For Thomas's part, the marriage was also a capitulation to convention. He already knew he was homosexual—he had just ended a four-year love affair with a young painter, Paul Ehrenberg. This sexual relationship was a departure from Thomas's usual pattern of platonic obsession. At fourteen he had become infatuated with an adolescent boy, one of his classmates; this first experience of passionate, unrequited love became an archetype in his later life and in his work. At twenty-five, Thomas no longer saw his homosexual desires as belonging to the caprice of his childhood, although the focus of his sexual passion would continue, throughout his life, to be adolescent boys. Decades later, when he reflected on his relationship with Paul Ehrenberg, he considered it to be the "central emotional experience" of his life. He wrote, "I have lived and loved. . . . I actually knew happiness, held in my arms someone I really longed for." At the time, the great joy of that union was tarnished by his self-loathing and disgust at his "abnormality."

"A punishment he imposed on himself" is what one of Thomas Mann's biographers called his marriage to Katia, claiming that "in marrying her he was building a dam to divert the course of his sexual energy, sacrificing his natural inclinations on the altar of his public image." He broke off with Paul Ehrenberg shortly before his wedding, and it would be more than twenty years before he fell in love with anyone again.

Was it a fear of his own dangerous passions? A need for the public validation that comes with marriage? An insurance policy against the potential life of penury he faced as an author? Whatever his motivation, Thomas Mann, on the rebound from Paul Ehrenberg, was suddenly very determined to marry Katia Pringsheim. First, he had to win over her skeptical father, who was not impressed by the critical success of *Buddenbrooks,* and who said to his daughter, "A writer isn't quite the thing, don't you agree? It's rather on the frivolous side." Thomas never grew fond of his future father-in-law, but eventually won the professor's approval for the marriage by appealing to their shared passion for the music of Richard Wagner.

With the financial support of the Pringsheims, Thomas could embark on a life of heterosexual respectability and material comfort. He genuinely saw the marriage as the socially proper and appropriate step to take, neither dishonorable nor deceitful. If not in love with Katia the way he had been with Paul Ehrenberg, he certainly was captivated by Katia's cultured background, her family's position in Munich society, and no doubt the prospect of regaining the privileges of wealth which had eluded him since the death of his father. His own happiness, and hers, did not enter into it.

Heinrich had insisted that a fling with a young girl would quickly cure Thomas of his "nonsense" with Paul Ehrenberg, but marriage to Katia Pringsheim was going too far. He suspected his younger brother of a calculated move for personal gain, something which so infuriated him that he refused to attend the wedding ceremony. Heinrich was more radical and less pragmatic than Thomas ever would be, and, with his penchant for literary caricature and ribaldry, he never achieved anything near Thomas's stature in the literary world. In fact, Thomas on occasion would have to bail his elder brother out financially. Despite Heinrich's early success with *Professor Unrat* (1905; later made into the movie *The Blue Angel,* starring Marlene Dietrich), he never had his heart set on fame, or as Thomas would call it, "greatness," in the way Thomas had. Even before *Buddenbrooks* was published, he admitted to Heinrich, "It was always my secret and painful ambition to achieve greatness."

Wrought with jealousies and competitiveness, Thomas and Heinrich's relationship as authors and brothers was deeply compassionate, extremely intimate, yet often estranged, and there would never be an easy camaraderie between them. Even as children they had once gone an entire year without speaking, something they would resort to again as adults. Nonetheless, it was Heinrich to whom Thomas first wrote, exactly nine months after the wedding, when Erika was born:

> Well, it is a girl: a disappointment for me, I will admit to you, as I had so wished for a son and continue to do so. Why? It's hard to say. I find a son more full of poetry, more a continuation and new beginning of myself under new circumstances.

Katia had been in labor for forty hours, so one might expect her to be relieved and overjoyed regardless of the child's sex, but she too was disappointed. All she said about the birth was, "It turned out to be a girl, Erika. I was very annoyed."

Thomas and Katia got their wish for a son one year later. The boy's christening as "Klaus Heinrich Thomas Mann" sealed his literary fate. The names Klaus and Heinrich represented Katia's and Thomas's closest brothers, but together the name Klaus Heinrich is also that of the prince in *Royal Highness,* the novel Thomas was deep in the middle of writing at the time of his son's birth. Young Erika kindly chose for her baby brother the less burdensome sobriquet of "Eissi" (the toddler's mispronunciation of "Klausi"), and henceforth, within the family, Eissi he would remain.

Whether or not his literary forebears had anything to do with it, Klaus seems to have been born a writer. He started writing before he could even hold a pen properly; his earliest pieces he dictated to Erika. No one, not even Klaus, was glad to learn that he had a literary bent. His family tried in vain to discourage him from writing, and he himself referred to it as the family curse. Decades after his death, Erika reflected sadly,

> Klaus was a dreamer. Klaus was a poet from the very beginning. And this of course was not at all what my father would have wished for his son. First of all, he knew that any child of his, if he wanted to write, would have a very hard time of it. But for Klaus, writing was as essential as breathing. Without writing Klaus simply couldn't live.

Thomas Mann's disappointment at the arrival of Erika and his joy at the arrival of Klaus were false starts—emotions totally at odds with the

Klaus with his sister Elisabeth. Thomas Mann (*in background*) was enraptured with the beauty of his son.

relationship he would soon forge with each. Klaus would be the source of continual disappointment to him, while Erika was the source of his greatest joy. Despite his initial preference for a son, and his declaration that "a girl is not to be taken seriously," Thomas's eldest and youngest daughters, Erika and Elisabeth, became his two obvious favorites, to the chagrin of the others. "When a man has six children, he can't love them all equally" would be his defense.

But this was a flimsy excuse for his erratic, often cruel behavior toward the remaining four. Monika, the middle daughter, claimed never to have had an intimate conversation with her father, or even to have had the feeling that she existed for him in his mind. Michael, the youngest son, recalled being beaten with a walking stick and other harsh punishments that prevented him from being able to forgive his father throughout his adult life. He was allowed to listen in on the stories his father read to his

Erika and Klaus with baby brother Golo. "Erika and I belonged together" (Klaus Mann, *Der Wendepunkt*).

sister Elisabeth, but it was made clear that they were not meant for him. And Golo, the middle son, who grew up to become one of Germany's most prominent essayists and historians, had not one compassionate or affectionate word for his father in his entire autobiography. In the midst of his large family Golo often felt awkward and lonely. Klaus's callous treatment by his father was by no means unique to him.

Of the six siblings, Erika eventually grew to be the one most devoted to their father. As children, however, Erika and Klaus fixed their devotion on each other, and no one, not their revered parents or their adored younger siblings, could come between them.

Erika and Klaus shared a bedroom, in which they cooked up elaborate schemes, private jokes, and tall tales. Together they created a fantasy world of their own making, a "complicated phantasmagoria," as Klaus labeled it, which involved sailors and princesses, voyages and battles—the ordinary stuff of common childhood play, only here the fantasy superseded reality, and the children pitted themselves against the formidable enemy of the outside world.

Sometimes their siblings Golo and Monika—the "middle couple" among the children—were allowed to participate in this secret world if they followed strict orders and didn't ask questions. And even their parents were occasionally drawn in when the particular fantasy called for it. Their father's participation was often without his knowledge; his role, although crucial, did not require his presence. At their summer house in Bad Tölz in the Bavarian lake district, the extensive house and gardens became an ocean liner, of which their father, "of course, was the captain, hiding most of the time, in the sanctum of his private cabin."

In *Escape to Life*, a book they wrote together in 1939, Erika and Klaus agreed that their youth had been magical, yet they "had enough imagination to be exceedingly naughty and always in hot water." They loved to tease their younger siblings, and hatch gruesome tales to frighten them. They enjoyed making up stories they would tell each other in public, often mimicking different accents, something Erika could do perfectly.

Klaus.

Erika.

Using a funny Bavarian dialect, Erika would sometimes describe a sadistic child who knifed a poor cow to death. There was no truth in it; they simply enjoyed horrifying their fellow travelers on the streetcar.

In 1913, to accommodate his growing family, Thomas Mann had a villa built at 1 Poschinger Strasse in the Herzog Park district of Munich, right on the banks of the idyllic Isar River. Unlike the previous apartment in Franz-Joseph-Strasse, which had been selected, paid for, and furnished by the Pringsheims, this home, reflecting his growing reputation as an author, he paid for himself (with the help of a mortgage). Three stories high, it held a grand piano, countless books, a large dining room, and Thomas's study, which led through French windows to a large, beautiful tree-lined garden. Erika and Klaus no longer had to share a room, and neither did Katia and Thomas. In an atmosphere of literary high-mindedness and material opulence, with servants, frequent travels, and distinguished visitors, Erika and Klaus spent their formative years. Klaus claimed that it was as typical a German bourgeois cultured home as one was likely to find.

The six Mann children have all described in one way or another their relationship to their father's study, a room in which none of them were welcome without an invitation or a summons. They were forbidden to make any noise outside his door between nine in the morning and twelve noon, which were his working hours, or between four and five in the afternoon, which was his nap time. If any of them were called to his study, it meant serious trouble—Katia handled all but the most serious of the children's infractions.

Katia was prone to nervous exhaustion and other vague ailments. Although she had domestic help, it was she who held her large family together and insured that the household ran smoothly. None of the births had been easy; they had taken their toll on her body, and she had two miscarriages after her fourth child was born, but she still went on to have two more. Her marriage was not sexually satisfying, and after the last

Katia Mann with her first four children in 1915: (*from left to right*) Klaus, Erika, Golo, and Monika.

child ceased to be sexual at all. In her old age, she admitted that she had married only because she wanted the children. Of the six, Klaus was and would always remain her favorite.

In 1912, seeking a tuberculosis cure, Katia paid her first of several visits to a sanatorium in the Swiss Alps, a clinic that would one day become internationally famous from her husband's novel *The Magic Mountain*. The visit lasted over six months—no wonder, when injections of arsenic were the prescribed treatment. One can only imagine the distressing effect of that seemingly interminable absence on her children, Erika and Klaus, then only five and six years old. Klaus wrote about having to have dinner alone with his father one evening, an awkward, painful experience. Thomas Mann's three sons all dreaded a meal with him whenever Katia wasn't present; they used to write notes down in advance in order to have something to say to him.

Erika was the one child Thomas found amusing, but he was not amused when Katia informed him that Erika had become a chronic liar, both for entertainment and to clear herself of the trouble she frequently found herself in. He summoned the eight-year-old into his study, much to her dismay. There, without rising his voice, he solemnly lectured her on the consequences of lying, and asked what kind of world it would be if no one could trust anyone else. Erika didn't respond; she simply ran out of the room. She fully intended to go on lying, but after this reprimand discovered she could not. Her father's manner was such that she was cured of lying—at least until she was a teenager, when the benefits of lying outweighed her fear of her father. Golo claimed that Klaus also lied outrageously, "but no one came down very hard on him, perhaps because he showed so much imagination."

Erika and Klaus were rarely seen without their bicycles, on which they explored all of Munich and the surrounding countryside. Although Erika became a world traveler, first by choice and then by exile, her favorite city remained Munich, because of the fond memories she had of her life with Klaus.

Unlike Klaus, Erika wrote very little about her own childhood. She did write many children's books and some of them, in the detail if not the plot, draw directly on her childhood experiences. For example, the brothers in her book *Muck, the Magic Uncle* play a scaled-down version of the ocean liner game, confined to the bathtub, but she used such bits and pieces as amusing anecdotes rather than to idealize their childhood (or their relationship) as Klaus did.

In a letter written a decade after Klaus's death, Erika made one reference to a childhood incident: One day, while out walking with their governess, she and Klaus encountered a little girl who was playing alone. It was inconceivable to her that the girl lacked a brother for a playmate. Perplexed, Erika blurted out: "Where is your Eissi? One *has* to have an Eissi!" Erika concluded the letter by saying she still believed one had to have an Eissi, which made it difficult for her to go on living without him.

Such references to her childhood attachment to Klaus are extremely rare. In her unfinished memoirs Erika refers only once to her relationship with Klaus—and it is an unpleasant memory at that. Her memoirs, which focus on the years 1933 to 1943, do not deal with her childhood; if they did Klaus could not possibly have been left out, so inseparable were the two during those years. The reference to Klaus is in a flashback to an event that occurred when they were in their teens, during one of their many bicycle escapades. After days of strenuous traveling, Erika and Klaus reached a mountaintop in the Austrian Dolomites. On the way back down, Erika lost control of her bike, fell off, and suffered a concussion. By the time Klaus found her, two hours later, she seemed perfectly normal. To her great irritation, he refused to believe her account of the accident; he was sure that she made him climb back up the mountain to look for her solely as a prank.

Erika wrote in her memoirs that she experienced a similar irritation when she first went into exile and found no one would believe her accounts of life in Nazi Germany. Although she admitted it is not an entirely fair analogy, and duly clarified that Herr B., the first person she encountered over the Swiss border, "to be sure, was not Klaus," she used the experience of Klaus's disbelief to illustrate how she felt about the suspicion and incredulity that greeted her in exile.

Such disloyal accounts do not appear in Klaus's autobiographical writings. As Klaus tells it, Erika and Klaus were always a united front, set against the stupidity of the outside world. Clearly the fantasy world of their childhood, which they created together, took on different meanings and dimensions for each of them later on.

Throughout his life, Klaus returned in his writings to the imaginative, interior landscape of their childhood as a means of taking refuge from the world. Erika not only did not seek refuge; she consistently placed herself in the eye of the storm. Daring and confrontational, she was better equipped, socially and emotionally, for the conflicts life presented, while Klaus, gentle and forgiving, had the more introspective and creative personality. After his death, Erika cursed the gods for taking the

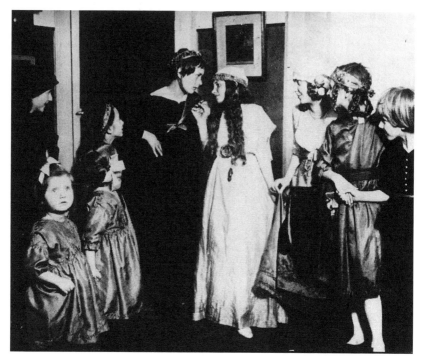

"I always wanted to go on the stage." Erika (*middle left*) as the Prince in a childhood production of Cinderella.

more gifted one of the pair; she was not just ranting at life's injustices, but speaking what she knew deep down to be the truth between them. They loved each other far too much for envy to factor in to their relationship, but they leaned on each other for the strengths they felt they lacked in themselves; in that sense they each completed the other.

Klaus's lifelong artistic collaboration with Erika began with theatrical events they produced for their family and their parents' friends in Munich and Bad Tölz. To round out the cast, they often dragged in Golo and Monika. Klaus immediately emerged as the writer of the troupe, and composed short plays and poems, while Erika outshined him with her outstanding acting abilities. Erika knew early on that the theater was her calling: "I always wanted to go on the stage. As there were four of us, we were a company in ourselves. When I had my black moustache on, I was very much like my father."

Erika claimed she developed her acting skills from their father, who would perform his stories with a wide variety of voices and personalities as he read to his wife and the elder children on special occasions in his study. If such things are inheritable, she also must have acquired something toward her dual careers in art and politics from her mother's side; Katia's mother had been an accomplished Shakespearean actress with the ducal theater in Meiningen (Katia's father, Professor Pringsheim, fell in love with her from his box), and her mother's mother had been one of Germany's leading suffragettes.

The theater was Erika's first love, and an interest in politics came only much later, when the Nazis foisted it upon her. Until then, "I was of the mistaken opinion that politics was a matter only for politicians," Erika admitted. The day would come when politics would curtail her acting career entirely, but it had already started to impinge on it when they were mere children. One afternoon in Bad Tölz, Erika and Klaus were in the midst of preparing for a grand theatrical production of one of Klaus's dramas, *The Burglars,* when world politics, taking the human form of their governess, interrupted them:

> The governess looked pale with malice when she suggested with one of her wry, hideous smiles that nobody would be interested in our spectacle, just now. "You'd better forget it," she said.

Erika and Klaus didn't care for the governess at the best of times and were furious at her suggestion that they had to relinquish their great enterprise for no good reason. When they demanded explanation, she smugly replied that war had been declared on Germany and Austria, and added, "Our magnificent Kaiser has taken over the supreme command both of army and navy." Klaus later recalled his emotional reaction to the news that World War I had erupted:

> The report of the governess left us flabbergasted. We sat in the grass and wondered. None of us had the faintest idea of what was actually meant. Could the Kaiser, in his capacity as supreme commander, simply forbid our show? We discussed it at length but finally drew the conclusion that this was too definitely beyond us. Only our parents could help.
>
> We found both on the terrace but not really together— strangely separate from each other. . . . Father did not seem to notice our presence when he said in a lowered and yet sonorous voice, "Before long a bloody sword is going to appear in the sky." After this, we did not have the nerve to ask any questions concerning our show.

The First World War began when Erika was eight, Klaus seven, and ended a little more than four years later. The family had some financial setbacks: their wealthy grandfather Pringsheim halved the amount of his monthly checks; their beloved house in Bad Tölz, the locus of their paradisiacal childhood, was sold for war bonds; and some of the household help had to be fired, including the ill-humored governess. Katia spent all day on her bicycle looking for coal and food on the black market. But the immediate consequence of the war on Erika and Klaus was that they were pulled out of the exclusive private school they hated, and would now attend the ordinary local schools. As the classes were segregated by gender, this meant the inseparable siblings finally were to be separated.

Erika adapted to the new situation better than did Klaus. Although neither performed well academically, Erika excelled at sports and showed leadership potential while Klaus was unathletic and dreamy—not exactly the requisite traits for popularity in a class of growing preadolescent boys. It didn't help that he could not even speak the local Bavarian dialect. None of the Mann children could, even though they were all born and raised in Munich, and to Klaus's ears it was nothing more than "guttural gibberish." Erika could mimic the dialect exactly when she wanted to, while Klaus sounded like a foreigner among his classmates—providing further cause for ridicule, especially in the xenophobic climate of the war years.

Like his father before him, Klaus found school bleak and uninspiring, the teachers petty tyrants. It was on account of his separation from Erika, he claimed, that he could not remember a single detail or incident from those dull, insignificant days. He was excluded from Erika's rebellious capers, into which she tried to incite her otherwise obedient classmates. He had to wait each day until they were home again to try to join in on the fun: their specialty was placing fake telephone calls, inviting a neighborhood housewife to a nonexistent dinner party or, on one occasion, flattering a local matinee star into a secret rendezvous. That matinee star, Bert Fischel, was good-natured enough to become a friend of theirs after he fell into their trap. Erika excelled at imitating voices—she often called herself an "ape"—so invariably it was Erika who made the phone calls, but Klaus enjoyed it so much he considered it a joint undertaking.

On the playground Erika assumed the role of "older brother" to defend her younger sibling from bullying. Fortunately she was tough and could fight as well as two boys put together, according to Klaus. She became goalkeeper for the girls' soccer team, and started a trend when she went barefoot to school, in order to spare humiliation for a schoolmate of hers whose family could not afford shoes. Not surprisingly, Erika "presently became the chieftain among the girls, while my own position in the male class remained somewhat precarious. . . . In short, they thought me a sissy."

In school they had learned that all other countries were "degenerate, stupid and criminal," that "we were invincible and our Kaiser was a super-man, next to God." The war became an exciting game for Erika and Klaus, one that even the grown-ups were willing to play. The goal, as far as they could make out, was to gather as many enemies as possible. The countries to be annexed by the Fatherland were promised as if they were toys or sweets. With the reduction in household servants and the curtailment of luxuries, the children's newfound liberty took on a "breezy and dangerous" quality, Klaus recalled, "the tough, unbound life without governess and dessert." Joyous farewell parties for various relatives—some cousin of the cook, perhaps, leaving for the front—rang throughout the house. Flags and military songs filled the streets of Munich, and everyone talked of imminent triumph, until the Kaiser "as unpredictable as valiant, changed his mind and postponed victory, just for the fun of warfare." When Germany finally lost the war in 1918, Erika recalled, they learned that "the Kaiser was not next to God, but in Holland, [and] it naturally was rather a shock."

Over the four long years of war, a rift slowly developed between Thomas and Katia Mann, or actually between Thomas and everyone around him. Katia's opinions about the probable outcome of the war dissented from Thomas's, and although she claimed that they never argued in front of the children, the children were astute enough to notice her loss of faith and his grim, stubborn confidence. Golo remembered that there were bitter clashes between them, painful to witness, in which their father "was no match for our mother's alert, legalistically logical intelligence." Thomas set aside his creative work and embarked on writing *Reflections of a Nonpolitical Man*, which caused him a lot of difficulty, most likely because it dealt with politics and he was, by his own account, nonpolitical. The responsibility that the war placed on authors was something he took seriously, calling it a "test of conscience"—if so, it was a test he failed miserably. Among many lapses of conscience to be found in *Reflections of a Nonpolitical Man*, he actually extols the sinking of the *Lusitania*—with its twelve hundred civilian passengers on board—because it was a British ship.

Heinrich Mann was one of very few Germans to speak out against the German war machine. The brothers' opposing political viewpoints strained their already difficult relationship, although Heinrich, separating his intellectual opinions from his fraternal devotion, still wanted Thomas to be the witness at his upcoming wedding. Heinrich, forty-three years old in 1914, planned to marry a young Czech actress (who had an uncanny resemblance to their sister Carla). Five days before the ceremony, Thomas broke his promise and asked Heinrich to find someone to take his place. The rift between Heinrich, the left-wing "man of letters," and Thomas, the nonpolitical "poet," was widening.

The brothers had been attacking each other in print for some time without mentioning any names: Thomas's essay "Thoughts in Wartime," which was written at the war's outset and became an intellectual manifesto for the German cause, managed to equate German militarism with German morality, defend the greatness of German culture and civilization, and weave in a clever condemnation of Heinrich's powerful, visionary, antimilitaristic essay, "Voltaire-Goethe," written four years earlier. Heinrich could not ignore that Thomas's philosophical rants were also personal barbs directed at him, even if most other readers of "Thoughts in Wartime" paid scant attention to the subtext.

Not long after the wedding, the two brothers met in Heinrich's modest apartment on Leopoldstrasse, and in front of several acquaintances had a heated argument about the war. Heinrich was pro-French (he had a deep, lifelong affinity for France, its culture, its language, and its political steps toward democracy); Thomas was blindly pro-German. Calmly and quietly, with a patience he reserved for his less politically astute younger brother, Heinrich told Thomas, "Don't you know that Germany will lose the war, that the German ruling classes bear the chief responsibility, and that the inevitable result will be the fall of the monarchy. . . ." Thomas stormed out.

Thomas did not speak to Heinrich again for almost a decade, not even to greet when they passed on the street, not even to congratulate Heinrich on the birth of his daughter. Heinrich himself could not understand how their political disagreement had so sharply veered into a personal one. Needing a brother more than an intellectual sparring partner (and sensing that Thomas wasn't a match for him intellectually anyway), he wrote, "You have underestimated your influence in my life as far as natural feeling is concerned, and overestimated it in terms of intellectual influence." But a previous attempt at reconciliation had failed miserably, so this time he decided against sending the letter.

Thomas also broke off with Katia's twin brother, Klaus Pringsheim, who believed that concessions would be necessary to secure the peace.

Indignantly, Thomas shouted at him, "Are we supposed to give them back Alsace-Lorraine?" In overhearing these exchanges, his children were privy to the subversive views of a minuscule minority that opposed itself to the overwhelmingly nationalist majority, and these seditious opinions became part of their political education.

The arguments they witnessed also left a more personal impression. If Katia's idyllic relationship with her twin brother, Klaus, had a formative effect on Erika and Klaus in childhood, Thomas's troubled relationship with his older brother Heinrich provided a cautionary model for them in adolescence. Not only would Klaus veer toward Heinrich's synthesis of literature and social criticism when he tried, as a young writer, to get out from under the yoke of his father, but from witnessing the brothers' terrible estrangement, Erika and Klaus were bound even more tightly together.

"We had once loved our father almost as tenderly as our mother, but that changed during the war. . . . For the most part we experienced only silence, sternness, nervousness, or anger"—so Golo admitted on behalf of all six offspring, once their father had died. The war changed Thomas, and changed his relationship to his children as well. He left his study only for mealtimes, wearing a gray, uniform-like jacket, his "service jacket" he called it. As the war dragged on interminably, the initial excitement it generated diminished along with the food supply. Whether it was not having enough butter and eggs, or whether it was the sacrifice of writing uninformed political tracts instead of the novels he enjoyed, he grew extremely irritable—so much so that the children were afraid to speak in front of him. On one occasion he hit Klaus simply for taking a snack when he was told not to. "I can remember all too well certain scenes at mealtimes," recalled Golo, "outbreaks of rage and brutality that were directed at my brother Klaus but brought tears to my own eyes." Klaus more gingerly conceded, "This wartime father seems estranged and distant, essentially different from the father I have known before and after those years of struggle and bitterness. The paternal physiognomy that looms up when I recall that period, seems devoid of the kindness and irony which both inseparably belong to his character." So typical of kind-hearted Klaus, he forgave his father's cruelty and even tried to justify the misguided statements in his father's book: "It is easier to understand this book, both its rampant fallacies and saturnine beauty, if one has witnessed and can recollect the circumstances to which it owes its existence." Even Katia would admit that her husband's *Reflections of a Nonpolitical Man* was an extended polemical attack on his brother Heinrich (Heinrich, hoping to heal the rift, decided never to read it), but Klaus blamed the inadequate food, the chilly temperature in his father's studio, his lack of political training, and the general harshness of the times for what he called a "political blunder of impressive proportions." One wonders if Klaus found similar justifications for the abusive behavior.

In early summer of 1915, when Klaus was nine years old, he very nearly died from a burst appendix. He underwent six separate operations, the fourth of which involved having his intestines removed completely, put on a table for examination, and then replaced. Miraculously, his heart held up throughout, but he suffered intestinal paralysis, and hovered over the line separating life and death so precariously that his mother Katia finally suffered from nervous collapse.

Within the family Klaus's survival became "a legend in the grand style." Qualities previously unassociated with him were now lavished upon him; the word "heroic" was used often. His father wrote to a relative, "We were already mourning good ol' Eissi when he stayed with us after all. That he pulled through is proof of a vitality with which I would not have credited that weak little dreamer."

By the time Klaus was twelve years old, his lifelong obsession with writing was solidly demonstrated. And by the age of sixteen, his oeuvre included at least twenty-five plays and novels—"which I cannot remember today without shuddering," he confessed years later. He scribbled prolifically, as if his life depended on it—and sent his younger brother Golo out as his agent.

> He used the nom de plume "Karl Trebitsch." I don't know why he picked that one. Then I—nine years old, barefoot—had to go to the Volkstheater and say, "I'm the nephew of Karl Trebitsch, and I'm supposed to ask what you think of his play." And I actually got to see some reader or other who said, "Now where did I put that trash?" And then he gave it to me, or rather threw it at me, saying, "All right, your uncle doesn't have to stop by. Here it is." I told Klaus this, and he said, "Well, after all, he knew where the manuscript was and didn't have *that* low an opinion of me."

Klaus tells it only slightly differently: he pressured Golo to approach publishing houses and local newspapers with his blue notebooks, telling Golo to pass them off as the work of his stepmother, Miss Natasha Huber. Golo never made it past the doorman. Together Klaus and Golo would rail against the cruelty and injustice of it all.

Already at this time Klaus had started to write about death, although he had by no means a morbid personality. Golo insists Klaus was always optimistic and full of adventure. Their sister Elisabeth has described Klaus as a lot of fun and extremely amusing: "Klaus was—it's strange because obviously he was a profoundly depressive person, but he always had the aspect of being full of sunshine, you know, and very open, and very very friendly. He did not have, on the surface it, this dark side at all." Their father felt that Klaus's fascination with death—which developed much later but Thomas couldn't say exactly when—"contrasts astonishingly to his apparent sunny, friendly, easy and worldly personality."

Klaus's brush with death had a profound effect on him, but he confined the "dark side" to his diaries and his literary endeavors. He referred often to having been so near to the borderline of death: "Its shadow had evidently marked me," he believed. One of his earliest plays was about a suicidal schoolboy, and one short story ended abruptly with the sentence, "I even believe that she laughed, as she jumped out the window." These early references to suicide were, according to Golo, "still child's play; later they would no longer be."

By age fourteen it was not enough just to write; Klaus was also driven by the desire to achieve fame as a writer. "I must, I must, I *must* become famous," he wrote in his diary, even though his literary talents were still not yet particularly evident.

Erika's talents on the makeshift family stage were far more apparent. "She had a very lively charm," Elisabeth recollected, and was "very, very funny; [she had] a kind of talent maybe similar to Peter Ustinov, or Peter Sellers, this kind of thing. She was extremely gifted." Golo confirmed that from early on Erika was "witty and self-possessed." He called her "my spirited, funny sister Erika, who could always put others in a good mood."

Even their preoccupied father couldn't fail to notice Erika's thespian gifts. He was captivated by Erika's charisma and invariably became gloomy in her absence. In his diary he commented that, in one domestic theatrical performance of *As You Like It,* "Erika was quite entrancing."

Thomas's observations of the teenaged Klaus were unfortunately restricted to his budding sexuality: "Am enraptured with Eissi, terribly handsome in his swimming trunks. Find it quite natural that I should fall in love with my son. . . . It seems I am once and for all done with women? . . . Eissi was lying tanned and shirtless on his bed, reading; I was disconcerted." Thomas Mann, a master of sublimating his forbidden passions into his art, saw in this infatuation the "germ of a father-son novella."

In Erika and Klaus Mann's "Portrait of Our Father," published in the *Atlantic Monthly* in 1939, the siblings described their father's epic novel *Joseph and His Brothers* as the least autobiographical of all his work. But even here, they found some of their father's familiar traits, and specifically recognized their father's face in "the thoughtful face of the father [Jacob] watching his son, young Joseph, with anxious yearning." Did Erika and Klaus, reading *Joseph and His Brothers* (with its strong erotic overtones), have an inkling that Jacob's yearning for his son intimated their father's infatuation with *his*?

Klaus and Erika were occasionally privy to their father's fixations on young men, although presumably this was something he shared with them only once they were grown, and even then one imagines he would not have mentioned his own son in this context. Klaus's story "The Father Laughs," written when he was seventeen, suggests he knew anyway without being told. Here, a widowed civil servant is sexually aroused by his "boyish" and "unfeminine" daughter, easily a stand-in for the androgynous author. The father symbolizes control, discipline, and sublimation, defining characteristics of Thomas Mann, while the daughter lives life to the full. When the father is convinced he is dying (from a psychosomatic illness), he and the daughter end up in a hotel room where the daughter teases and seduces him with "her soft, metallic voice, so coquettish that the blood froze in his veins." When he abandons his restraint, it becomes "a duet where she sets the tone." In the morning, they burst into irrepressible laughter, a motif in Klaus's writing that has recently been interpreted as a "forbidden and subversive force represent[ing] liberation and release . . . from societal norms." Provocatively sexual, unapologetically incestuous, Klaus's story hints that he *was* aware of being the object of his father's sexual obsession.

The teenaged Erika may well have tried to protect Klaus from their father's lust and rage. As the eldest child, she was the first to outgrow her subordinate role. With her ample charm and cleverness, she was able to diffuse and at times challenge Thomas's authoritative airs, and force him to reckon with her as practically an equal. She always spoke her mind and had little fear of the consequences. Her courage provided a shield for Klaus. The imaginary world they created for themselves as children had already bound Erika and Klaus irrevocably to one another, but their desperate loyalty to each other against the increasing havoc of their family tightened that bond into something that was virtually sacred.

Adolescence, that awkward phase when one's skin erupts and one's body plays all sorts of unwelcome tricks, was kind to Klaus in one way:

he maintained his extraordinary beauty throughout. Erika had to pass through the dark tunnel like most unfortunate teenagers. She emerged at the end of it, however, in better emotional form than he did. Adolescence stripped Klaus of his childlike innocence way before he was ready to give it up.

Klaus railed loudly and often against the harsh intrusion of reality into the self-constructed myths of his childhood. He had long believed, for example, that his uncle Erik (eldest brother of Katia) had died by falling off a horse in Argentina; that his aunt Carla (Thomas's youngest sister) had died suddenly of apoplexy. He often visualized his two grandmothers, dressed in black mourning clothes, running into each other's arms, blinded by grief. It was a milestone in his loss of innocence when he learned that Erik, banished by his father to an Argentinean farm after his gambling bets soared out of control, married a woman who had her eye on their steward and on her husband's large estate. As Klaus would be left to wonder, "Who knows what actually happened among those three human beings, the uncle, his wife and the South American steward—isolated in a vast and savage country? The only palpable fact is that the native couple got the better of the foreigner. . . . Nobody ever traced the gruesome details of his tragedy." For Aunt Carla's part, apoplexy had never fully satisfied Erika and Klaus as an answer. But to learn that their actress-aunt swallowed poison and acted out her agony before an imaginary, applauding audience while her mother pushed in vain on her bedroom door did not offer satisfaction either. (Twenty years later, Thomas's other sister Lula, a morphine addict, would also kill herself, although by hanging. Thomas always felt Klaus had the genetic makeup of his two sisters.) "Don't attempt to unveil the secrets hidden from you by the grownups," Klaus warned. "Enjoy the cloudless skies of ignorance as long as they are granted to you! . . . What you forfeit is irreparable and valuable beyond words—your paradise."

The rudest awakening by far was closest to home: Klaus called it "the decline of Jennie." Despite the deprivations of the war years, the Manns continued to employ Jennie, the maid who had been with the family for as long as the children could remember. She had been the maid in the Pringsheim home when Katia was growing up, and made the move when Katia did, almost as though she were part of the dowry. She rocked the children to sleep and advised on all domestic matters; her character was beyond reproach. And as she fell from grace, Klaus felt the secure world of his childhood collapsing.

The first warning signs went unnoticed: Jennie insisted one cook after another be fired for dishonesty or theft, until she finally insisted on running the kitchen herself. The last of the series of cooks, as she departed, put Katia on alert: it was Jennie herself who was the culprit. The matter might have been easily settled, had not Thomas been aroused from his study by all the commotion—a serious event in itself, which stunned all parties involved. Klaus recalled Jennie opening the door of her room to prove her innocence: "'You'll feel very sorry for having suspected me,'" she said, "a statement that seems almost insane in its glaring absurdity, considering the sight in store for my parents behind the mysterious door. There it was, the motley collection of things stolen from us in the course of the years." When Thomas picked up an old bottle of his favorite Burgundy, and greeted it as though a long-lost friend, Jennie, realizing she was trapped, struck out at the master of the house.

Klaus was surprised by his own reaction to this startling event—he was delighted: "This truly was revolution!" As if the kleptomania weren't enough, reports started coming in from the neighborhood, claiming that every night she could be seen with a different soldier or officer; how could the Manns allow such scandalous behavior? This only enchanted Klaus further: "I began to admire Jennie. . . . Why should she not change her lover every other night . . . ?" Klaus's heartfelt rendition of the story, in which significantly Erika does not appear, used the figure of Jennie to give voice to his own rebellious feelings toward his father, as well as to articulate a growing awareness of himself as a sexual outlaw, both signs of his passage out of childhood. When the case landed in court (the departing cook had called the police in the middle of the altercation), "Jennie triumphed because she represented,—and with what skillful élan!—the underprivileged class. She lied with gusto and flamboyant eloquence. Everybody was smitten with her popular wit. She stole the show. My parents gave a pitiful performance." Klaus relished her flair and her defiance. She was far more colorful and outrageous than his staid parents.

It was only her "bleak epilogue" which broke his heart and made him mourn his prior innocence. In rain or snow, she returned each evening to haunt her former home, rummaging her bag as though she had lost her key. With each passing night, her clothes became more threadbare, her hair increasingly wild. Drunk, furious, miserable, she would raise her fists, spit, and murmur some curse in the darkness. Then she would slowly shrink into herself, pull her torn shawl around her neck, and turn away. "It was this freezing, pathetic gesture—that helpless attempt to protect herself against the chill of the night—which struck me most deeply and painfully. . . . Something dwindled and paled in view of this sodden wreck that had once been our dexterous playmate. Something irreplaceable crumbled and faded away, hollowed out, corroded by unknown, relentless forces. . . . What sort of reality was it that got the better of our myth, our childhood?"

Klaus began to show signs of defiance himself, channeled into his copious writings from that time (they no longer exist). Thomas did not encourage Klaus's literary endeavors; on the contrary, he found them to be pretentious and embarrassing. Katia came upon one of Klaus's blue notebooks, left open in his room, and it caused a minor family drama. When she reported her findings to her husband, he reported in his journal that Klaus showed "such an unhealthy coldness, ingratitude, lovelessness, deceitfulness—to say nothing of the callow and silly literary and radical posturing—that his poor mother's heart was deeply disappointed and wounded. . . . I will never play the infuriated father. There is nothing the boy can do about his nature, which is not of his own making." Thomas did not often interfere with family matters, but when he learned that Klaus intended to send out some early short stories to publishers, he determined that this was "a folly from which he must be dissuaded."

The private musings by Thomas about Klaus in his diary hint at a complicated father-son relationship which was troubling on both sides. Klaus was never known to exhibit jealousy, and therefore one can only guess whether Klaus ever had jealous feelings about the huge literary success of his father, a success that eluded the son throughout his life. It is also possible that Thomas had an occasional jealous thought of his own. Klaus came of age in a much freer society than that of his father, and was never one to hide his sexual passions in the pages of a secret diary. Unlike his father, Klaus was not tormented by the need to conform to society's rules, and judged his actions by his own moral standards (exceptionally high ones at that). Yet as much as Klaus was able to reject the need for approval by bourgeois society, he could not dismiss the need for his father's approval, and this was in short supply. Thomas Mann paid painstaking attention to his art but relatively little to his wife and children, and never did see how he replicated his own father's disappointment in his sons—even though he examined, with so much poignancy, his own uneasy relationship with his father in *Buddenbrooks*.

"We seldom saw our father," acknowledged Erika and Klaus. "In spite or because of that, we felt him as a great power in our lives, as the final authority from which there was no appeal." It was not exactly for this reason that they bestowed him with his family title of "The Magician," which is what they called him throughout their lives, although surely the name stuck because it fit so precisely.

Klaus insisted that the name derived from an incident involving a ghost who frequented Klaus's dreams when he was five years old. On a rare visit with the children at bedtime, Thomas banned ghosts from their bedroom. "Tell him that a children's bedroom is no place for a decent phantom to hang out and he should be ashamed of himself," is what he advised. The ghost's submission to Thomas's authority was "imposing proof of Father's almost superhuman insight and influence," and henceforth he was "Der Zauberer" (or "Z.")—the Magician.

Erika later corrected for posterity Klaus's fanciful version, replacing it with a rather banal but likely more accurate account. According to Erika, she and Klaus were invited to a costume party at the home of the playwright Christa Winsloe (author of *Mädchen in Uniform*). They roped their father into coming along even though he hated such events and claimed he had no costume. Erika decked him out in a turban made out of towels, and he went as a magician. And from that night onwards, for more than half a century, he was "The Magician."

His moniker also alluded to one of his best-known books, *The Magic Mountain,* on which Thomas labored for twelve years, from 1912 to 1924 (although he made little progress during the First World War). This colossal work hovered over the childhood, adolescence, and early adulthood of Erika and Klaus, and after publication came to dominate their father's already substantial reputation. It was the novel that introduced Erika and Klaus to their father's world, when they were invited as teenagers to sit in on his readings of the work-in-progress most evenings. Obsessed with disease both literally and figuratively, *The Magic Mountain* conflates love and death, a theme so pervasive in German literary tradition that it has earned its own name, *Liebes-Tod.*

In the writing of *The Magic Mountain,* Thomas relied heavily, at times even *verbatim,* on amusing, descriptive letters written to him by Katia when she was convalescing from a tubercular infection in a series of sanatoria in the Swiss Alps. *The Magic Mountain* is precisely set in such an allegorical place. The protagonist Hans Castorp leaves his normal orderly life for this mountaintop, far removed from the pedestrian concerns of ordinary people living below, and falls irredeemably in love with Clavdia Chauchat, a Slavic woman he meets there, whose disease both attracts and repels him. Yet impelling the novel, as many critics have pointed out, is a current of repressed homosexual passion, diverted to a woman. It is a memory of an unrequited fixation on a young boy that dominates Hans Castorp's (and his creator's) sexual life.

Weighing in at over seven hundred pages in the English edition (and longer in German), the book moves at an excruciatingly slow pace, building tension from silent longing to sexual consummation. Thomas wrote the narrative's long-awaited climax, the love scene, only shortly after he entered Klaus and Golo's bedroom, and found his handsome eldest son "totally nude and up to some nonsense by Golo's bed. Deeply struck by his radiant adolescent body; overwhelming." The father in him would never act on his lust for his son, but the author in him knew just how to transform it into great literature. Perhaps he was a magician after all.

Thomas nonetheless "remained a stranger to his son," Klaus wrote in his autobiography. As Klaus struggled with finding his own young voice as a writer, the process was complicated by this stranger's shadow over him. Torn between resistance and respect, Klaus was driven to make his own mark in the world. Protest against his father's authority pulled more strongly in him than did gratitude and emulation. Klaus was, at heart, too much of a rebel for the struggle between his conflicting emotions to have it otherwise. But the matter was never resolved; he could neither fully accept nor fully repudiate his inheritance. Looking back on those formative years, he wrote in a faraway third-person voice: "Fame and authority of the father become a stimulus, a thorn, an obsession to the striving son."

Klaus himself admitted that "it is no easy job to be the child of a genius," and launched immediately from there into an account of one such child's suicide. The child in question was the eldest son of the famous Austrian poet Hugo von Hofmannsthal, a neighbor and friend of the Mann family. The night before the funeral, the poet had a terrible dream about his inability to catch a silk hat just beyond his reach. Strangely enough, he really did drop his hat the next morning as he walked behind his son's coffin. As he stooped to pick it up, he collapsed, never to stand up again. "It was a tragedy on the great, antique scale. Hugo von Hofmannsthal was killed by his dreams and his grief." Such stories, mixing together suicide, poetry, and the complexity of the father-son relationship, held endless fascination for Klaus.

It was unfortunate that the striving son had set his sights on the same career as his famous father. Katia felt that being his father's son made life difficult for Klaus, especially as people assumed it would be just the opposite. In this regard Erika fared better; within the family, theater was her domain alone. It was only because of her enthusiasm and insistence that Klaus found himself acting alongside of her.

On the first of January 1919, Erika, then thirteen years old, and Klaus, twelve, founded a theater troupe, the "Laienbund Deutscher Mimiker," together with their close friend Ricki Hallgarten. It was a formalization of the amateur acting they had been doing all along, now raised to a new status. In a magazine article she wrote a decade later about the Mimik-bund, titled "Kindertheater," Erika explained that she, Klaus, and Ricki "were the founders, executive committee, and ensemble. There was no manager; we planned everything communally." Golo was enlisted to play a role in *Minna von Barnhelm;* his performance was so memorable that Katia recalled it when she was ninety: "'Accept my tears and the reward of Heaven.' [Golo was] incomparable as the Lady in Mourning, eight years old and lisping."

Soon Golo's participation wasn't enough and they went out into their neighborhood of Herzog Park to meet the growing demands for the cast. Their friends Lotte and Gretel Walter took acting parts—their father, the great conductor Bruno Walter, musical director of the Munich Opera House, had become a close friend of the Manns after he called to complain about Klaus pulling Gretel's hair. Ricki Hallgarten, a promising artist, painted the sets. Serving as in-house theater critic, Thomas reviewed their first performance, *The Governess* by Theodor Körner. The Mimikbund's repertoire extended from Shakespeare, Lessing, and Molière to Klaus Mann himself. Erika and Klaus no longer constituted a self-sufficient and isolated entity, but established themselves as an indivisible couple at the heart of an artistic community, a social configuration they would often repeat as adults. The Mimikbund players were replete with talent and trouble in equal measure. Several would come to a tragic end.

Erika and Klaus's passion for the Mimikbund grew in direct propor-tion to their boredom with school. Their grades were poor and their imaginations stifled. To their parents' disapproval, they started cut-ting classes to mingle with bohemian circles in downtown Munich, but the final blow was when Erika and Klaus were caught and arrested for shoplifting. In April 1922, the siblings, by then fifteen and sixteen, were packed off to a country school in the Rhön region that, as it turned out, had a more life-affirming approach to education. Erika and Klaus were thrilled to be reunited in class once again.

Bergschule Hochwaldhausen was an experimental youth community in which students and teachers sought out a purer pedagogical experience in nature, far removed from the constraints and demands of industrializing society. Initially, the philosophical impulses behind this free school movement were liberal and liberating, especially when compared with the austere and punitive teaching methods of traditional schools. But its emphasis on long marches, German folk songs, and the cult of the body would later be all too easily absorbed by the Hitler Youth. Klaus was one of the first to detect the reactionary undercurrents in its romantic assertions.

The German Youth Movement, of which the free school movement was part, had its roots in the nineteenth century but witnessed a booming revival after World War I. The youth who came of age in Germany during the war shared a basic distrust of authority—the false promises and rampant lies of the German government made a deep if inchoate impression on them. Although Erika was only twelve at the end of the war, and deeply shocked at first to learn the Kaiser was in Holland, she quickly got over it: "After a very short time indeed I was glad to realize that a new life had begun, that the things we had been told were obviously wrong and that we should not think of them any longer." She found this realization to be true not only for herself but for her entire generation. Explaining why the youth movement suddenly found fertile ground in the late 1910s, she wrote: "After the War, there was deep disillusionment. . . . Everywhere, what had been valid yesterday was no longer so. One had been cheated by this War. Too long had its laws been obeyed in good faith. All that was over. Of a sudden, everything and anything was permissible."

Both Erika and Klaus were introduced to the ideals of the German Youth Movement, the openness and sensuality of which appealed to them. What excited them most, among the permissible "everything and anything," were the new sexual mores. According to Erika,

> The "Youth Movement" rejected even bourgeois clothes; they wore loose frocks and sandals and spent their nights around campfires. . . . Girls slept with boys; boys with boys; girls with girls; teachers (who called themselves "comrades") with male and female pupils.

Klaus, already sexually experienced from a young age (according to Golo), was immediately attracted to the fellow "deviates" at the school, while Erika, who in today's parlance would be called an "enabler," took the most disturbed students under her wing: "I gathered around me all those who were greedy for immoral and varied novelties," Klaus would later write, "but Erika took care of those who were problematic, overwrought, those fully off their rockers."

Despite the inevitable distractions of such complicated schoolmates, Klaus responded to the freer educational approach and his life started to be dominated by intellectual interests. Erika returned to Munich because it was time to take her *Abitur,* something she only did "out of pure love for Mother." Klaus joked that it was a scandal she was allowed to graduate, since she knew nothing.

When Erika left for Munich, Klaus left Bergschule Hochwaldhausen for another, even more progressive country school, the Odenwaldschule, which had been founded in 1910 by Paulus Geheeb. Located in the hills outside Heidelberg, Odenwaldschule was a democratically run experimental community with a solid educational reputation. Geheeb, a veteran of the youth movement and a pioneer of the free school movement, made a deep impression on Klaus, who wrote to him from Berlin eight years later, "I can't imagine my life without that year in the Odenwaldschule; or imagine the Odenwaldschule without you. Therefore I can't imagine my life without you." Klaus later portrayed him in a short story, "Der Alte," as a boarding school headmaster who seduces the eldest female students. Geheeb called Klaus "shameless"—apparently everything and anything was permissible, as long as it was kept quiet.

In this liberated educational setting Klaus acknowledged his passion for another boy, Uto, who could neither understand nor return Klaus's feelings. Again Klaus did not keep quiet; he immortalized Uto in several books:

> There was one lad among them whom I liked to watch in particular. His name was Uto. He was sturdy and deft but by far not the strongest or most dextrous one of the lot. Nor was he especially handsome. But I loved his face. He had the face I love. You may be smitten with many faces when you live long enough and possess a responsive heart. But there is only one face you love. It is always the same. You recognize it among thousands. And Uto had that face.

Klaus did not remain long at Odenwaldschule and, to the irritation of his parents, never made his *Abitur.* He told the unsuspecting Uto that his parents wanted him home, which was a blatant lie. The truth was more complicated: "I couldn't bear it anymore. Uto was so much stronger and lighter than I was, and I envied him. He was all vigor and serenity: no problems existed for him. But to me, the cosmos was but one problem, impenetrable and disconcerting. I could not decipher the hints and signs of my destiny."

As his personal crisis over Uto veered into a metaphysical crisis, Klaus returned home, but he would not remain long in Munich either. Always one to seek out geographic solutions to his problems, Klaus came up with a plan and presented it to Erika.

In addition to introducing the teenaged Erika and Klaus to the pleasures (and heartaches) of homosexuality, the German Youth Movement of the postwar years altered Erika and Klaus's self-perceptions in another way. As Germany's younger generation came into its own, so did the younger generation of the Mann family. No longer were they only the precocious offspring of Thomas and Katia Mann; now they deemed themselves to be important individuals in their own right. They had the audacity to live life on the edge, flamboyantly and in the public eye. The more outrageous they dared to be, the more their father washed his hands of them. To Heinrich he called them "those bad, unbridled children! May God awaken reason in them with time!"

The new, postwar generation did not just break with the traditions and the values of their elders; it put a match to them and laughed as they went up in flames. Germany during the Weimar Republic, the first German democracy, was the most modern and certainly the most exciting place in Europe. In style, outlook, and attitude, Erika and Klaus Mann came to represent this new generation as much as anyone.

So there was only one thing for the siblings to do: leave the bourgeois family home in Munich and head for the cultural capital of Europe, Berlin—the city Klaus referred to as "Sodom and Gomorrah in a Prussian tempo."

CHAPTER 2

JOURNEY WITHOUT SLEEP

WHEN ERIKA AND KLAUS MANN arrived in Berlin in 1924, Germany's turbulent experiment in democracy was less than six years old, and only Berlin was youthful enough to be its capital. A new city by European standards, one which did not become strategically important until the 1840s with the opening of Prussia's railway network, Berlin began to take on some of the characteristics of an international metropolis only in the last quarter of the nineteenth century. Even then, Victor Tissot, a French journalist on assignment in Berlin, warned that visitors should leave the city within twenty-four hours or risk dying of boredom.

Seemingly thrown together overnight so it could face the industrial revolution arriving in the morning, Berlin lacked the elegance and beauty of Paris, Vienna, or London. Furthermore, any connection Berlin had to Germany's imperial past was severed by the First World War, so that even today it cannot claim to have its own political or artistic legacy any more than it can claim its own cuisine. Berlin's only tradition is its lack of tradition, its need to rebuild and reinvent itself with each generation, and its ability to thrive as a metropolis despite its sense of geographic dislocation and historical discontinuity.

Culturally, Berlin in the Roaring Twenties was a Wild West sort of place where new ideas did not have to wrangle with old, tenacious ones before staking a claim. An influx of immigrants from Russia had brought Soviet art and theater to Berlin, where it induced the birth of German Expressionism. With so much new building to do, and relatively few old buildings standing in the way, Berlin found itself to be the home of a new architecture. The International Modern Style showcased countless new housing schemes and industrial sites, theaters and cinemas, offices and municipal buildings by the likes of Walter Gropius, Erich Mendelsohn, and Mies van der Rohe, among others. Instantly Berlin was considered, and magically became, cosmopolitan, urbane and exceedingly modern. Its central role in the avant-garde movements of the twenties was not limited to architecture; it extended to the visual arts, art photography, photojournalism, cinema, experimental theater, music, and fashion. Whatever else might happen to you in twenty-four hours, you would no longer die of boredom. Berlin held a mysterious aura, a strange fascination that drew people to it, especially adventurous and thrill-seeking young people like Erika and Klaus Mann.

The arrival of Erika and Klaus in Berlin, when Klaus was seventeen and Erika eighteen, was a rite of passage into adulthood; it marked the beginning of their professional lives. They dived right into the uninhibited gay nightlife, the experimental theater scene, and the extremely liberated social milieu with which Berlin in the twenties is synonymous. Erika came to study acting under the great stage director Max Reinhardt, and Klaus intended to launch himself as a professional writer. They settled into two dreary rooms in the Uhlandstrasse, and proceeded to find everything exciting, bewildering, and "gorgeously corrupt."

Klaus was already fascinated with Berlin from a previous visit, and was determined to make a go of it. He had tried to move to Berlin six months earlier, without Erika, before she had finished her *Abitur* and before a drastic currency reform relieved Weimar Germany of its notorious inflation. In November 1923, when Klaus turned seventeen, one dollar was equal to 4.2 million marks, and it took an entire suitcase of cash to buy a loaf of bread—not the most auspicious moment to leave the family nest and strike out on one's own. On arrival in Berlin, Klaus refused to wash dishes or operate an elevator. Such work was not demeaning to him, but neither was it amusing, and Klaus insisted on being amused. He hit on a solution: he would perform in one of Berlin's many music halls and cabarets. At least he had had some experience in this arena: he fondly recalled his amateur theatricals, performed with Erika back in Munich when they were mere adolescents. Why not give it a try on the glitzy Berlin stage? One of the more risqué songs, written by their friend W. E. Süskind for an Oscar Wilde parody that Erika directed, had a chorus that seemed appropriate:

Perversion's really swell, my boy,
Perversion keeps you well, my boy,
Perversion beats the standard brand,
Perversion isn't hard to stand.
Perversion is beyond compare—

Klaus begged a cabaret artiste he knew, Paul Schneider-Duncker, for a recommendation, and the man obliged by putting through a call to the proprietress of Tü-Tü, a cabaret known for its homosexual clientele. Klaus heard Schneider-Duncker tell her how handsome and gifted the lad was, a real genius, and Klaus was hired on the spot. He showed up at Tü-Tü a few hours later in borrowed clothes, a tuxedo that hung on him and patent leather shoes that pinched his toes. "The Tü-Tü crowd greeted me coolly. They sized me up with their eyes, which revealed an effort to conceal their contempt. . . . In a very shaky little voice [I] began:

Perversion's really swell, my boy—
Perversion keeps you well, my boy—

Not a hand stirred. . . . It was the most embarrassing situation of my life." Schneider-Duncker had played a trick on him, as Klaus learned years later. He had called the proprietor right back and told her that this "raw youth" he had just recommended was clueless; he was a highbrow "Dichterkind" (child of a poet) with the " 'meshugener idea he has to do music-hall. Treat him so that he loses the taste for it.' —I lost the taste." Humiliated, Klaus fled to Munich the very next day.

Still seventeen and still a highbrow *Dichterkind* when he returned to Berlin in early 1924, Klaus was fortified by the constant companionship of his sister, as well as by the Rentenmark, which was introduced in late 1923 to rescue the disastrous economy. Together Erika and Klaus discovered a new, wild music called jazz originating from America, its "galvanizing rhythm" uniting Berlin's unruly youth as if it were a "great balm and narcotic." There were other narcotics to discover, and Erika and Klaus encountered marijuana, morphine, and cocaine in the back rooms of Berlin's nightclubs, just as easily obtainable as if they were in the harbor saloons of Marseilles or the speakeasies of Harlem. Klaus developed a taste for cocaine, as prevalent as champagne, and not much more expensive. He was in seventh heaven. "I had the time of my life. To be in Berlin was a constant thrill in itself."

Unlike the earnest youth of the free school movement who had made such a strong impression on them when they were still students, Erika and Klaus found Berlin's youth to be single-mindedly devoted to "violent pleasures and excesses" which neither Erika nor Klaus could totally embrace. As much as they were drawn to the bohemian life, they were both deeply romantic and acutely moral at heart, and the appeal of decadence remained largely an intellectual posture. Klaus attended an orgy that turned out—he later admitted—to be little more than staying up all night, singing, drinking, dancing, and driving to the lake district as the sun came up. Erika felt the decadence of Berlin's youth was based on a deep sense of disillusion, cynicism, and resentment caused by the dishonesty of the war years, a pessimistic worldview she understood but didn't share.

In the Roaring Twenties, the new fashion that was scandalizing New York and Paris—hemlines above the knee—was not even considered daring in Berlin, as so many women opted to dress like young men instead, in suits and ties. Homosexuality had gone from perverse to chic virtually overnight, and was no longer a subject confined to whispers. Berlin's Institute for Sexual Research, established by Dr. Magnus Hirschfeld, promoted homosexuality as a legitimate "third sex" rather than an aberration. Gay bars, drag balls, and social clubs sprung up all over Berlin for both men and women (and those in between). Tourists could find them in guidebooks and go slumming on the "queer circuit" until dawn. Rent boys and professional streetwalkers, male and female, had proliferated with the failing economy, and found no shortage of clientele. Among the counterculture youths of Berlin, the only taboo on the books was to believe in something, anything, beyond the immediate gratification of pleasure.

Erika believed in herself. She had a genuine passion for acting, but it was no longer enough to act just for the fun of it. She came to Berlin armed with fierce ambition, determined, "body and soul," to become an actress. She planned to take Berlin by storm by securing the title role in an upcoming Max Reinhardt production of G. B. Shaw's *Saint Joan.*

The problem with Erika's plan was that she had signed up to begin Reinhardt's acting school less than four months before the scheduled premiere. The Magician did not want to crush her spirit and wrote to her somewhat ironically, "It wasn't a bad idea to aim for Joan, but of course it was slightly premature." The coveted role went to the famous stage actress Elisabeth Bergner. Erika did appear on the stage alongside her—as an extra.

Erika would play Joan two years later, in Munich, but for now she was confined to smaller roles that did not interest her. She was "first actress" in Pirandello's *Six Actors in Search of an Author,* and the princess in Carl Sternheim's *Oscar Wilde*—not exactly starting at the bottom, but Erika expected to start at the top. She played her little parts "ten times, fifty times, and a hundred times, each time a little differently, until finishing the season no longer interested me, and I implored Reinhardt to let me go." She left the troupe and by March of the following year had signed her first theater contract, for her first major role, in a play by Klabund. The only catch: it was in Bremen.

While Erika diligently built her acting career with mostly matinee roles in the provinces, Klaus jumped immediately into the spotlight as a writer, thanks partly to his youthful arrogance and partly to his famous surname. He began by submitting literary essays under a pseudonym to the highly respectable journal *Die Weltbühne,* but his editor quickly dispensed with the anonymity:

> Unfortunately, the editor soon found out my identity and insisted on featuring my name, which provided a tiny sensation and probably was the pivotal mistake of my literary career, for from now on I was labeled the precocious son of a distinguished father. . . .

Klaus would repeat this pivotal mistake over and over again. He found himself trading on his father's fame when it might work to his advantage and distancing himself from it at all other times. His younger brother Golo saw this contradiction in Klaus's relationship with the Magician, noting that "he suffered from the feeling that he was in his father's shadow, but at the same time directed as much of the brighter light on himself as he could." Even if the trap was partly of his own making, it was one from which he could never get free.

That Klaus had chosen a literary career was a source of amusement for the press. A cartoon published in *Simplicissimus,* a Munich satirical journal, showed Klaus Mann in short pants, leaning gleefully over his father, who is seated at his writing desk, looking annoyed. The caption

"The precocious son of a distinguished father." Klaus circa 1925.

read, "I am told, Papa, that the son of a genius is never a genius himself. Therefore, you can't be a genius!" Bertolt Brecht compounded the joke when he wrote in an essay, "The whole world knows Klaus Mann, the son of Thomas Mann. By the way, who is Thomas Mann?" Klaus was still young enough to be flattered by such notoriety; he was still, he reflected, "too vain and immature to reject the offering of a shoddy halo which I confounded with fame." His own lapses in judgment contributed to the spectacle. His father had signed a copy of *The Magic Mountain* (1924) "To my respected colleague—his promising father." Klaus casually showed the dedication to a friend and soon found it repeated, *ad nauseam,* in the press, much to Klaus's embarrassment. Klaus must have realized the perverse logic at work in such ridicule: it insinuated that Thomas Mann, a vestige of an earlier age, was ripe for displacement by his son Klaus, a symbol of the rising generation, but it was Klaus who was the real butt of these jokes. He was trapped in the role of *Dichterkind*, the promising son of a great man who will never measure up to his father's stature, nor have his work judged by its own literary merits.

The shoddy halo did not pay the rent, low as it was for Erika and Klaus's gloomy accommodations. Cabaret was out of the question, so Klaus found paid work as a second-string theater critic for the daily "Zwölf Uhr Mittagsblatt" ("12 O'Clock Page"), and enjoyed enormously the sudden influence he wielded as a mere eighteen-year-old, to praise or damn the leading stage performers of the day. Klaus admitted to feeling he was a sham as he sat among the distinguished "gentlemen of the press" in the theater on opening night. The job felt like another prank of his, "another trick to bamboozle the grown folks." Often he tried to see how far he could go before being called on it. Once he was extra nasty for no particular reason about a popular stage actor, Ferdinand von Bonn. "There was nothing Mr. von Bonn, or anybody else, could do about it: the critic of the 'Zwölf Uhr Mittagsblatt' just didn't like his performance. Had they known how I inwardly chuckled! The big hoax! It worked!"

Erika and Klaus's move to Berlin signaled the beginning of the constant traveling that would characterize their adult lives. No sooner were they settled there than Erika was performing in Hamburg or Bremen or Frankfurt. Her travels at this time, and indeed throughout her life, were primarily dictated by the demands of her work, first as an actress and later as a lecturer and journalist. Meanwhile Klaus's travels were more a case of unquenchable wanderlust. Less than six months after his arrival, Klaus left Berlin for his first big trip outside Germany. With W. E. Süskind (author of the "Perversity" song, who would write more distinguished pieces later on), Klaus traveled to London, which only depressed and confused him, and to Paris, a city he would love for the rest of his life. In Paris he traded companions: Süskind went back to Munich exactly on the day they had planned to return, for "he was an orderly boy. I was not." Klaus picked up a young man in Paris and traveled with him to Marseilles, Tunisia, and inland to the Sahara, all of which bewitched him. He finally forced himself to move on, to Palermo, Naples, and Rome, where Italy's recent embrace of Fascism repelled him. After Klaus's death the novelist Christopher Isherwood said of him, "He had traveled widely and continuously—so much so that the huge upheaval of the Emigration [the mass exodus from Europe during World War II] seemed, as far as he was concerned, to be no more than an extension of his normal way of living."

Klaus's first novel, *The Pious Dance,* published in 1925, can be read today as one of the first ever "coming out" novels, an earnest, unapologetic, and extremely candid autobiographical story of a young homosexual man. The protagonist Andreas leaves behind his fiancée, the daughter of a great artist, and comes to Berlin, where he encounters a run-down boardinghouse, a seedy cabaret, and the captivating face of a reckless young man with whom he falls in love. Buried in the middle of the book is a sentence eerily prefiguring Klaus's own future predicament: "He who is too deeply associated with death will be homeless on earth."

The book is dedicated to Pamela Wedekind, daughter of the playwright and poet Frank Wedekind. Wedekind's unconventional plays were scathing attacks on the hypocrisy of bourgeois morality. He achieved fame, although not fortune, with his overtly sexual plays *The Earth Spirit* (1895) and *Pandora's Box* (1903), both of which emphasize the depravity that results when a misguided and sanctimonious society tries to suppress or deny the power of sexuality.

Wandering between Zurich, Paris, and London, Frank Wedekind lived a bohemian life, at times reduced to performing his ballads on the cabaret stage to pay for his next meal. He finally settled down at age forty-four and married Tilly, a gentle, childlike eighteen-year-old girl with whom he already had a young daughter. The family set up house in Munich, where Wedekind became a close friend of Klaus's uncle Heinrich. It was in Heinrich Mann's home in 1923, five years after Wedekind's death, that Klaus first met the daughter.

Thomas and Katia Mann, still reeling from Klaus's announcement that he was never returning to school, now learned that Klaus planned to marry Pamela Wedekind, although he wasn't even eighteen at the time. "How will you support her?" they murmured, clearly stuck in their old-fashioned, patriarchal ideas about gender roles in marriage. Klaus's reply did little to assuage them: he would become a ballet dancer.

Katia was genuinely worried; she had high hopes for her eldest boy. The Magician took it somewhat in stride, as he did most of the scandalous reports he received pertaining to Erika and Klaus. The ironic detachment he was so known for in his writing and his adult relationships manifested itself now in his relationship with his eldest children. Klaus later wrote about his father's bemused reaction to the latest career plan:

he "had no prejudices against the profession as such but only wondered if I was fit for it. Wasn't I rather on the gawky side?"

As flippant as Klaus was about a career as a dancer, he was only slightly more serious about marrying Pamela. He had proposed in a letter—didn't she think it a nice idea?—and was as surprised as his parents when she sent a postcard back with the word "yes." When Klaus returned to Berlin in 1924, Pamela remained behind in Munich, and later joined an acting troupe in Cologne. For short visits with the siblings, she flew to Berlin by small propeller plane, still a novel form of transportation.

A pleasant but not particularly attractive young woman, with pale white skin, thin lips, a long hook nose, and arched, tapered eyebrows that gave her face a perpetually questioning expression, Pamela Wedekind did not have any of the qualities that Klaus described as essential ingredients for his falling in love. (Of course, these were qualities he sought, and found, in a succession of young men, so perhaps he held women to a different measure.) Despite being verbose on the subject of his physical attractions, he never once mentioned anything physically attractive about Pamela. Her voice was metallic, her fingers broad and blunt. The kindest he came was to say that her face was "but a softened and rejuvenated version of the paternal features" as seen in her father's death mask, hanging on the wall of Wedekind's studio. It seems from all Klaus has written about the engagement that his fascination for the father was greater than his love for the daughter.

Frank Wedekind had deftly managed to be at the vanguard of the Roaring Twenties even though he was already dead two years before the decade began. His expressionist stage effects and his focus on the primacy of sexuality were well ahead of his time, and only came into vogue with the subsequent generation. Klaus's affection for Pamela cannot be separated from his desire to recapture the essence of her absent father, whom both Klaus and Pamela adored. Perhaps his yearning had a symbolic dimension as well: Wedekind may have been a stand-in for his own inaccessible father.

It was in fact Erika, not Klaus, who was physically attracted to Pamela. Although not a classic beauty, Pamela did share a quality with the Lulu of her father's famous dramas: ostensibly passive, she served as a catalyst for other people's desires. A weak personality in relation to the more forceful Erika and the more imaginative Klaus, Pamela quickly succumbed to Erika's advances.

Erika's letters to her lover show a dimension to her which Erika, a consummate actress, kept hidden from most people who knew her. What Klaus once wrote to her when they were children—"I know that you don't like it, when so much is revealed"—held true throughout her life. Unlike Klaus, Erika did not often articulate her innermost feelings, and especially did not expose her weaknesses, self-doubts, or moments of despair. Instead, she came across as adventurous, ever-confident, charming, and full of vitality. A revealing letter Erika sent Pamela in August 1925 from Bremen, where she was acting at the Schauspielhaus, gives a rare glimpse into a moment of personal insecurity and suggests a certain trust between the two women:

> But you don't know how unhappy I am. I don't really believe myself that I'm simply less talented than all the rotten two-cent actors in Bremen. I can't possibly be that untalented. But I'm just not suited for the theater, I simply don't really fit, it's awfully dreadful, for what else in the world should I do?

The intimate relationship between Pamela and Erika became the centerpiece of Klaus's next work, a romantic play called *Anja and Esther*, completed at the end of 1924. Specifically written with his sister and his fiancée in mind for the title roles, it was "a play about young people of course. . . . A neurotic quartet of four boys and girls . . . were madly in love with each other, in the most tragic and mixed up fashion."

Set in a "home for fallen children" where no one is ever reformed, *Anja and Esther* pits the seductive but dangerous real world against the safe but claustrophobic world of adolescent fantasy. Klaus himself preferred this protected fantasy world, and dwelled in it far longer than most children do; by the time it eventually collapsed, he had developed few inner resources to cope with the difficulties of real life and would take refuge in escape. In his play, the intense, delicately balanced relationships between the confused foursome are threatened by the appearance of a handsome and mysterious stranger, Erik. Erik is virtually interchangeable with the reckless young man with whom Andreas falls in love in Klaus Mann's novel *The Pious Dance*. His intrusion into their cloistered world will have devastating consequences.

Kaspar, clearly homosexual and modeled on Klaus, is the brother of Anja, who is fiercely in love with Esther. Esther abandons Anja for the mysterious Erik, and leaves the school with him, taking Anja's beloved brother Kaspar with her. As Esther prepares to leave, she acknowledges to Anja the intense sibling relationship between Anja and Kaspar, the intimacy of which echoes that between Klaus and Erika: "At first you'll feel rather hard done by when you miss your brother Kaspar. You were, after all, more closely bound to him than you knew yourself. In so many things you are alike, and your differences cancel each other out in so happy a manner that one can hardly imagine one of you without the other."

The perverted Old Man who runs the school personifies unchecked sexual greed; with no mothers around to watch over their children, he is able to prey on the young girls at the school. Some literary critics have seen Klaus's depiction of the Old Man "as a token of Klaus's inward psychological conflict with his father," but such an interpretation seems too facile. His father's sexual obsession with Klaus was surely inappropriate, but it was never unbridled, and it was Thomas himself, not Katia or Erika, who held the reins tight. The Old Man is more likely based on Klaus's mentor Paulus Geheeb, whom he physically resembles. Klaus depicted Geheeb in other writings as a seducer of female students; there may well have been a basis in reality. (In *Anja and Esther*, the school itself is a parody of Paulus Geheeb's Odenwaldschule.)

Thomas is alluded to elsewhere in the play as the offstage, absent, but blameworthy parent. Esther screams: "I say the parents are to blame!! . . . With their unforgivable lack of scruples, they brought us into the world. They had a firm foundation beneath their feet, which we had to lose. *They* had their little griefs to curl up in, their little foibles that were warm and cozy. But we have to feel jeopardized at every moment as no generation ever felt jeopardized before. . . . Now the morality of these fathers turns away in terror from the dubious generation they have wronged."

Thomas Mann, as a spokesman for his own pro–World War I generation, may be blamed by his children for the insecurity of their postwar generation, but as a closeted homosexual he is also guilty of hypocrisy. Speaking of Kaspar and Anja's father, Esther says, "If anyone is our enemy, he is. . . . The fact that he represents the highest, perhaps the most perfect type of the species . . . makes him only that much more dangerous, that much more detestable. I don't care if he is Anja's father, she has *nearly* nothing in common with him. . . . Oh, I can hear the clever and well-chosen words he'd use to keep us apart, to proclaim that our passion, our pleasure is immoral."

Of course Thomas Mann would say no such thing. His repression of his own homosexuality might have to do with self-loathing, but he never repudiated his children for their sexual preferences. If anything, his children's participation in the intoxicating world of Berlin in the twenties must have provoked in him both envy and enticement. Erika and Klaus often joked with their parents about their own sexual inclinations, and their father, on rare occasion, even joked back. The nature of Thomas's gentle gibes reveal a touch of regret or jealousy, in that his children could live out their sexual lives in a way that their father could only fantasize. In a joint letter to Erika and Klaus, the fifty-two-year-old Thomas entreated Klaus to stay away from a seventeen-year-old youth named Klaus Heuser, on whom both father and son evidently had their eye.

> Dear Children!
> . . . Yesterday I wrote in such detail about Kläuschen Heuser, who is already gone once more. . . . The matter of *this* Klaus, as he uses to distinguish himself from *that* Klaus, i.e. Eissi, is certainly overestimated. I call him Du [the informal address for "you," the sign of a certain familiarity] and at our farewell, with his express consent, I pressed him to my heart. Eissi is ordered to stand back voluntarily and not disturb my sphere. I am already old and famous, and why should you two alone indulge yourselves?

Thomas had no real intentions of indulging himself—even though his locking eyes with the son of Professor Werner Heuser, of the art academy in Düsseldorf, while vacationing on an island in the Baltic marked the first time he had fallen in love since his aborted affair with Paul Ehrenberg almost twenty-five years earlier. (He had several unrequited passions in between, including one for the ten-year-old Polish boy Wladyslaw Moes, the real-life inspiration for the fictional fourteen-year-old Tadzio in *Death in Venice*.) Thomas compared his love for Klaus Heuser with his love for Paul Ehrenberg so many years before, finding that "the K.H. experience was more mature, controlled, happier." He invited the boy to Munich several times, and visited him in Düsseldorf, but it was only in Thomas's dreams that their intimacy went beyond "Du" and a hug. As if to defend his secret fantasy life over the flamboyant and publicly proclaimed indulgences of his children, he ended his discussion of Klaus Heuser by pronouncing, "The secret and virtually silent adventures of life are the greatest."

Anja and Esther did cause a minor scandal in the Mann family home when Klaus read it to them after dinner one night—Aunt Lula, Thomas's sister (the morphine addict mentioned earlier), particularly disapproved of how "conspicuously fond" the two young women were of each other.

The Magician found the play "very strange indeed" but had no problem with Anja and Esther's relationship. To Aunt Lula he merely dismissed it as "a sentimental friendship, between schoolmates."

If *Anja and Esther* was "very strange indeed," Klaus's next work, a collection of stories called *Before Life Begins* (accepted for publication in 1925), Thomas considered downright bizarre. Klaus had gathered some of his earlier unpublished short stories and finished them off by writing a cluster of disturbing tales about Kaspar Hauser, the legendary boy who lived in a pitch-dark cave for his first sixteen years, and who was murdered shortly after his liberation. Thomas commented to Erika, "I read Kläuschen's book with concern. A lot of it is quite strange. But, among other things, he has quite a 'Magician' complex [i.e., 'father complex'] here."

With these stories, and his simultaneously written first novel, *The Pious Dance,* Klaus developed a style of fiction writing that would cause him considerable grief later in life: drawing on actual experiences and personalities very close to home. Not surprisingly, this was also an established technique of his father's. As Katia said of her husband, "everything was based on reality, even down to the details, but no one besides Thomas Mann would have been able to make them into *Death in Venice.*"

Thomas Mann's celebrated novella *Disorder and Early Sorrow,* written in 1925, is a closely drawn portrait of his own family life, specifically focusing on his eldest children, Erika and Klaus (in the story named Ingrid and Bert), and on his youngest, Elisabeth and Michael (named Ellie and Snapper). Dr. Cornelius—a character so closely resembling the Magician himself that it seems disingenuous of the author to refer to him in the third person—openly prefers both his daughters, and defends his preference by asserting that "the heart will not be commanded."

In Professor Cornelius's household, economic distinctions have been blurred by the social upheavals of the time—the story is set in the notorious inflation year of 1923. The bourgeois parents are reduced to wearing worn-out clothes (although the wife remains largely out of sight); the servants are embarrassed by their servitude because only recently they belonged to the middle class. The representatives of the younger generation revel in the social breakdown and push it even further. When Ingrid and Bert invite their bohemian artist friends to the house for a casual dance party, the boys wear rouge and the girls wear pants, social etiquette is tossed aside, and the collapse of sexual roles compounds the collapse of class distinctions. Boys dance with boys, girls with girls, and four-year-old Ellie dances with one of the male guests, Max, before she is shoved off to bed against her will. Both Ellie and her father find Max "as pretty as a picture . . . just charming to look at . . . with kind dark eyes." Cornelius, who loves his little Ellie with the same obsessive adoration that Thomas felt toward Elisabeth, is helpless to comfort his hysterical daughter, who is experiencing for the first time the torments of unrequited love.

Observing the older children from the distance of the hallway, Dr. Cornelius cannot help but compare the talents, achievements, and future prospects of the male guests with those of his own son, and is "gnawed by envy and chagrin": "He tries to be just; he tells himself that, after all, Bert has innate refinement; that probably there is a good deal more to him. . . . But paternal envy and pessimism win the upper hand." It was agonizing for Klaus to read in his father's novella such a harsh depiction of himself. He was still stewing twelve years later when he itemized in his diary his father's many betrayals of him, from "the depiction in *Disorder* up to the present situation."

Critics have read Klaus's own fictional family portraits from that time as a "strategic literary response or a 'counter discourse' to the father." In Klaus's novella *The Children's Story* (1926), the father, an emotionally remote, authoritarian philosopher, is long deceased. His four children enact the blithe fantasy world of the Mann siblings' own childhood in Bad Tölz. Their mother, Christiane, meets Till, a man who embodies everything the absent father does not: he is a joyful and warm surrogate father to the children, and an ideal sexual and intellectual partner to the mother. Finding a real person who could serve as an inspiration for this character was a struggle for Klaus, but he was equally unable to summon him up out of thin air. Klaus traveled to Paris in search of his muse and found him in René Crevel, the gay surrealist poet, part European man of letters and part impish boy. To Klaus he had "the eyes of an archangel." Besotted with René, Klaus returned to Berlin to finish his book.

After the inadequate or outright negative responses by Thomas to his previous works, this time Klaus wished his father "wouldn't bother reading the novella at all." The Magician did read it, however, and wrote to Erika that it genuinely made him laugh, but also raised doubts for him now and then. Whether the doubts pertained to the book's literary merits or his own unflattering portrayal, he doesn't say. And he seems not to have mentioned the story at all to Klaus directly. Within their relationship, one critic has noted, "there could be no question of mutual confidence, of friendship or cordiality, let alone intimacy. Instead, there were tensions, inhibitions, and guilt feelings. Time and again it became evident that neither could change his nature and that no understanding was possible. All his life the son courted the father's sympathy and recognition." It was not forthcoming.

In developing his own individual voice as an author, Klaus sought to evade his father's influence as much as possible. He was drawn to very marginal themes, those that would come to dominate his own life: homosexuality, drug addiction, suicide. He wrote rapidly, prolifically, and as a consequence often sloppily, being far too restless and unstable a personality to embrace the disciplined, flawless approach for which Thomas Mann was so famous. Like Thomas, Klaus wrote very close to his own life, but whereas Thomas, in the words of one of his biographers, "experienced next to nothing and wrote about almost everything," Klaus lived life to the full—some might say too full. Klaus searched for his erotic muses among the gay demimonde, and actively sought literary models beyond his father, notably in Heinrich Mann, Jean Cocteau, and, most of all, André Gide.

In 1925, Gustaf Gründgens, the twenty-six-year-old rising star of the Kammerspiele in Hamburg, telegraphed Klaus out of the blue with the idea to perform *Anja and Esther* in Hamburg, with Erika and Pamela playing the title roles (fulfilling Klaus's original intentions). Gustaf proposed that Klaus play Kaspar, while Gustaf would direct and take the role of Jakob, another of the youths at the school who was attracted to Esther. Gustaf would have been more suitably cast as Erik, the ruinous stranger, but none of them could possibly foresee the havoc Gustaf Gründgens one day would strew over Klaus Mann's life.

Klaus never forgot his first impression of Gustaf. Wearing a faded leather overcoat and worn-out sandals, Gustaf was so light-footed when he bounded into the Mann siblings' hotel room that Klaus took him for "a neurotic Hermes." In his eye he sported a monocle, the height of contemporary fashion, and managed to look chic despite a certain shabbiness. Coming from a lower-middle-class background, he was handsome and proud, yet somewhat nervous and insecure around the lofty Manns—Klaus would come to learn that Gustaf was more "himself" on the stage than off it. If Klaus had been flattered by Gustaf's telegram, when he met him in person, he was smitten.

Gustaf, smitten as well, publicly proclaimed that "the younger generation has found its poet in Klaus Mann. Everyone accepts this as fact." In an article titled "About Klaus Mann" published in the Hamburg journal

Der Freihafen, Gustaf marveled at Klaus's play, calling it astonishing and brilliant and insisting one must love its creator.

Gustaf Gründgens soon became Klaus's lover, as well as Erika's fiancé—although she continued to carry on her passionate affair with Pamela, who was still Klaus's fiancée. In other words, the offstage entanglements between the foursome which developed during the production of *Anja and Esther* were as confusing as those enacted in front of the audience. For reasons she kept to herself, Erika actually went ahead and married Gustaf shortly after their engagement was announced. A skeptical friend of the groom demurred that the marriage was advantageous, career-wise, for Erika, although Gustaf's motives seem even more mercenary. He was fascinated not only by Klaus's play, but also by the Mann siblings themselves, their famous literary roots, their sophistication, their high bourgeois self-confidence to which they never gave any thought. Like Klaus, Gustaf was entirely homosexual, but unlike Klaus he was eager to repress his homosexuality. Marrying Erika seemed like the perfect solution to that problem, enabling him to gain the respectability of the Mann family name at the same time.

It was a mismatch from the very beginning. Even Erika's mother could see that this new role of married man "didn't suit him at all." The novelist Sybille Bedford, a close friend of Klaus's, has suggested that Erika married Gustaf only because he was Klaus's lover. It is equally plausible that Klaus proposed to Pamela only because she was Erika's lover. No rivalry between Erika and Klaus can be discerned in these marital arrangements; instead they express, albeit indirectly, the intensity of their feelings for each other. Sybille Bedford has surmised that "all their [Erika's and Klaus's] own attachments and their own amorous and sexual life, was very much dictated by their enormous attachment to one another. Which of course was impossible. Which of course they also romanticized, but I'm quite sure nothing of the kind ever happened between Klaus and Erika."

The available evidence provides a less definitive answer to the question of incest. Klaus's diaries give contradictory signs; more than once, he would be disappointed by a male lover and write longingly about Erika in the same sentence. The cryptic letters between the siblings (Erika often addressed hers to Klaus as "my love" or "my lover") hide as much as they reveal about the subject. They reflect an intense love which may well have been exaggerated for dramatic effect, and are peppered with baffling references and secret allusions; it is extremely difficult to decipher Erika and Klaus's intimate private code. Sybille Bedford was convinced they "were in love with one another," but that a relationship was impossible because "Klaus could never sleep with a woman." She also questioned the authenticity of Erika's homosexuality, seeing it as a by-product of her subconsciously merged relationship with her gay brother. Although there is no clear evidence of actual sex between the siblings, there are many indications of a psychosexual dynamic in their relationship, which one could call "emotionally incestuous."

Thomas and Katia may not have known the full extent of their children's relationship, whatever that extent was, but they did know that Erika's relationship with Pamela took precedence in her heart over that with Gustaf. Just before Erika's marriage, the Magician wrote to her and sent his greetings, not to her betrothed as one might expect, but rather to "deine Freundin" Pamela.

Although the foursome of Erika, Klaus, Pamela, and Gustaf were at their closest ever, Pamela wisely chose not to attend the wedding. Erika described the event in a letter to Pamela written two days later:

> Many many greetings, my beloved Goddess, from the wife. . . . Yes, Pamela, the wedding was a big shock. . . . All of a sudden the minister told me, now sign here Mrs. Gründgens. That was a big shock, but then it all went well. . . . Kläuschen Pringsheim [Katia's twin brother, Klaus] was flirting with Gustaf, who was performing as though he were the typical groom. . . . And now we're at the Kurgarten Hotel; nobody here would believe we are married.

It was no accident that Erika chose the elegant Kurgarten Hotel in the fashionable resort town of Friedrichshafen for her faux honeymoon. Situated on the white sandy shores of the Lake of Constance, the closest Germany comes to having its own Riviera, the Kurgarten Hotel was the first-class hotel for the region, known for drawing the high bourgeois and literati set, the group Gustaf was determined to join and Erika, already a member, was determined to mock.

The choice of hotel held another irony for Erika: only one month earlier, she had checked into the Kurgarten with Pamela, *incognito*. Although Erika was the one with a penchant for dressing in men's clothing and had the far stronger personality, they switched roles in order to raise the stakes for the stunt they were about to pull. Pamela donned a bowler hat, jacket, and tie, and carried a walking stick to pass herself off as a man.

Erika Mann and Pamela Wedekind.

In her letter, Erika made reference to the deceit before reassuring her lover that her wedding to Gustaf had changed nothing between them:

> But that we (you and I!) are listed in the hotel list of last month, me as an actress and you as Mr. Wedekind from Munich, is really wonderful. My Pamela, please please come soon. I would love it awfully, because I love you beyond measure. . . . Everything tender, Erika

Although Klaus was only nineteen at the time, he considered his relationship with Gustaf Gründgens to be one of the most important in his life. Klaus later recalled that Gründgens "sparkled with ideas," "captivated audiences," "looked strikingly attractive," and "was all talent, no substance: the most ingenious performer I have ever seen." In the rehearsals for *Anja and Esther,* Gustaf paid scant attention to his own part and focused instead on the daunting task of turning Klaus into an actor. "More bitchy, Klaus!—if you know what I mean . . . not so stiff! More life! Take two steps to your left, just before you have to say this line . . . two bitchy little steps—look—like this. . . ." His clever interventions spurred Klaus on to master his role (which was after all directly based on Klaus himself), while his graceful demonstrations would seduce the enamored Klaus still further.

Anja and Esther premiered in Hamburg on October 22, 1925. The media seemed genuinely charmed by the fact that the offspring of Germany's esteemed authors had written and now were performing a play. Headlines proclaimed, "Children of famous poets stage a show in Hamburg," and audiences queued up at the box office. Both "famous poets" missed the sensational theatrical debut—Frank Wedekind had been dead now for almost a decade, while Thomas Mann did not want to leave his writing desk. He wrote to a friend, "Should I, can I forbid it? But that

The original press photo from Klaus Mann's first theater piece, *Anja and Esther.* *From left*: Gustaf Gründgens, Erika Mann, Pamela Wedekind, and the author.

would be madness. . . . Let us look on with our very best wishes, but at a distance. For not even ten horses would bring me to the premiere." He did, however, attend its much more modest opening in Munich, featuring an entirely different cast (since the two productions ran simultaneously). In Klaus's hometown, the play was merely met with a reception of "chilly curiosity."

Anja and Esther garnered an onslaught of publicity across Germany. The Hamburg show was the main tent in the media circus, especially after Germany's most popular magazine, *Die Berliner Illustrierte Zeitung*, ran a group photo of the cast on the front page—the most spectacular publicity one could hope for. The photo they used showed the foursome in baroque costume, their eyes wild as if they had escaped from Dr. Caligari's asylum instead of a home for fallen children. But the magazine decided that Gustaf Gründgens, the play's director as well one of Germany's most promising young actors, didn't have famous parentage and was not yet famous enough himself to be included. The editors cropped him out of the photo, even though his flaming purple wig and demented expression made him the most curious figure in the group portrait. To make matters worse, they replaced his corner of the frame with an inset of yet another picture of the remaining three, this time in street clothes, with Klaus in the middle of the two women, their arms all interlinked.

Gustaf was sitting with Klaus, Pamela, and Erika in the theater's little restaurant when he saw the printed magazine cover for the first time. A smile froze on his face and he sat motionless and silent, a "beautiful performance of dignity and grief," according to Klaus, who showed less dignity by gloating. Throughout the seemingly interminable Nazi years to come, whenever Gustaf's face was featured on the cover of countless popular magazines, Klaus would remember this awkward moment in the theater restaurant and feel certain that Gustaf had plotted his revenge, then and there.

The disproportionate attention the play received was partly due to the famous surnames involved and partly due to the play's "homosexual decadence," which incited brutal condemnation. The sexual tolerance for which the Weimar Republic is famous coexisted with traditional and even reactionary forces, mobilized to squelch that tolerance at every opportunity. One right-wing paper called Klaus "a felon against the German people." When the play was about to open in Vienna, some journals managed to combine the famous surnames angle and the "homosexual decadence" angle into a single tabloid headline, and circulated a rumor that Thomas Mann refused to read the play on the grounds of obscenity. He denied the claim publicly without defending the play, insisting, "I am no boarding-school mistress."

It could not have been a good career move for Erika to follow one scandalous role with another, yet that is exactly what she did when she appeared in Klaus's next play, this time a comedy, written for the same foursome. She was being offered important roles by now and was in demand on the stages of the Kammerspiele, Staatstheater, and Volkstheater in Munich. Her marriage to Gustaf Gründgens, if nothing else, improved her acting skills—not only because the marriage itself required a certain degree of craftiness, but also because professionally he was the perfect mentor for her.

Klaus Mann's *Revue zu Vieren* (Four in Review) opened in Leipzig in April 1927, followed by a tour. Not quite a "succès de scandale," it was merely a flop. Klaus wrote, "We sneered at the critics, quarreled with our agent, roared over our fan mail, and ruined our reputations." He doesn't mention, however, that Pamela and Gustaf themselves found the play to be terrible, Gustaf abdicated his director's role, and the tightly knit foursome started unraveling. Only Erika stood by Klaus, as she always did, no matter what.

As their professional relationships collapsed, so did Erika's short-lived marriage to Gustaf Gründgens. (Separated in the summer of 1927, they finally divorced on January 9, 1929). A cynical explanation would point out that Erika's theatrical career had flourished to the point where she no longer needed Gustaf as a stepping-stone; that Gustaf had finally realized his marriage to Erika would not bestow upon him her father's impeccable social credentials, which were rising steadily to keep pace with his literary successes. A more considered appraisal would have to put Erika and Klaus's relationship as a primary factor. If Erika really did marry Gustaf because he was Klaus's lover, what should she do now that Klaus was suffering a different infatuation every day of the week? Erika's affair with Pamela Wedekind ended at the same moment that Klaus's engagement to her was called off—when Pamela announced that she was planning to marry the aging playwright Carl Sternheim, who had been a contemporary of her own father's (although not in Frank Wedekind's league). Pamela had met her betrothed through his daughter Thea (nicknamed Mopsa). The same age as Pamela, Mopsa was a good friend of the Mann siblings and had done the set design for Klaus's *Revue zu Vieren*.

With all the father complexes flying around their group, this new arrangement might not have been so disruptive, except that Klaus and Erika both felt betrayed. They knew Sternheim well from Erika's experience acting in his play *Oscar Wilde* a few years earlier (which Sternheim also directed), and they hated him for his "flippant aggressiveness and quarrelsome arrogance."

Erika's star was rising: she finally was asked to perform a role she had long coveted, that of Queen Elisabeth in Schiller's *Don Carlos* at Munich's State Theater. Klaus's star was falling: he had nothing but a big pile of bad theater reviews from his most recent flop. Both were aching to get away from it all. They began to plot a scheme as they walked along the shore of Lake Starnberg, outside of Munich. Klaus narrated the scene in his autobiography:

> "I don't know what's wrong with me," [Erika] complained. "Everything works out nicely, and I still feel low." There was a short stillness before she added: "The Lake Starnberg is fine, Munich is fine, and the State Theatre. But I'd rather be somewhere else. Ten thousand miles from here."
>
> "Not a bad idea," I said. "There are plenty of things to run away from."

Klaus recalled a letter he had neglected to answer, sent by the publisher Horace Liveright several months earlier, who had published an American edition of Klaus's novella *The Children's Story*. The letter had inquired, in the most noncommittal terms, whether Klaus might consider a lecture tour to the United States sometime the following year. After his conversation with Erika, he cabled back the publisher:

> Enchanted by your friendly invitation which reached me only today STOP Ready to leave in four weeks with well-known actress Erika Mann who happens to be my sister STOP Intend to spend winter in U.S....

Erika and Klaus turned their imminent transatlantic journey into the hottest news item, and everyone fell for the glamour and excitement of the story. They rhapsodized over their chance to see the "land of stunning mixtures and contradictions: the vast country from which publishers sent friendly cables and Chaplin bewitched the world, and handsome pilots embarked, with nonchalant heroism, to their lonesome flights across the ocean." But immediately the American publisher shot back a less than friendly cable, chastising Klaus for not letting him know sooner and insisting that the trip be postponed for one year. Impossible, Erika and Klaus decided; it was too late to postpone it and still save face. They cabled once more, with even more audacity: "So happy . . . intend to arrive New York about the first of October."

On October 7, 1927, the Mann siblings sailed second class across the Atlantic. Just when they gave up hope of it ever appearing, the famous gray skyline was discernible in the early morning mist. The only touch of color in the panoramic scene was the yellow glow of Liberty's lamp.

Their friend Ricki Hallgarten, the neighbor from Herzog Park with whom they had put on the local theatrical productions almost a decade before, was waiting for them at the pier. A few months earlier, Ricki had left his friends and his wealthy, highly intellectual Jewish family in Munich without explanation, to make his way without any support in New York City. Dark, handsome, and sulky, his head crowned with wild black curls, Ricki was "savage and delicate, somewhat like a neurotic gypsy," according to Klaus. He was bisexual, took strong likes and dislikes, and seemed to be able to live however he pleased. When he came to greet Erika and Klaus at the pier, he was doing short-term stints as a dishwasher and errand boy, both so low paid that he occasionally had to spend the night on a park bench. Klaus later reflected on his predicament:

> True, in his particular case such hardships were the result of desperate romanticism, rather than of inescapable circumstances. However, they were actual and painful enough; besides there were many among his friends who had to bear the same sort of life, by no means out of any masochistic whim. We met quite a few of them . . . all subjected to the same callous system that allowed anyone to become President of the United States or to starve to death.

Ricki was not the only one waiting for Erika and Klaus to disembark. To their surprise, a cluster of journalists was at the pier, but Erika and Klaus were too teary-eyed from Ricki's embrace and too excited by their arrival to manage any words in English. Even more journalists showed up at their hotel, the Astor. There they amused the press with their charming stories, some of which were true—for example, Sinclair Lewis really had tried to dissuade them from making the trip because of

Prohibition—and some weren't, such as that Erika and Klaus were twins. Above a double portrait, the afternoon headlines proclaimed them as "The Literary Mann Twins"—which the siblings had thought up earlier that day, partly as a lark, partly out of panic that they would not be considered exceptional enough as they were.

Since Horace Liveright was not prepared for Erika and Klaus's arrival, and since, at first, they could barely speak English, the lecture tour did not amount to very much. Boni and Liveright did hire a lecture agent on their behalf, one Mr. Friede, who was pressed into organizing their tour on short notice. Mr. Friede was a sharp-looking young man with a trim mustache and a seductive smile, or so Klaus thought. While he tried in vain to secure engagements, Erika and Klaus were free to explore the city, sit in smoky bohemian dives in Greenwich Village, and marvel at the curious macabre Broadway shows on offer. The best by far was *Dracula*, which Erika and Klaus loved so much that they agreed to admit it, belatedly, to the intimate circle of legends and myths that was the stuff of their childhood. They practiced their English by turning to each other at any occasion with "My poor Lucy looks very tired today" or "And how is the patient now?"

When Mr. Friede called them into his office to admit defeat, Erika and Klaus could not stop exchanging sympathetic looks and repeating their lines about poor Lucy. Possibly taking their peculiar behavior as an incomprehensible threat, or simply fearing the two had lost their minds, the agent offered them one thousand dollars to break the contract. As he said farewell and bid them a safe trip back to Europe, he almost collapsed from the news that they had no intentions of going home; they were headed cross-country to California and would set up their own lecture tour along the way.

With sheer nerve and one thousand dollars, the two set off by train for California. They were astonished by the vastness of America as it went by their window, but were not daunted by the challenge that lay ahead. They were armed with ample letters of introduction; just as they were leaving Germany, everyone they knew suddenly found an American cousin somewhere in the family tree. After all, it was 1927, not 1929, and wherever they went, they were welcomed with open arms and open pocketbooks—and plied with food and drink, regardless of Prohibition. They met everyone from H. L. Mencken, with whom they shared a bottle of red wine and a meal of lamb chops in his apartment at the Algonquin Hotel in New York, to Greta Garbo, who, wearing a sloppy raincoat and drinking whiskey, enchanted them at a lavish dinner party at the home of the great German actor Emil Jannings in Hollywood. Despite encountering such hospitality, they still had some close financial scrapes:

> Not one cent was left for the hotel bill which assumed disquieting proportions. The manager—so utterly suave in the beginning—had already paid us a rather embarrassing visit. We tried to convince him that we were, indeed, the most popular and trustworthy creatures on earth. It was out of sheer eccentricity—we intimated—that we delayed that trifle of a payment. "You know how young people are," we said apologetically, as if the reluctant payers were not we ourselves but a couple of capricious millionaires in whose services we had got used to a lot of crazy things. . . . But the manager made it very clear that it made no difference whether it was a sophisticated whim or plain poverty that prevented us from meeting our obligations. What a tiresome fellow!—utterly devoid of charm and imagination.

Unlike Ricki Hallgarten, the "literary Mann twins" were not cut out for poverty. Whenever they were stuck for funds, Klaus would write articles and Erika would write letters to organizations, seeking lecture engagements. They often arrived in town with no change in their pockets, figuring that "the taxi driver can pay the Red-Cap, and the doorman of the hotel will be only too pleased to pay the driver."

During what was developing into Erika and Klaus's trip around the world, the siblings were the closest they ever would be in their adult lives. They were more outrageous and daring together than either would ever have been alone. Their relationship as young adults still retained the fairy-tale happiness of their childhood, and they relished the absolute freedom they felt as they traversed the globe with no sense of responsibility to anyone else. They made many friends (and a few enemies), but none who would infringe upon or threaten their primary relationship with one another. Klaus often thought of this early experience of constant travel as a "dress rehearsal of exile," without acknowledging one crucial difference. Klaus spent most of his exile years apart from Erika, trying to recapture the emotional closeness and imaginative fantasy world they once shared.

The idea for their first co-authored publication, *Rundherum: Abenteuer einer Weltreise* (Roundabout: Adventures of a Trip around the World), came about late in their travels—they had long left mainland USA and, by way of Hawaii, arrived in Japan. They lingered at the Imperial Hotel in Tokyo for more than six weeks, "kept in that luxurious prison by the evil spell of our unpaid bill." Klaus hated Japan as he had hated Italy five years earlier: viscerally. He had a constitutional repulsion to Fascism and Fascist countries. Finally, Erika and Klaus were rescued by their father's publisher, who sent money on the condition that they co-author a book about their experiences.

Klaus had jested with Erika that one day she'd "be a writer all right. Wait and see. It's a curse with us." Erika had held out admirably, steadfast in her commitment to her acting career, until dire financial straits finally forced her to sign the book contract with the S. Fischer publishing house in Berlin. It marked the beginning of Erika's second, considerable career. There was now yet another writer in the Mann family, this time primarily of journalism, political essays, and children's books.

From Japan, Erika and Klaus moved on to Korea, China, and Russia. The distance between Harbin and Moscow made their American cross-country trek seem like a quick jaunt. The book advance did not see them all the way home (most likely they broke their budget on the Russian vodka), and they were forced to turn to a fellow traveler in Siberia to hold them over until Moscow. Klaus felt his guardian angel was in good form: the stranger turned out to be Bernhard Kellermann, a popular German author and remote acquaintance of Thomas Mann.

Erika and Klaus arrived back in Germany in the summer of 1928, ten months after they had left. They ended the story of their world trip by describing the jolt they felt at being back in Berlin after so long—the sensation of seeing their homeland, for a momentary flash, through the eyes of foreigners:

> After Moscow, Warsaw was a sinful luxurious paradise, with lit cafés and boulevards full of people. Touched and thankful, we enjoyed the comfort of Hotel d'Europe and we felt embraced by good old Europe. Less enjoyable was the first encounter with Prussia. When the train staff changed at the border in the early morning dawn, we ended up under the whip of the German police *par excellence,* exactly the image that prejudiced foreigners would conjure up. Now we had to stop laughing and sit up straight. . . .

The sensation of estrangement passed and immediately they felt at home once more. As soon as they saw the Gedächtnis Kirche, Berlin's famous church and central landmark, the whole trip seemed like a dream. [It was as if] we had never seen the Woolworth Building with Ricki, never eavesdropped on Chaplin in the restaurant, never dined with Louise in Honolulu, never with his Excellency Solf in Tokyo. . . . That we were mourning with the Chinese over Chang Tso-lin, was only in our imagination. The same for our negotiations with Bernhard Kellermann in the middle of Siberia. We never strolled anywhere else but between Uhlandstrasse and Lützow Ufer, or had any other music in our ears than the old shouting, "BZ am Mittag" "BZ am Mittag"! [*Berlin Times,* Midday Edition!]

The conclusion of *Rundherum* managed to condemn Prussian authority (as Bavarian bohemians, they found Prussia itself loathsome) while establishing that they viewed wild Berlin and not staid Munich as their hometown of choice. They wanted recognition in their own right, as the standard-bearers for the new generation, fully autonomous and independent of their parents, and only in trendy Berlin—despite its Prussian environs—could they achieve that status.

Their trip, however, did not end as Erika and Klaus had led their readers to believe. They returned not to Berlin but to the family home in Munich and were met at the train station by their mother, father, youngest sister, and brother. Stuck in between childhood and adulthood, they were too old to be precocious. Yet they still engaged in childhood pranks, and they still relied on their famous father's colleagues and acquaintances, such as Bernhard Kellermann, to bail them out. The Magician's opinion of them still mattered to them, and mattered a lot. That Thomas Mann took the time to greet them at the station touched Klaus deeply, "a most unusual gesture on his part."

As he had throughout the entire *Anja and Esther* scandal, Thomas responded to his children's foolishness with a calculated absentmindedness, as though he were too preoccupied to notice. When the younger siblings asked the older siblings for their most wonderful experience, Erika and Klaus flashed on their financial desperation in Siberia and announced in unison: Bernhard Kellermann! Their parents, uncomfortable with the shameless audacity of their eldest children, exchanged glances but said nothing. Katia, ever astute, thought they seemed "a little ridiculous" as they awkwardly clung to the machinations of their childhood, "Not like a couple of grown-up globe-trotters, really."

Their return to Germany marked the beginning of an extremely productive period for Erika. She moved from stage to silver screen just as the talkies came in. She played the drama teacher in the early lesbian classic *Mädchen in Uniform* (Girls in Uniform), and also had a small role as an English tour guide in *Peter Voss*. She wrote numerous magazine articles, a play (*Plagiat* [Plagiarism]), and a second travel book with Klaus, about the Riviera you won't find in guidebooks, featuring illustrations by Matisse. She wrote a children's book (*Stoffel fliegt übers Meer* [Stoffel Flies over the Sea]) illustrated by their friend Ricki Hallgarten, and together with Ricki wrote a children's play, *Jans Wunderhündchen* (Jan's Miracle Puppy), which premiered in December 1932 in Darmstadt with an as yet unknown Lilli Palmer in the cast.

Klaus continued to write, and his literary output was prolific. Ever since childhood, he had written constantly, indeed almost desperately. Shortly after their return from the world trip, he came out with a volume of short stories (*Abenteuer* [Adventures]) and a novel (*Alexander*). Two of his plays premiered in 1930 and a collection of essays was published in 1931.

While Klaus worked at his writing table, fashioning himself and his sister into an endless variety of fictional counterparts, Erika became a symbol of the daring new woman of the Weimar Republic: the kind of woman who wore short hair, had affairs with men or women, and wrote witty, charming pieces in the popular press. She had no ambition to be the proverbial great author her father was; she had no need for writing as salvation, as her brother had. Instead she aimed only to be, as she spelled out in one magazine piece, the "new kind of female writer, who . . . doesn't confess; she doesn't write her soul out of love, her own fate stays silently to one side, the woman reports instead of confessing. She is acquainted with the world, she knows judgment, she has humor and cleverness, and she has the strength to set her own self aside; it is almost as if she translates her life into literature, not into an extraordinary, high literature, but still into one that is useful, respectable, often loveable."

Erika was vivacious, full of humor, and did not take herself overly seriously—and her short pieces for the popular press had all these characteristics as well. Young, stylish, and modern, Erika took her "new woman" image yet one step further: she happened to look dashing behind the wheel of an automobile, and it turned out she could handle that wheel rather well.

Erika's little Ford took the siblings on several great expeditions, which they financed by writing magazine articles along the way. From

Dashing Erika behind the wheel of her Ford cabriolet.

the northern tip of Finland to the French Riviera, they "zigzagged Europe together, in an unending flight, as it were." Later they would claim, unconvincingly, that it was all the talk about Jewish conspiracies and the disgrace of the Versailles treaty that kept them on the move, but they were seeking adventure more than running from sinister forces.

In 1930 Erika and Klaus left Europe through the southern tip of Spain, and crossed over to Morocco. They were convinced that their experience of Fez would be false if they didn't at least try the magic drug hashish—so try it they did, at three times the potency recommended by their Arabian guide. Klaus was content to let it lead him wherever it may, despite the ghastly feeling that he had "burst literally asunder." Erika, with stronger instincts for self-preservation, demanded they leave their hotel room at three a.m., in slippers and dressing gowns, and so they groped and shuffled their way like blind dancing puppets to the hotel lobby, which seemed to be an interminable distance away. The concierge delivered them to a local military hospital, where they eventually regained their senses.

Klaus was a terrible driver and useless when it came to changing a tire. So when Erika was planning her next driving adventure—the most demanding one of all—she decided to leave Klaus behind. But the trip she

Klaus and Erika circa 1930.

was planning in June 1931 required a passenger, preferably one of whose company she would never tire; it was to be, as she called it, a 10,000-km "journey without sleep." She decided on Ricki Hallgarten, who had given up washing dishes in New York to be a painter in the countryside outside Munich.

Erika had entered them in a trans-European car race sponsored by the Automobile Clubs of Germany. Starting off in Berlin, they covered the routes in ten days, which meant she and Ricki drove through the night. It wasn't enough just to drive, refuel, and study the map, however; Erika also reported on the race for a newspaper, calling in her articles from their stops along the road. In one report, she commented that she would have given away pearls (had she had any) in exchange for sleep. The only sleep she managed was a few stolen moments whenever Ricki took the wheel. They came in first place, and Ford gave her the two-seater cabriolet convertible she had been driving as a gift.

If racing competed with acting for precedence in Erika's heart, her loyalty to Klaus had an even stronger pull. Again she found herself in one of Klaus's complicated interpersonal dramas; this time it was *The Siblings,* based on Cocteau's *Les enfants terribles,* and no one, least of all Cocteau, seemed to care for it. He felt it was a clumsy grafting of his novel onto their father's famous incest story (*Blood of the Walsungs*). In Klaus's play, the incestuous sister and brother—Elisabeth and Paul—are trapped in the fantasy games of their childhood, turned cruel and dangerous. Elisabeth manipulates Paul's mental condition to the point where she ends up convincing him to let her shoot him, falsely promising they would go together:

> PAUL: Press the silver object against my temple.
> ELISABETH: Tight against your temple. Do you feel it? Try to open your eyes.
> PAUL: I can't—
> ELISABETH: Think hard—concentrate. You are floating upwards. We're going to have the same dream.
> PAUL: The birds are flying up with me. Have you got a grip on The Silver Thing? The Doves—The Room is beautifully arranged. We are touching each other—at last.

This bizarre incest play opened in November 1930 at the Munich Kammerspiele, and in Klaus's words was "rather a flop, and a pretty noisy one too." As with *Revue zu Vieren* three years earlier, the press was vicious toward Klaus, and hinted at what only the pro-Nazi newspaper *Der Völkische Beobachter* would state directly: "If [Klaus] were not the son of Thomas Mann, this play surely would never have made it to the stage." Only the remarkable actress Therese Giehse, in the role of the virtuous and good-natured Bavarian maid, came away with any praise from the critics; the increasingly right-wing press in Germany found her a relief after all the other decadent and licentious characters.

In 1930, Erika and Klaus each found new partners with whom to replicate the foursome dynamic they had once created with Pamela

Wedekind and Gustaf Gründgens, but this time it was without engagements, weddings, or other heterosexual displays. Klaus and Ricki, friends since childhood, became occasional lovers, as did Erika and Annemarie Schwarzenbach, who was given the pet name Miro by Erika and Klaus. The beautiful, androgynous, eccentric, and troubled daughter of a Swiss noble family, Miro was an aspiring novelist and journalist. Three years younger than Erika, she had just returned from graduate study in history at the Sorbonne in Paris, and her first novel, *Freunde um Bernhard* (Bernhard's Circle), was about to appear in print. Annemarie fell desperately and incurably in love with Erika and would tell her so at every opportunity. Erika, for her part, cared deeply for Miro and felt a strong sense of responsibility toward her, but it couldn't be called love. Erika became, as she was for Klaus, a sort of protective "older brother," which is how Annemarie addressed Erika in her many letters.

Annemarie's connection with Klaus also ran deep. The photographer Marianne Breslauer, who became close to the siblings around this time, has described their friendship as

> something very wonderful and very pure and in a way much easier than Annemarie's friendship with Erika. . . . Erika was so overwhelmingly attractive and Annemarie was so terribly attracted [to her]. And on the other side was Klaus. They were very much equal to each other, very much interested in the same things. Also very politically interested. Klaus and Annemarie were close friends and of course there was no sex between them at all, but I always thought it would be good for them to get married. But of course this was probably a crazy idea.

Annemarie and Klaus were kindred spirits who had their writing, their homosexuality, and their left-wing politics in common. Increasingly, they would also share an impulse toward self-destruction and a perilous temptation to drugs.

In 1932, Klaus wrote a novel, *Treffpunkt im Unendlichen* (Meeting Place in Infinity), which returns to the structure of a complicated foursome; here the characters are Sebastian (an autobiographical figure) and Sonja (modeled on Erika), a dancer named Gregor Gregori (modeled on Gustaf Gründgens) and his former girlfriend Greta. The story begins in a Berlin train station, where Sebastian is departing for Paris and Sonja is arriving from Munich. Gregor is also at the station, not to see Sebastian off as

Sebastian had hoped, but to greet his future wife Sonja, whom Sebastian doesn't know but who will turn out to be his soul mate. Klaus created an array of semiautobiographical figures in addition to Sebastian; one of these, a homosexual novelist named Richard Darmstaedter, repeatedly attempts suicide until finally he succeeds.

When nothing works out for Sebastian in Paris or for Sonja in Berlin, they escape to Fez, where they encounter each other and consume too much hashish. Despite their seemingly ideal bond, Sonja dies from an overdose, one of many literary examples of a recurring theme of Klaus's—what biographer Fredric Kroll has termed "nonpossession," the impossibility of achieving reciprocal, requited love, because it is dependent upon mutual possession, something Klaus could not possibly endorse. This theme of nonpossession was a leitmotif of Klaus's life as well as his work, and manifested itself in his chronic restlessness, his sense of dislocation, and his inability to maintain a lasting relationship.

The inseparable foursome, Klaus and Ricki, Erika and Annemarie, were soon planning their greatest adventure yet, an expedition to Persia in two cars through the Balkans and Asia Minor. Ricki undertook most of the elaborate preparations, everything from purchasing tents to securing newspaper contracts to finance the trip (despite the fact that Annemarie and Ricki both came from families of incalculable wealth, and Erika and Klaus weren't going hungry either). He decided that the purchase of a gun was necessary to protect them against Persian robbers.

As the date for departure grew nearer, Ricki occasionally would make baffling, cryptic remarks. He'd inquire nonchalantly whether Klaus would enjoy a sudden windfall of cash, say ten or fifteen thousand marks, without any effort, which gave Klaus the uneasy feeling that the unpredictable Ricki was taking up theft, just as a lark. Or he'd ask Klaus to try on his expensive new shoes, to make sure they'd fit. Or he'd suggest abruptly that the other three embark without him; they could meet up in Bucharest a little later on.

Odder still, Ricki suddenly would break from his usual playful, joking demeanor and launch into wild diatribes about the increasingly dangerous situation in Germany. He'd scream at the siblings, "Everything is lost! We are doomed! The whole lot of us. The Nazis will swallow my little dog Wolfram and Erika's car and your books, Klaus, and my pictures too." Often the diatribe would end with a perfect imitation of Hitler's shouts and prances, which broke the tension and sent Erika and Klaus into shrieks of laughter. But at other times his performance would simply run out of steam. He'd mutter something incomprehensible about the siblings being right, it's just not worth dying on Hitler's account, or else, frustrated by their blindness, he'd hammer away at them with the question "Don't you realize what is happening?"

On May 4, 1932, the day before their scheduled departure, the two couples drove to the grounds of a leading Bavarian newsreel company. Dressed in grease-monkey overalls, bursting with excitement and pride, they were filmed for a newsreel story about their great adventure. The propinquity of the siblings to the venerable Thomas Mann, Erika's growing fame in her own right as an actress, and the sheer audacity of such an itinerary in 1932 all served to make the story newsreel-worthy.

For the filming, the newsreel director wanted Erika and Annemarie to sit primly in the car, while Ricki and Klaus were instructed to squat alongside the wheel and pretend to repair some imaginary damage. This kept the foursome in gales of laughter: Erika was a certified auto mechanic and Klaus didn't know the carburetor from the camshaft. After the film shoot, they spent the rest of the gloriously sunny day together, and as they separated late that night, they confirmed their plans to meet at three o'clock the next day to begin the expedition. For Ricki the appointed hour never arrived. At noon he fired the gun, allegedly bought to dissuade robbers, into his heart.

Erika and Klaus received the terrible news by telephone while they were sitting with a coffee and cigarette after lunch. Annemarie was already with them, and her beautiful sad face went stark white. Erika exploded in an avalanche of tears. But it was saddest of all for twenty-five-year-old Klaus. He who wrote relentlessly in his diary could only manage to mark the day with the letter *R*.

Years later, when Klaus was finally able to write about Ricki's suicide, what he wrote underscored his own predicament: "Many people think life dreary but bearable, whereas a delicate minority is smitten with life but cannot endure it."

Erika and Klaus drove to Ricki's house the following day. They went directly upstairs to his room as they had so many times before, for unannounced visits that were greeted with a hug and a grin. This time they were met with his lifeless body stretched out on his bed. Klaus was not surprised by his total stillness but by how shriveled and withered he looked; he found himself thinking that to die simply means to dry out. He was called back into the moment by a sudden shriek from Erika. She pointed to the wall above Ricki, which was speckled with blood. The siblings clung to each other and when Klaus spoke, his words sounded meaningless, his voice shocking even to himself: "He must have hit . . . his heart." Klaus shuddered, sensing an ominous sign, a premonition in the blood stains above him, "the scattered fragments of a mysterious pattern—a last message, a warning, the writing on the wall."

CHAPTER 3

THE LIGHTS GO DOWN

THE YEAR FROM JANUARY 1932 to January 1933 was a pivotal one for Germany, and consequently for the entire world. It was the year in which Germany's unstable Republic might have been saved. It was the year in which the National Socialists, until recently a relatively small group of right-wing extremists, became a center-stage political party with a huge herd of followers. How did it happen? How *could* it happen? The many failures of the fragile Weimar Republic, still in its infancy in a country unaccustomed to democracy, have often been delineated, but also crucial was the curious appeal of the Nazi ideology, which played to people's worst fears, resentments, and insecurities. Its corresponding campaign of physical terror against working-class organizers, Communists, Social Democrats, Jews or those thought to be Jewish, and non-Germans of all sorts was a crusade which, far from alienating the general populace, held a magical allure, especially among the young.

The National Socialist Party was not the only extremely right-wing outfit jockeying for power in the endgame of the Republic, but it distinguished itself by its violent pogrom-like excesses rather than by its ideology. Nor did it surface entirely from a subterranean existence in January 1932—Nazi-provoked violence was evidenced as early as 1926—but in 1932, especially during the election campaigns of that summer and autumn, the bloodshed was escalated, a peculiar campaign strategy that managed to elevate brutality to a form of "military chic."

As the Nazis swelled their ranks, the majority of decent Germans carried on with their daily lives, neither oblivious nor sufficiently alarmed. Even within the highly intelligent Mann family, only Klaus and his uncle Heinrich were fully on alert and tried to rouse their compatriots. Heinrich Mann was one of the most articulate, passionate, and prolific political writers against the Nazi menace throughout the years of the Weimar Republic. Klaus, equally astute, was considerably less effective, preoccupied as he was by his own personal problems.

After Ricki Hallgarten's suicide, Klaus, Erika, and Annemarie (Miro) canceled the grand Persian expedition but left town in May 1932 anyway, needing a diversion from their heartache. It was a miserable holiday even though Venice was the destination. Klaus and Miro felt abandoned by Ricki. They shared his "longing for death [which] pursued him as a relentless assassin pursues his victim."

Erika didn't have any wish to accompany Ricki into death, but rather mourned her own powerlessness. Throughout her life, she tried to summon up enough strength not only for herself, but for the more vulnerable, tormented souls who clung to her, Klaus and Miro especially. Writing to her father from Venice, she called Ricki's action "his deadly impertinence" and bemoaned that she had been "unable to understand or predict him in that instance." More than that, her considerable personal "strength . . . was not enough [to stop him] after all and that is sad." She ended her letter by saying, "Ricki would have loved it here. Oh, one of the many pleasures he robbed himself of."

In the weeks following Ricki's death, Klaus and Annemarie consoled themselves by increasing their drug consumption, while Erika threw herself into her work with abandon. Annemarie, as well as their old friend Thea Sternheim (daughter of the aging playwright Carl Sternheim, whom Pamela Wedekind had married in 1928), both provided Klaus with limitless supplies of various drugs. Klaus reported his escalating daily intake in his diary—"Eucodal. Cocaine. Eucodal and cocaine. 3 x eucodal and morphine"—and monitored their effects as though he were conducting empirical scientific experiments. He found it interesting, for example, to compare the difference in his reaction to pure morphine and to eucodal: "the physical shock from the morphine—le coup de révolver—was stronger, although the euphoria was virtually the same." Heroin, his newest diversion, was still too unnerving for Klaus to

Annemarie Schwarzenbach (*front*) with Erika in Venice, 1932.

list outright; for that he used the code name "tuna" among his friends and in his diary, or he merely wrote "genommen"—that is, he had "taken" it. Not surprisingly, it wasn't long before Klaus's experimentation slipped over into addiction.

Erika was by far the most cautious one in their group, when it came to drugs at least, and although she also tried everything from prescription drugs to heroin, she regularly pleaded with Klaus to stop his "petty bourgeois vice": "Don't do it, Hulda,* don't do it, especially when times seem so 'friendly and inviting,' one should not give in to it." On at least one occasion, she and Miro took some unidentified pills which caused a terrible reaction, not unlike the negative effects of heroin. They had to call the doctor at three in the morning and confess all; it was a "Fez-like"

---

*Erika and Klaus frequently made up nicknames for each other and for themselves. "Hulda" was probably an attempt by Erika to infuse some levity into a serious warning.

déjà vu, she wrote to Klaus. For Erika such experiences were enough of a deterrent; for Klaus it was already too late to heed such warnings. As the drug dependency of Klaus and Miro deepened, Erika slowly but surely withdrew from them both.

Erika found a more suitable partner in the stage actress Therese Giehse, whom she had first met in 1927, when Giehse appeared in a play by Heinrich Mann. In 1930 the two actresses became close when they acted together in Klaus's disturbing incest play *The Siblings*. Portly, brash, and self-confident, Therese Giehse was a mentor for Erika in all matters relating to the theater, and Erika relied on her judgment. For her part, Therese simply adored Erika. They became lovers, further unsettling Erika's already unbalanced romance with the lovesick, drug-addicted Annemarie Schwarzenbach, although not ending it altogether. Erika's two lovers couldn't have been more different: the lanky androgynous young waif bent on self-destruction and the matronly, gregarious thespian squeezing the most out of life.

Therese Giehse was a truly great performer, and was later to become famous for her work with Bertolt Brecht, particularly in the title role of *Mother Courage*. Marianne Breslauer, a close friend of Therese, recalled her dazzling transformation on the stage:

> She was a fabulous person. I must say she impressed me like nobody else because she was, to be quite honest, a more or less unattractive, fat woman of Bavaria, but she was a genius. And when she came to the stage, you couldn't resist her anymore. . . .

About a year before Hitler came to power, when Therese Giehse was starring nightly in a production at the Munich Kammerspiele, Klaus happened to stop in to the nearby Carlton Tea Room in downtown Munich. There he caught sight of Hitler and his cronies eating an enormous pile of strawberry tarts. Klaus too had a fondness for strawberry tarts, and had been about to order one, until the repulsive sight of Hitler turned him off them for good. Ironically, Klaus chose the cozy tea room because the café opposite it was packed with S.A. henchmen.

Taking a seat a few feet away from Hitler, Klaus watched him with cold curiosity. He wondered what Hitler's fascination could possibly be for so many people, while at the same time wracking his brain for whom he reminded Klaus of, other than a gluttonous rat. Klaus studied his hideous face and suddenly flashed on the resemblance he had been seeking:

Hitler looked virtually identical to a sex murderer named Haarmann, a serial killer in Hanover who had lured forty or fifty teenage boys to their defilement and death, and whose trial and execution in the mid-1920s caused a sensation. Considering that Haarmann's face had been front-page news all over Germany when he was finally caught, the rising popularity of his "identical twin" was all the more baffling.

All of a sudden Klaus overheard someone at the next table mention his dear friend Therese and her current production. Klaus stopped musing on the duplicity of human nature and started eavesdropping in earnest. "I rather like Frau Giehse," he heard Hitler announce. According to Klaus, Hitler spoke "with a weird sort of politeness, very much as if a madman tried to behave in a nice, civilized way, just to fool his guardians." One of Hitler's accomplices protested that Giehse was ever so slightly Jewish; she probably had a drop or two of Jewish blood. At this Klaus laughed uneasily to himself: Therese was entirely Jewish, and proud of it, as well as a passionate anti-Fascist. But Hitler was quick to dismiss the charge as vicious gossip. "After all," he barked, "I know the difference between a German artist and a Semitic clown."

Klaus was grappling intellectually with the threat of Fascism as early as 1927, when he wrote "Today and Tomorrow: On the Situation of Young European Intellectuals," an essay against nationalism and in support of pan-Europeanism. In it he warned that high-minded ideal-ism is not always what motivates the radicalism of youth; many of his generation were promoting barbarism and retrogression with a passion and commitment that should have been put to a better cause. Aside from Ricki Hallgarten, whose outbursts were fleeting and heard only by his immediate friends, Klaus was the only one of his circle—indeed he was one of the few of his entire generation—to recognize the growing Nazi threat. Erika considered him to be something of a political visionary. But Klaus had self-doubts about whether he had the right to pose as the progressive, anti-Fascist voice of his generation. After all, what was he actually doing to further the cause? He never attended a political meet-ing. He never joined a liberal or anti-Fascist organization. Merely writing about the plight of democracy did not seem to contribute all that much to its defense.

Although Klaus loathed the Nazis with his entire being, his eternal optimism kept him from registering the magnitude of the danger. For too long, Klaus viewed Hitler merely as the "gluttonous rat" he observed in the tea room, someone who would never rule Germany; certainly he could not believe the Nazis would sweep his country like an epidemic with no antidote. Years later, Klaus berated himself for this blind spot: "Was there no bloody aura around [Hitler's] head to warn me? No writing on the wall of the Carlton Tea Room? . . . It's not Hitler who is mysterious . . . but the Germans are. My mistake is not that I underrated Adolf Schicklgruber but that I overrated the Germans." Klaus's unwarranted faith in humanity would often lead to deep disappointment, but he never abandoned that faith.

Despite his optimism, Klaus had an uncanny premonition about exile. He ended his 1927 essay with a prophetic statement, although he was slightly off on his dates:

> We must not fall into a fashionable Fascism, in which somehow aestheticism becomes the *dernier cri!* Does 1930 belong to the military dictatorship? Good, then we will live that time in exile—by 1935, this much is certain, presence of mind must be regained.

The headline of September 14, 1930, "National Socialists gain 6 million votes, increase from 12 to 107 seats in Parliament," was a shock, much worse than even the most committed pessimists had predicted. Receiving 18.3 percent of the vote, the Nazis were now the second largest party in Parliament. Still the news did not rally the opposition; it was met, even among Klaus and Erika's own circle, with what Klaus described as defeatism and uncertainty.

Erika did not comment on the landslide victory until several years later. Looking back, she didn't blame the swelling numbers of deluded Nazi supporters, seeking redress for their personal grievances, for the Nazi Party's parliamentary victories; rather she charged the more mainstream electorate, including herself, with careless liberalism, skeptical individualism, and gullible pacifism. The good-intentioned people of Germany displayed "short-sighted egotism, lack of imagination and insight into the psychology of the enemy, false love of peace, lack of moral feeling, lack of voluntary discipline, lack of responsibility for the whole, a crippling mixture of skepticism and vague gullibility and a lack of spirit"—all these personal failings on a collective scale were responsible for digging the grave of democratic Germany.

The elder statesmen of the Mann family were already unpopular with the Nazis well before they came to power. For years Heinrich tried desperately to reconcile the divisions among the Left and bring together a People's Front against Hitler, although by 1931 he already knew in his heart that the Republic was doomed, that such an anti-Fascist coalition would never materialize. He kept working doggedly for it nonetheless, even after the appointment of Hitler.

Although generally much less outspoken and more conservative than his older brother, Thomas also came under attack when he tried to deliver his celebrated "Address to the Germans" at one of Germany's largest concert halls, the Beethoven Hall in Berlin, one month after the upsetting 1930 election results. During his speech he appealed to civilized Germans of all political inclinations to unite against the rising danger of National Socialism—only to be interrupted by a mob of Nazis who had packed the balcony. The mob was led by Arnolt Bronnen, a playwright and close friend of Bertolt Brecht who had wavered between the Nazis and the Communists throughout the twenties until the Nazi appeal finally held greater sway. Mr. Bronnen's membership in their club had been temporarily in jeopardy when a rumor circulated accusing him of being a Jew whose real name was Bronner. Bronnen, born Bronner, rescued his reputation at his mother's expense. As Klaus tells it,

> The ingenious son publicly accused his late mother (a pure Aryan) of having cheated the late Mr. Bronner with an unknown gentleman of guaranteed non-Jewish blood. Who gave a damn whether Frau Bronner was faithful to the Jew who happened to be her husband. . . . Nobody cared about the disgrace of one anonymous woman—her ambitious son less than anybody else. Having slandered his mother, he was entitled again to speak—or rather, to shout—as the guardian and representative of the national honor.

Bronnen and his cronies succeeded in creating a considerable disturbance in the crowded hall. Thomas tried to carry on with his speech but was inaudible over the hecklers. From the audience, Bronnen charged Mann with being a liar, a traitor, and an enemy of the people. Thomas cut his speech short and was smuggled out of Beethoven Hall. As luck would have it, his good friend and neighbor, the conductor Bruno Walter, was conducting that autumn 1930 season in the neighboring Philharmonic Hall, and had become familiar with its private passageways and catacombs. He escorted Thomas through an anteroom into Philharmonic Hall and out the back where, conveniently, his car was parked.

Although Erika had been in the audience for this humiliation, and was proud of her father's attempts to persevere in the face of it, she was the one family member to remain resolutely apolitical. She felt that acting, not politics, was her business—and "people should mind their own business." Once the shock waves of the 1929 Wall Street crash reached Europe and unleashed a worldwide Depression, even Erika could not fail to contemplate on occasion the growing unemployment and poverty, and their accompanying social problems in Germany. The economic crisis was exploited to enormous advantage by the Nazis, who blamed the country's woes on dishonest Jewish businessmen and the shame of the Versailles treaty. But neither the sudden upsurge of the Nazi Party nor the plight of others less fortunate succeeded in rousing Erika to action, not even to go barefoot or engage in other displays of solidarity with the poor, as she had done during World War I when one of her classmates lacked shoes. Now her single-minded ambition and her rising fame as a stage actress set her apart from the masses. Those moments of political reflection invariably ended with her deciding it was "none of our business."

Ironically, of the entire Mann family, it was young apolitical Erika who became, as Klaus would write, the Nazi's "pet enemy." She may well have remained completely indifferent, had the Nazis not forced her into taking a stand against them. When they did, everything changed for her, literally overnight.

A women's pacifist group in Munich invited Erika, in her capacity as a leading stage actress, to read a poem at their public meeting on January 13, 1932. That morning she was lying in bed with a high fever, and the family doctor paid her a house call, but by evening she insisted on getting up and fulfilling her commitment. Despite her lack of interest in political matters, she considered herself a pacifist: "Of course, I was a 'pacifist.' War was shameful; war was impossible—there would never be war again. I was convinced of that without doing anything on my part to work for peace." Erika knew many antiwar poems by heart and would occasionally recite them at poetry readings. So it was not all that unusual that she was listed on the program to read an antiwar poem by Victor Hugo.

Klaus and Erika made their way downtown to the Union Hotel. As Erika listened in the wings to the event's main speaker, the French pacifist Marcelle Capy, she found herself in agreement with all the woman said and yet at the same time strangely detached. She certainly never thought that the great questions of world peace and democracy being raised by Madame Capy only a few yards away were her personal problem or responsibility. From behind the curtain she looked out on the audience, and saw that the great hall was filled to capacity. It seemed as though the audience consisted mostly of middle-aged women. But she also recognized "'intellectuals' with horn-rimmed glasses, the young people of the Youth Movement in frocks and sandals, and, in smaller number, representatives of the 'progressive students.'" After Marcelle Capy's speech, logical, sincere, and intelligent as it was, the audience merely applauded politely. Erika distinctly felt that they too weren't particularly "uplifted by her message even at the end."

Finally, Erika's own name was announced. She walked onto the stage and began to recite the poem. Her voice sounded confident and convincing as she delivered the lines. Therefore she was somewhat surprised to perceive growing restlessness among the audience.

Erika raised her voice and continued, applying a more militant tone to the pacifist lines of the poem, lines which proclaimed, rather inoffensively, that war is unworthy of humanity. At that, a few youngsters in the gallery booed at her. From the orchestra, women hissed back at them, demanding quiet. Greater noise came from outside; it seemed to be a dispute between the ushers and a group demanding admittance. Erika, disturbed by all the activity, reflected on her father's dignity in the face of similar behavior and kept on reciting nonetheless.

Suddenly the doors flew open. As Erika recalled it, "Thirty or forty young men in brown shirts of the National Socialist Storm Troops rushed into the hall. . . . One of the brownshirted lads had come close to the stage. To this day I can still see his face distorted by hate, with the narrow forehead upon which fell a greasy lock of blond hair."

The young man took over Erika's platform. "Do you hear that?" he asked the audience. "Did you hear how she insulted our glorious fighters? Our soldiers are 'criminals,' she said, and 'it is a shame to die for the fatherland.'" He turned his attention back to Erika, and started screaming at her: "You are a criminal, yourself! Jewish traitress! International agitator!"

Erika appealed to logic. She hadn't insulted the soldiers; she wasn't even the author of the poem. But her arguments were useless and the commotion in the audience swelled out of control. Hand-to-hand fighting broke out in the gallery. Six storm troopers pulled a young man in glasses, ostensibly a Jewish intellectual, out of his seat and beat him to a pulp on no provocation.

As Erika described it, "In the hall, everything became a mad scramble. The Storm Troopers attacked the audience with their chairs, shouting themselves into paroxysms of anger and fury. Their numbers seemed to grow. Part of our audience took sides with the attackers whose conviction they could not possibly have shared. They were simply infected with the mass madness. Women fled, crying. . . . The chairman shouted 'Police, police!' But there were no police around."

Erika's dramatic account of the evening understates the extent to which she personally was at risk. It seemed to Klaus that the storm troopers brandishing clubs and guns were headed straight toward her through the crowded room. In a feverish daze, Erika failed to perceive the danger she was in or move out of its line of fire, and "was literally almost murdered." The police arrived in the last possible moment and dispersed the crowd. Erika waited in the emptied hall until the streets were completely cleared. She was badly shaken, and felt "sick at the pit of my stomach."

Whether or not it was actually a life-threatening situation, this evening marked the turning point for Erika, personally and professionally, and its direct consequences for her were considerable. The next morning's headlines denounced her as an agitator, and the open-air theater where she was engaged for the upcoming summer season cancelled her contract. Very sorry, the manager said, but of course she would understand that she was now more a liability than an asset. The Nazi Party threatened to boycott all of their performances if she had a small role in even one of them.

Erika understood all too well. She first turned to the actors' union, confident that they would back her up. But its president, a personal friend of hers, made it clear that they, too, simply couldn't afford to: the actors' union did not want to do anything to upset the Nazis, in case they did manage to come to power. "You are an actress, aren't you? As long as you don't mix in politics, you have nothing to fear. Don't sue them, will you?"

Erika jumped at the suggestion and immediately sued the theater for damages. For good measure she also sued the Nazi newspaper, *Der Völkische Beobachter*, which called her a "flatfooted peace hyena" with "no human physiognomy." The judge reviewed several portraits of Erika and, after much indecision, finally ruled in Erika's favor, declaring her features legally "human." The successful lawsuit did nothing to reinstate her acting career. Soon after the verdict was delivered, according to Klaus, Goebbels personally "declared war against the Mann family."

The direct, personal experience of the attack shook Erika out of her complacency: "I realized that my experience had nothing to do with politics—it was more than politics. It touched at the very foundations of my—of our—of the existence of all." She now felt obligated to do something against the Nazi threat. But—what could she do? She was twenty-six years old, belonged to no organization and had no experience with social activism. So she called a meeting in her little room in the Hotel am Zoo in Berlin.* Erika invited a select group of six acquaintances representing different social groups and political ideologies: a Communist, a Social Democrat trade unionist, a pessimistic poet, a humanitarian Christian, an apolitical young gay man, and the moderately liberal son of a Jewish banker. She felt optimistic that this small group would find some common ground and help her decide on a course of action.

The room was impenetrable with cigarette smoke (she didn't open the windows for fear of the neighbors overhearing) when the meeting, after much argument, drew to a close. Erika duly considered the position of each friend and granted that each had made a certain amount of sense. Nonetheless, "despite different arguments, they all were agreed on one point: for the time being, nothing should be undertaken. It was unnecessary, inopportune, unpacifistic, unchristian, premature, or simply hopeless to undertake anything." Soon after this meeting took place, a dispirited Erika left Berlin for good, and returned to her family home in Munich.†

In March 1932, Hitler ran for president against the incumbent Paul von Hindenburg, an election that represented an ideological showdown pitting democracy against dictatorship, except that no one could get very excited about eighty-year-old Field Marshal Hindenburg. As Klaus put it,

> The would-be dictator represented everything we abominated, whereas his competitor . . . did the Marshal represent anything we were fond of? . . . But who would be so choosy, with Hitler almost in power? . . . So we accepted the cynical and reasonable slogan of the Social Democratic party: "Drink a schnapps—and vote for Hindenburg!" It was not just one schnapps we swallowed. After

*Erika described this event in her essay "Don't Make the Same Mistakes," but I have been unable to verify it or identify any of its participants. It sounds somewhat contrived and it is possible she made it up for rhetorical purposes.

†Erika recalled the fates of these six friends: the Social Democrat became a hounded refugee; the Christian was beaten to death; the poet committed suicide by jumping out of a window during the "Night of the Long Knives"; the Communist "converted" to the Nazi ideology after extensive torture in a concentration camp; he subsequently accepted a highly paid position under Hermann Göring. The young gay man became a bomber flyer for the Nazis, and later, still working for the Nazis, was admitted into the United States by way of a false passport stolen from a Jew. Aside from Erika, only the banker's son fared reasonably well—he wrote to her from Palestine, full of remorse and self-accusation.

having consumed quite a few of them, our minds were stimulated enough to fancy the obtuse general as a sturdy paladin of all republican virtues.

In a runoff election Hindenburg won 53 percent of the vote in contrast to Hitler's 36.8 percent. The Republic was granted a temporary stay of execution. But despite Hindenburg at the helm, the Reichstag elections six months later made the Nazis the majority party in Parliament, with 33.1 percent of the vote, far eclipsing the Social Democrats and everyone else. Even with two-thirds of the country opposing them, the Nazis were unstoppable now.

On the morning of January 30, 1933, Klaus boarded a train for Munich, never imagining he too wouldn't be returning to Berlin anytime soon. He had arranged to stop along the way in Leipzig, in order to meet with a theater director who was interested in staging one of Klaus's plays. But something seemed eerily wrong as Klaus arrived at the Leipzig railroad station. The director was waiting there but he looked pale, worried, and distracted; it was clear to Klaus that their meeting was not going to take place as scheduled. Cryptically, the director whispered the terrible news: "The old gentleman has appointed him." Old gentleman? Finally the baffled Klaus understood. That morning, while he dozed on the train, the aging (some say senile) President Hindenburg, in a gesture of appeasement, appointed Adolf Hitler as Reich Chancellor.

Wretched and confused, Klaus boarded the next train to his family home in Munich, where Erika had been living for the better part of the last year. Munich was about as far as one could get from Nazi headquarters in Berlin without leaving Germany altogether. The Gestapo had not yet replaced the conventional police in Munich and enthusiastic crowds could still, without fear of arrest, flock to see Erika Mann's popular anti-Nazi literary cabaret, *Die Pfeffermühle* (*The Peppermill*).

Erika's composer friend Magnus Henning had first proposed the idea of a cabaret to her in the winter of 1932, and Erika, out of work for the better part of a year following the poetry-reading incident, responded with the immediate enthusiasm that was characteristic of her effervescent personality. She rounded up a troupe of ten young actors from Munich, the most prominent of whom was Therese Giehse. The Magician came up with an ambiguous name, "The Peppermill"; "gay and harmless, it sounded," Erika explained. They seemed unable to find any songs whose lyrics weren't either completely meaningless, or if they had a po-

Erika and Klaus (*in foreground*) with friends in Munich, beginning of 1933. "This last month in Munich assumes in my recollection a savor of grim and feverish merriment. Everyone kept drinking and dancing . . . to forget the sinister reality" (Klaus Mann, *The Turning Point*).

litical edge, too grim and didactic, so Erika was forced to write them herself, something she had never done before, and had them quickly set to music. Klaus helped out by supplying a few of the numbers, but this was Erika's baby, or rather the joint custody of Erika and Therese, not a shared venture with Klaus. With Erika as master of ceremonies, the show opened to an overwhelming response on New Year's Day, 1933.

It is virtually impossible to translate the show's lyrics into English, so riddled are they with oblique attacks on the Nazi regime, hidden in innocent fairy tales and droll cabaret skits. The staging of the performance, however, underscored its political edge, and even with its coded text the audience was fully cognizant of the intended meaning. One number titled "The Morale Singer," sang by Therese Giehse in traditional Bavarian costume, contrasts the female job of social cheerleader with a woman's escalating private doubts. It goes something like this:

Maidens in uniforms
God, they're sweet
Yes, and this paradise, my fatherland

No, my hunting hat
disturbs me too much . . .
Forgiveness, forgiveness I just can't.

Erika had to acknowledge that the show's initial success was primarily due to the eminence of some of the actors—notably herself and Therese Giehse—rather than to its political message. "Those among our spectators who were moved—knowingly—by the urgency of our appeal, were very much in the minority. Yet I incline to think that some of our success rested upon the heartfelt concern which hid behind our jests."

Erika Mann: writer, director, lead actor, and master of ceremonies for *The Peppermill*.

Erika and Klaus, circa 1932. (Photo courtesy of Rowohlt Verlag Archiv, Reinbek bei Hamburg.)

Erika's intimate relationship with Therese Giehse broadened into a fruitful creative partnership; she was at a strong point both personally and professionally. Klaus felt that his sister's success had the unintended consequence of taking her away from him. At the time he wrote, "This life, which actually should only be shared with my sister Erika; something denied to us. . . ." Klaus later reflected that in the two years prior to exile, he was more despondent and more alienated "in that estranged country of mine" than at any other point in his life. In June 1932 he had written in his diary that he "thought about suicide," but by February 1933 he expressed the urge in more desperate terms: "In the mornings, nothing but the wish to die. When I calculate what I have to lose, it seems negligible. No chance of a really happy relationship. Probably no chance of literary fame in the near future. . . . Death *can* only be regarded as deliverance." He noted that only his ties to Erika and his mother were keeping him from death's embrace.

Annemarie Schwarzenbach was also in poor condition. She and Klaus received a steady supply of morphine from their mutual friend Thea (Mopsa) Sternheim, who had developed a serious drug addiction herself. Annemarie wrote to Erika from Berlin a few days after *The Peppermill* premiere in January, spelling out her dependency on both the drugs and the siblings:

> Concerning this (the sins), I am not contemplating them seriously or being tempted by them anymore. Because, E. dearest, I will not, cannot and do not want to carry on in this ruinous yuletide mode. Even my character is not strong enough to be allowed to use it without endangering myself. And with you and Klausy I always felt strong enough (to use morphine). I wouldn't want to spoil that for myself. In Berlin and wherever else, I will not do otherwise unless you are there. I hope I can stick to this.

An odd promise—to stay away from morphine unless Erika and Klaus were nearby—and of course she couldn't stick to it. Very quickly she reached the stage where, she admitted to Thomas Mann, she hadn't "the slightest enjoyment from the drug, but only feels impossibly bad if she does *not* take it." Thomas didn't talk to his son about Klaus's own addiction, but did write about it dispassionately in his diary. The first entry merely states, "I hear he takes morphine, though in moderation." Six months later, another diary entry: "Klaus unwell, morphine reaction. Dr. Stahel saw him, but naturally he could only deal with the deprivation symptoms by giving him a shot. Klaus believes he is capable of maintaining control over the drug, achieving a balance between voluntary withdrawal and occasional use. . . . He does not have a desire to stop using it altogether." The Magician seems not to have noticed that for Klaus, voluntary withdrawal and occasional use were no longer options.

Like Annemarie, still hopelessly in love with Erika, Klaus was also unlucky at love—except that he didn't think it was down to luck at all, but rather was "my fault, my failure." He kept choosing men who could not reciprocate, either because they were heterosexual or, like his new Finnish friend Hans Aminoff, they were desperately trying to be.

Klaus noted that for several months he "had only had sex for cash; I had to pay. Sailors, masseurs, hustlers." The other relationships, where he had hoped for something more, all came to nothing. Hans Aminoff forced himself to enter into marriage and parenthood, even though he knew they weren't right for him; Klaus was despondent over it: "Worse is the shadow, the disappointment about Hans is casting over everything . . .— that's how it is. . . ." (Four years later, when Klaus ran into Hans and a young boyfriend in a gay bar in Amsterdam, Klaus felt hurt and envious; he still had lingering feelings for Hans.)

Reflecting on the problem of his attraction to what he called "normal"— i.e., heterosexual—men, he wrote in his diary: "I seldom have a response to gays, I never really have; but to live with those who are basically normal is impossible in the long run." He had short-lived affairs with young men who intellectually were no match for Klaus, but "their faces seemed so innocent, and sometimes they were handsome." One working-class boy, Willi L., was good-natured and naïve, his ignorance as boundless as his sexual energy. He had no job, no home, no ambition, and most of all nothing to believe in. Klaus enjoyed asking him taunting questions: "You know, of course, that Johann Wolfgang von Goethe was a mighty general fighting the Chinese, in the war of 1870?" Willi would shrug it off: "Okay, so what?" Klaus was more saddened than surprised to see him one day, looking more handsome than ever, clothed in the black uniform of the elite Nazi storm troopers. Klaus realized with a jolt that this innocent kid wasn't immune, indeed no one was, "certainly not a derelict youth who possesses nothing to counterbalance the swindle. The Devil got his soul because the angels didn't bother to catch it."

The affair ended casually but abruptly. "Good-bye then, Willi," Klaus muttered. And Willi responded, "Look after yourself. And if you ever need an influential friend in the party—well, you know where to reach me."

After the fiasco with Hans Aminoff and the disappointment with Willi L., Klaus pursued a hopeless infatuation with a striking performer in *The Peppermill*'s troupe, Hans Sklenka, and dreamt that his father had a secret gay relationship with one of *The Peppermill*'s musicians.

The Peppermill ran for the first two months of 1933 in the cozy little Bonbonniere, more a pub than a theater, situated next door to the local Nazi Party headquarters in the Hofbräuhaus. The response to the show was so favorable that Erika found a more spacious theater in the Bavarian district of Schwabing that could better accommodate the packed audiences. This theater, called "Serenissimus" (Serenity), wouldn't be ready for a couple of weeks, however, so some of the troupe headed off for a short break in the Swiss Alps.

While they were away, the Reichstag, the nation's Parliament, went up in flames, and with it the country's remaining civil rights. Instigated, most historians now believe, by a special SS unit, at the time the fire was blamed on the Communists. A slow-witted Dutch vagrant, supposedly acting in their employ, was tried and executed. It was an audacious stroke of genius for the Nazis: the fire both destroyed the seat and symbol of the constitutional government and offered a perfect excuse to clamp down immediately on all opposition. The building was still smoldering the next morning, February 28, 1933, when the commandant of the Prussian police, Hermann Göring, instructed his "men" to shoot suspected Communists and Socialists on sight. His rogue band of teenage boys, suddenly given official sanction, went on a shooting spree. At noon, President Hindenburg, convinced by the fire that a Communist revolution was on its way, signed the historic diktat which gave the new regime unlimited emergency powers, including the right to arrest all suspected dissenters and imprison them in a concentration camp, without arraignment, right of trial, or chance of parole.

Skiing in the Alps, Erika had a premonition that their days in Germany were numbered. On March 10, when she and Klaus returned to Munich ready to resume rehearsals, the atmosphere in the city had changed drastically. Only one day before, the Nazis had taken over the state parliament in Bavaria—previously a democratic stronghold—and started rounding up political opponents.

The siblings were met at the Munich train station by Hans, the family chauffeur, who behaved rather strangely as he warned them that they were in danger. He told them they should make plans to leave Germany again, right away. On the short drive home, Erika witnessed people being arrested on the streets and felt certain she would soon be among them. She realized it would be suicidal to reopen an anti-Fascist show now, even if the manager of the new theater was a Nazi man himself and had offered to put two "brown shirts" at the door to protect them. Obviously he didn't quite register the meaning behind the satire, or he simply cared more for the guaranteed box office profits than for whatever transpired on stage.

Several years later, Erika wrote a book, *The Lights Go Down*, about the strange quality of life in Germany during the early days of the Nazi regime. After collecting literally hundreds of firsthand experiences, she chose ten stories which she felt were representative of what life was like under the Nazis for "ordinary people"—people who were neither exceptionally powerful nor exceptionally heroic, but just wanted to go about their daily lives. Her original idea was to write "Middletown: A Nazi Version," borrowing from the "small-town America" literature of Sherwood Anderson, Sinclair Lewis, and Thornton Wilder. Although she peoples them with stock figures at times bordering on stereotype, the stories in *The Lights Go Down* are examples of Erika's best writing, and reveal her talent as an author to apply measured storytelling techniques to her urgent moral agenda.

In the first story, "The City," a line drawing of the town center and a caption underneath it establish the setting; the caption reads: "Life was going on in our city. The old market place, with its painted houses grouped around the usual equestrian statue, hadn't changed for centuries; to the casual visitor it was a scene of peaceful enchantment." The casual visitor of her story, an unnamed American, strolls into the city one night and finds it beautiful and serene; he thinks he'll stay awhile. But soon he encounters the local townspeople, whose baffling, even bizarre behavior betrays his first impression. Incredible though it seems, they all genuinely believe that the local manufacturing plant is making shiny "peace angels" instead of munitions. Two young men dressed as storm troopers berate him for wandering outside instead of listening to Hitler's loudspeaker address; they practically have him slated for a concentration camp before they realize he is a visitor. He wanders into a bar and finds people mouthing slogans; he is unsure as to whether the statements are sincere, ironic, or some sort of code. The bartender announces that "the world belongs now to the master race," while his customer, an older woman, tells the stranger, "If you're making any kind of report, I'm one hundred percent behind the Führer." The story ends with the man deciding to cut short his stay in this weird place. He falls asleep in his hotel room and dreams of "an enchanting mountain village, tiny as a child's toy, but a gigantic hand arose and covered it."

The saddest story in the collection is called "Last Journey." In it a woman, Frau Murks, and her eighteen-year-old son Friedel live in Hamburg, while another son, Max, her favorite, is off at sea in the German navy. Friedel works on what he facetiously calls "The Garbage Front"—collecting wastepaper from the neighbors and policing how much paper they use or waste. His mother craves a taste of coffee or chocolate but "found nothing odd in the fact that in the midst of peace there were no 'peacetime' goods obtainable anywhere in Germany." She receives a postcard from the son embarking for America, and she writes back asking him to bring her some roasted coffee as a special treat. As Christmas approaches she dreams of him visiting her and bringing the coffee, but on Christmas Eve another man shows up at the door instead. His name is Paul, and he is Max's closest friend. He has come with the terrible news that Max attended some union meeting in New York, was reported on by the ship's cook, and was subsequently shot, killed, and thrown overboard by four Nazi storm troopers. The mother can't absorb this news; she goes into a state of shock. "There was something ghastly and unnatural in the silence and immobility which had come over Frau Murks since she first saw the stranger. One might have thought she was in a faint, were it not that she sat so upright, with wide-open eyes." Only at the sight of the roasted coffee Paul has brought her is there a flicker in her eyes and a whimper from her throat: "'Thank you, Max,' said the mother, and again the mad light glimmered in her eyes. 'Thank you, my big boy.'" At this point Paul becomes Max for her; she lurches into insanity, where she is joyfully reunited with "her son."

A carefully researched and referenced document based on ten allegedly true individual experiences, *The Lights Go Down* reads like an odd collection of short stories bordering on science fiction—so much so that Erika felt compelled to reiterate its factual basis in the book's epilogue. Titled "The Facts," the epilogue insists that "all of the stories, tragedies, persons, events, developments . . . *are* facts; nothing has been invented, everything has actually happened and there is not a single incident which has not been brought to the attention of the author either by those who experienced it themselves, or else by the most trustworthy witnesses."

One person who could easily have been a bizarre character in Erika's book was the family chauffeur, Hans. Klaus and Erika later discovered why Hans was behaving peculiarly when he saw them for the last time: it turns out he

> had been a Nazi spy throughout the four or five years he lived with us—a stool pigeon appointed by the Braun Haus to report on all goings on in our family. But this time he had failed in his duty, out of sympathy, I suppose. For he knew what would happen to us if he informed his Nazi employers of our arrival in town.

Erika and Klaus's parents were relaxing at that moment in Arosa, Switzerland, following a series of lectures Thomas Mann had given in Amsterdam, Brussels, and Paris on the subject of Richard Wagner, to commemorate the fiftieth anniversary of the composer's death. Erika and

Klaus instantly decided that if Munich was no longer safe for themselves, it could not be safe for their parents either, and telephoned them in Arosa to insist they not return. It was a bizarre conversation, and one that none of them would ever forget although each would remember it differently. Katia was sure it was she who had called her children and asked them whether they advised staying away; she had already received alarming reports from her brother-in-law Heinrich, who had slipped out of Germany with only a small withdrawal of cash, and surprised them one late February night in Paris, where Thomas had just finished a lecture.

According to Erika's version, Thomas and Katia were completely unprepared for the news. Erika tried to argue that the weather was bad in Munich, that it would be far better to stay put in Switzerland. Unfortunately, the Magician argued, the weather was also bad, probably even worse, in Arosa. Then Klaus chimed in: "We are having spring cleaning and the house is in a terrible mess." It was an expensive phone call by the time their meaning was made clear.

On March 12, 1933, the Nazi flag became compulsory decoration for the entire country. The very next morning, as Swastikas flew ferociously over their beloved Munich—looking, according to Erika, like a skin disease on her hometown's beautiful face—the siblings left Germany once more. Klaus recalled,

> My luggage consisted of two suitcases, a typewriter, a topcoat, and a bunch of magazines and books. I had packed a few things, as though it were just for another journey. In fact, I hardly expected to stay away for more than a couple of months. Not that I ever considered returning to a Germany dominated by Hitler—certainly not. But I took it for granted that the Nazi farce wouldn't last.

For the rest of their lives, Erika and Klaus would insist that their departure from Germany was voluntary, that it was not due to their Jewish lineage on their mother's side, nor to their leftist political leanings, which might have been forgiven by the Nazis as it was in so many other cases. Rather it was a matter of avoiding suffocation: "We could not breathe the air in Nazi Germany. . . . You might as well suggest that a reasonable man ought to adapt himself to syphilis, or that he should overcome his prejudice against poison." Klaus assumed that, "according to the fantastic racial arithmetic adhered to by the Nazis," he and Erika would be considered "Aryans." Yet, according to released Gestapo documents, the Nazi regime's so-called literature office, which far more resembled the secret

Erika and Klaus shortly before exile.

police than any cultural concern, and which tracked Klaus's movements during his time in exile, referred to him, obviously without his knowledge, as "the half-Jew."

Klaus claimed he would be classified "Aryan" by the Nazis in order to emphasize that he went into exile out of personal conviction; it was not an attempt to disown his Jewish ancestry. He had been raised a secular Protestant, had a lifelong attraction to Catholic mysticism, and cherished the Jewish branch of his family tree. He once wrote that "there is nothing in my life for which I am more thankful than for the drop of Jewish blood we have in our veins." Without it, "we would probably have been rather boring, bloodless creatures. Naturally even as we have turned out, we all have our horrible faults. But at least we are not so dreadfully boring." Erika on the other hand never acknowledged in any way the fact that she was half-Jewish (although both sides of her maternal lineage had converted to Christianity long before her birth). "I was neither Jew nor Communist," she insisted.

Despite his definitive claims to being classified "Aryan," Klaus could not have been so confident of his grasp of Nazi arithmetic. His doubts surfaced in his dreams, in which his mother separated from his father in order "to spare him [Thomas] the race-disgrace." Katia married an old Jewish man in this dream and went with him to America, where the man decided—Klaus's unyielding temptation—to take his life with sleeping pills.

When they later published accounts of their rapid escape from Germany, Erika and Klaus often gave the impression that they left together, to visit their parents in Arosa. A letter written by Thomas the morning of Erika's arrival indicates that in fact he was expecting them both. Instead, Erika had driven her two-seater Ford across the border by herself, in order to explain the situation to their parents and bring them some items from the house. When she arrived, Thomas didn't comment in his diary on the absence of Klaus; he simply wrote that it was "no mere accident but rather one of those 'blessings' of my life" that it was his two most beloved children, Erika and Elisabeth, who were by his side. (Elisabeth, now fifteen, had joined her parents earlier in the month for a skiing vacation.) Klaus only makes a brief appearance in the Magician's diary two weeks later, with the phrase "annoyed with Klaus."

Rather than go to his parents in Arosa, Klaus took the overnight train to Paris, a city he worshiped like a lovesick admirer. He was drawn to the Parisian literary world, particularly the male homosexual writers René Crevel, André Gide, and Jean Cocteau. He also befriended the lesbian circle known as "the women of the Left Bank." He describes in his diary visiting booksellers Sylvia Beach and Adrienne Monnier, the "two Joyce-ladies" (the first publishers of James Joyce's *Ulysses*), in their apartment one evening. These first steps in their life of exile mark the moment when Erika's and Klaus's paths began to diverge, the beginning of a faint crevice in their steadfast relationship. The very day he arrived in Paris, Klaus wrote in his diary, "Feeling of loneliness always, whenever SHE isn't there."

Arriving in Arosa, Erika was faced with the formidable task of preparing her parents for the possibility of losing everything that was left behind. Therese Giehse followed Erika into exile two days later (to the great dismay of the Munich Kammerspiele, where she was then starring nightly to sold-out shows), and arrived in Arosa full of horror stories about people back home. She tried to impress upon Erika's parents the dangers to which they would be exposed if they were to return to Munich.

Thomas and Katia only had with them what they had taken for Thomas's lecture tour and a short vacation in the Alps, supplemented by a suitcase of clothes that Erika had brought along for them in her car. A section of the manuscript Thomas was working on, *Joseph and His Brothers*, was still sitting on his desk in his study at home. Erika took it upon herself to return to Germany one last time, in mid-April 1933, in order to smuggle the handwritten manuscript out of the country. Wearing dark glasses (which only made her more conspicuous), she arrived in Munich to find a Nazi celebration in full swing in the center of town. She hid at the home of some friends and made her way at night to Poschinger Street. Having sneaked into the house, she kept the lights off, located the manuscript, wrapped it in newspaper, and hid it among the tools under the seat of her Ford. In a Bavarian accent she chatted amicably with the border guards, and arrived safely back in Arosa the next day.

Thomas could not bear to leave behind the grand family home filled with all of his treasured possessions, including his gramophone and his extensive library. More than anything else he feared the discovery of his diaries, stashed in a key-safe in his study, which depicted among other things his infatuation with a long line of adolescent boys, including his own son. It is not clear why his utterly trustworthy daughter Erika wasn't instructed to grab these as well, but probably her clandestine rescue mission was too early in the Mann family exile for Thomas to realize that he wouldn't be returning any time soon. In fact such a realization wouldn't dawn for quite some time. That the diaries were locked in a safe was reassuring at first, but by the end of the month he was riddled with anxiety about their fate. "My fears now revolve first and foremost almost exclusively around this threat to my life's secrets. They are deeply serious. The consequences could be terrible, even fatal." Even sleeping pills couldn't help his deep anxiety, which Katia, without being told the diaries' contents, seemed to understand.

This time the middle child, Golo, then a student of history at Heidelberg University, was instructed to return to the family home in Munich. Thomas sent him the key to the safe and warned him, "I count on your discretion not to read [the diaries] yourself." Upon arrival, his car was stolen although it was immediately returned—completely stripped. Fortunately he had already managed to ship out a suitcase containing the troublesome diaries. He assumed they were safe, but the suitcase mysteriously disappeared as well and wouldn't reach its destination for several weeks. Thomas had ghastly nightmares of the Gestapo agents reading his diaries, and imagined that "they'll publish extracts in *Der Völkische*

Beobachter, they'll ruin everything and me too." The German border police, it turned out, did deliberately hold up the delivery, but they were only interested in the financial papers Golo had included, and removed some of them for their own files. Worn out with nervous tension, Thomas was finally reunited with his "life's secrets" when the suitcase was delivered by the rail freight service at the end of May.

Erika and Therese, virtually inseparable from the moment of exile onwards, had already left Erika's unsettled parents in Arosa and driven to Zurich, where the troupe of *The Peppermill* had started reassembling. They made plans to reopen *The Peppermill* in about six months, thereby launching its new life as a German cabaret in exile. It needed some drastic rewriting; its cryptic political message could be decoded and made explicit now that they were outside of Germany—or so Erika thought. For one skit she wrote,

> Colorful the web of lies
> That holds our great Reich firm entwined.
> Lie just once, you're not believed.
> Lie all the time, you cannot fail.

The new *Peppermill* in exile was "a very risky undertaking," Erika reflected years later. She couldn't possibly have imagined at the time how risky.

CHAPTER 4

PATHETIC SYMPHONY

1,200th hotel room, I greet you.
I greet my home of the past half hour . . .
My home for 2, 3, or 14 days.
Will you be kind to me?
Will you allow me to rest?

WHILE STILL LIVING in Germany, Klaus wrote this poem forecasting precisely the nomadic life awaiting him in exile. When he and Erika left Munich on March 13, 1933, they didn't choose a destination, settle down, and try to establish a new home and a new life for themselves. It was not in the personality of either of them to even consider such an obvious course of action. Instead they embarked on the oxymoronic life of the "permanent transient" and carried the idea of home around with them. Home meant, and could only ever mean, their family home in Munich, the locus of their idyllic childhood, and now that it was off-limits to them indefinitely, their idea of home became infused with tangled feelings of absence, displacement, nostalgia, alienation, longing, and anger.

To Erika and Klaus, exile was compulsory whatever the personal cost, in order to avoid suffocation in Nazi Germany. To their friends, however, their decision to go into exile seemed like a choice—and the wrong choice at that. Klaus read a letter sent to him by his old friend W. E. Süs-kind, who pleaded passionately for Klaus's return:

> Come back! Better today than tomorrow! If it were dishonorable to be in Germany now, do you think I would stay? Don't you know me—don't you trust me anymore?

Klaus answered him: "I shall not come back. I do not distrust you. I feel sorry for you. There are things which nobody can touch without polluting, indeed poisoning himself." His reply ended that friendship.

Without entertaining for one moment the idea of returning, Klaus must still have received such letters with mixed emotions. The reality of exile—loneliness, homesickness, immigration problems, poverty, struggles with learning new languages—fell far short of the romantic idea of exile, a time-honored fate for writers throughout history.

For almost four years Klaus drifted around Europe alone, without an itinerary. At any time he might be spotted in Paris, Amsterdam, Cannes, Budapest, Prague, Sanary-sur-Mer, Mallorca, Zandvoort, Zurich, Bern, Salzburg, or Vienna, always with a cigarette in one hand and a pen in the other. He wrote in his diary, "All the suitcases are too small. Heaps of collected papers. Don't know, where to. Feeling of homelessness . . . Six suitcases, and still leaving things behind. Oh, Poschinger Street!" In place of that grand family villa, Klaus now lived in an endless succession of hotel rooms, all of which seemed to have the same furniture, reading lamp, and worn carpet. As soon as he checked in, he would unpack his small pile of favorite photographs and display them to quell his loneliness—photos of Erika, his mother, Katia, Miro, Ricki Hallgarten, and André Gide. Klaus missed his friends and family, but he was also pining for someone with whom to fall in love. In July 1933, Klaus wrote in his diary,

> Thought about how sad I am to be alone. . . . But Erika has Theres[e], [she] had Pamela. By the rules of our bond, I too should be permitted to seek relationships elsewhere. I reflect on all the failed or half-failed attempts. . . .

In his more self-pitying moments, he saw himself as "an uprooted vagabond whose name has been forgotten in the country from which he comes." Traitor that he now was considered to be, his name was hardly forgotten in Germany, but the vagabond part of his lament was dead right: the many letters Erika wrote to him during those early exile years featured a different address on virtually every single envelope—or even several different addresses per envelope, as the letter would often have to be forwarded to catch up with its roving recipient.

How did Klaus survive? Next to Erika, his mother, Katia, was his most frequent correspondent, and his letters to her never failed to ask for money. In June 1933 Thomas and Katia settled temporarily in the south of France, in Sanary-sur-Mer in a large house Erika and Klaus found for them. In October Klaus wrote, "Hope to receive November money regularly—I am not, like my sister, able to manage without it, on the contrary—alas." In subsequent letters he would often itemize his financial needs: an outstanding dentist bill, a new pair of shoes, a typewriter ribbon. His expensive drug habit was never mentioned, although his mother was certainly aware of it.

It was not that he was slothful—on the contrary, he was extremely industrious. Sybille Bedford, who as a teenager befriended Erika and Klaus in the south of France, and who would later become one of England's most prominent memoirists, claimed he was more active against Fascism in 1933 than some European countries. But the work was simply not lucrative: writing and editing. Just two months into exile he started hatching the idea for an ambitious project, called *Die Sammlung* (The Collection), the very first of many German-language literary journals for émigrés to crop up during the thirties. He brought to it a strong sense of individual responsibility and commitment, such as he had not demonstrated previously. The last vestiges of the intellectual pranks and frivolities that had marked his literary beginnings a decade earlier now vanished for good. Klaus wrote poignantly about the obligation he felt, as an anti-Fascist German writer, to do whatever he personally could against the Nazis:

> Neither [personal] pleasure nor pain ever makes me forget the inexorable gravity of the situation and the weight of my responsibility. Every anti-Fascist German writer must exert his whole strength today to the very utmost, and I know that, for particular reasons, I am under an especially great obligation.

Although Klaus assumed this obligation virtually as a sacred calling, and devoted himself and his writing unstintingly to the anti-Fascist cause, the "particular reasons" for his especially great obligation were so agonizing to him that he could not help but bridle at the injustice of his own situation. He continued,

When the son of a great writer writes books of his own, many people shrug their shoulders. . . . Even in the rest of the world, the mixture of condescending patronage and hyper-criticism with which people usually approach the son of a great writer rather hinders than helps him. But he has to come to terms with it. Everyone has to come to terms with his own fate, and every fate has its complications.

With *Die Sammlung* Klaus was trying to make his own mark, independent of his father. The journal was intended to give voice to his own generation. Still, to garner the support he needed, he first turned to the more established authors of his father's circle. In May he wrote to Hermann Hesse:

There is the possibility for me to edit a magazine in Zurich together with the young Swiss poet Annemarie Schwarzenbach. . . . It should be a fortnightly literary journal, called "Die Sammlung." Naturally it must be oppositional in its basic attitude, but not about daily politics—that we must leave to others—; above all else we would like it to be a forum for the "European Youth"—so far as this entity still exists. . . .

Klaus ultimately decided to edit it alone, make it a monthly rather than biweekly, and base it in Amsterdam instead of Zurich. Annemarie Schwarzenbach did agree to subsidize the honoraria paid to its writers, a significant gesture on her part because, although far wealthier than Erika and Klaus, she was notoriously tightfisted (when the bill came in restaurants she could be counted on to say that she had forgotten her wallet). She complained that Klaus was willing to accept her financial contributions but refused her literary ones—although pieces from Annemarie did appear occasionally in its pages.

Klaus decided on Amsterdam because he found a publisher willing to take it on: Friedrich (Fritz) Landshoff, a German Jewish émigré whom Klaus had befriended a lifetime ago, in the heady days of Berlin in the twenties. Despite the conciliatory attitude of Holland toward Nazi Germany, Fritz Landshoff had managed to create a German-language division, called Querido Verlag, within a Dutch publishing house and devoted it to publishing those German books which were forbidden in the Third Reich. Consequently, Querido was one of few European outlets for important German authors banned in their homeland—until Landshoff was forced to flee the Nazis a second time, and moved to New York in 1940.

Querido not only published *Die Sammlung* for two years, but also published the many books Klaus wrote in the mid-thirties, despite there being little market for any of them. Klaus's deep friendship with the loyal and charming Fritz Landshoff served as a lifeline for Klaus during these endless dark days. Klaus lived for a while in the same modern brick hotel on Jan-Willem-Brouwer-Straat as Landshoff and their mutual friend Hermann Kesten, but the offices of Querido were the closest he came to having a real home anywhere in the world during the long years he spent wandering around Europe without a passport, an income (aside from the allowance from his mother), or his beloved sister. As Erika was preoccupied with *The Peppermill* and her relationship with Therese Giehse, Klaus depended heavily on this "brotherly friendship," as he called it, with Fritz.

Klaus put together an impressive editorial board for *Die Sammlung* consisting of Heinrich Mann, André Gide, and Aldous Huxley. The board members each wrote something for the journal, and future issues would include contributions from Albert Einstein, Bertolt Brecht, Jean Cocteau, Ernest Hemingway, René Crevel, and Boris Pasternak, among others. The journal quickly developed into a leading voice for German émigré writers and intellectuals, and even more quickly embroiled Klaus in a heated political and familial controversy.

Thomas Mann, along with several other prominent German authors living in exile, had agreed to have his name listed as a future contributor. But when the first issue arrived in his mailbox in September 1933, he was shocked to see that it featured scathing attacks on the Nazi regime by both Klaus and Heinrich Mann (what else did he expect of them?). Heinrich had written a provocative essay, "Moral Education through German Uplifting," and Klaus, in his editorial, explained why this literary journal would have to veer into the political realm:

> The true, valid German literature [i.e., German literature in exile] ... cannot remain silent before the degradation of its people and the outrage which is perpetrated upon itself. . . . A literary periodical is not a political one. . . . Nevertheless, today it will have a political mission. Its position must be unequivocal.

Thomas must have scowled reading these words. He felt tricked by his brother and his son: they led him to believe the journal would be

Klaus Mann with his publisher Fritz Landshoff.

relatively apolitical, and certainly would not take such a strident anti-Nazi stance.

At this time Thomas Mann was trying to maintain a precarious balance in his professional and personal life. He was living in exile (by default rather than by deliberate choice), yet privately he had moments of ambivalence regarding the Nazi program. As much as he abhorred its brutality and ignorance, he admitted in his diary, with some degree of shame, his approval of certain elements, especially concerning what he referred to as "the fuss over the Jews." In late March he objected to the systematic boycott of all Jewish-owned businesses yet found the boycott "idiotic" and "inconsistent" for not also targeting "the Jewish banks." Yet when it came to trying to transfer some of his money out of Germany into Switzerland, he entrusted the dangerous job to "the little Jew Tennenbaum." On April 10 he wrote in his diary, "But for all that, might not something deeply significant and revolutionary be taking place in Germany? The Jews: It is no calamity after all . . . that the domination of the legal system by the Jews has been ended. Secret, disquieting, persistent musings . . . I am beginning to suspect that in spite of everything this process is one of those that has two sides to them." By mid-April he started to see that intellectuals, Jewish or not, were treated with suspicion by the Nazi leaders, and this strengthened his resolve against the regime. He noted with alarm that "they are beginning to clamp down on intellectuals; not only the Jews." A fortnight later he wrote, "I could have a certain understanding for the rebellion against the Jewish element were it not that the Jewish spirit exercises a necessary control over the German element, the withdrawal of which is dangerous; left to themselves the Germans are so stupid as to lump people of my type in the same category and drive me out with the rest." In the final analysis, his opposition to the Nazi government was solidified by the regime's lack of respect for Thomas Mann.

Of course he never mentioned these thoughts even to his Jewish wife, who was eager for him to speak out against the Nazis even though it may have put her aging parents, still living in Germany, at risk. Katia was always far more astute than her husband when it came to political analysis, but her position on this subject was also determined by maternal considerations. Katia, much more than Thomas, was a strong advocate for her children—especially for wistful Klaus, her unmistakable favorite, who had never fully let go of her apron strings. Erika could fend for herself, but even so, to the highly perceptive Katia the widening rift between her eldest children and her husband must have been painful to watch.

If in the first few months of exile Thomas had wondered to himself whether there might be "something deeply significant and revolutionary" happening in his native country, ultimately he found the evidence against it too damning. In May 1933, still thinking he might be able to return to Germany in the foreseeable future, Thomas Mann wrote to his friend Albert Einstein,

> Basically I am much too good a German that the thought of a lasting exile wouldn't weigh very heavily on me, and the virtually unavoidable break with my country depresses and frightens me terribly. . . . That I would be forced into taking on such a role

must mean that something exceptionally wrong and evil had to happen, and, in my strongest belief, this "German Revolution" is completely wrong and evil.

Publicly Thomas Mann made no such statement. He tried to keep quiet and not make waves, in order that his books not be banned by the Nazis—he was still financially dependent on his sizable income from Germany.

This equivocal position was one his publishing house strongly encouraged, not without its own selfish motives. Fischer was a Jewish-owned publishing company in constant danger of being shut down. It had asked its émigré authors to, according to Thomas Mann's diary, "be exceptionally cautious; we are to keep absolutely mum lest trouble come to the firm." Fischer had passed hands five years previously from the ingenious founder, Samuel Fischer, now in his seventies, to thirty-five-year-old Gottfried Bermann Fischer, a former surgeon who was not born for the profession in the same way his father-in-law, Samuel, was and whom Thomas would never fully trust. It was a complex symbiotic relationship that developed between them: Bermann Fischer flattered his leading author obsequiously and showed him only positive reviews; Thomas Mann queried each royalty statement as if he were being cheated, yet followed Bermann Fischer's advice to the letter when it came to his public statements, even at the expense of his relationship with his children.

Fritz Landshoff of Querido offered to publish Thomas Mann's next book, *The Tales of Jacob*. Had Thomas accepted the offer, Querido instantly would have become an influential force in international publishing (which would have helped Klaus and his literary journal as well). Bermann Fischer fought desperately to hold on to his top-selling author, and finally persuaded him that the sustained appearance of his books in Germany was a triumph for all humanity. Even the retired Samuel Fischer felt that his son-in-law's position was wrong, and that all their authors should simply flee Germany. On the financial side, and it may well have been this argument that won Thomas Mann over, Bermann Fischer contended that publication in Holland instead of Germany could only mean lower sales.

On May 10, when ritual bonfires of "un-German" books were held in Berlin and Munich, the works of Thomas Mann were not among those deemed dangerous to the German psyche. The fact that books by Freud, Upton Sinclair, Heinrich Mann, and Erich Maria Remarque went up in smoke, at Berlin University no less, did not make Thomas Mann revise his position. Bermann Fischer considered Thomas Mann's exemption from the book-burning an encouraging sign—whether for the judiciousness of the regime or for the continued existence of his publishing house, he didn't say.

Erika and Klaus were troubled by their father's steadfast reliance on the unscrupulous Bermann Fischer's judgment—they were not concerned about his accounting, as their father was, but rather wondered what concessions to the Nazis he must have been making, as a Jewish publisher, to stay in business in Germany. They found the Magician's reluctance to take a strong stand against the Nazi regime to be unconscionable, although it must be pointed out that his two eldest children (now twenty-six and twenty-seven) were still financially dependent on their father and had no qualms about accepting his money.

The copy of Klaus's anti-Nazi journal that arrived in September set off fireworks in Sanary-sur-Mer. For two days Thomas and Katia discussed, as Thomas wrote in his diary, "the matter of *Die Sammlung,* which seems to be a blow to the Fischer publishing house and a serious danger for the Jacob book. What is more, Klaus has played a trick on us by including Heinrich's article in the first issue." To Klaus himself, the Magician simply wrote that "the character of the first issue of *Die Sammlung* did not conform to its original concept. That is true, as you know."

The list of authors agreeing to be future contributors to *Die Sammlung* was picked up by the Nazi's "Office for the Furtherance of German Writing" and reprinted in a German trade magazine, the *Börsenblatt,* with a warning to German booksellers: if they carried émigré journals, *Die Sammlung* in particular, they would be guilty of intellectual treason. Since Thomas Mann's name was on this list (indeed was the most prominent name on the list), Bermann Fischer was able to convince him that soon his books would not be sold or read in Germany. Thomas was extremely "aware that my books are not written for Prague and New York, but for Germans." Reluctantly, he sent a telegram to the *Börsenblatt,* which subsequently was widely reprinted in other journals, distancing himself from *Die Sammlung* on the grounds that he had been duped. He tersely announced, "Can only confirm that the character of the first issue of *Die Sammlung* does not correspond to its original program. Thomas Mann."

German-language newspapers in Prague and Vienna quickly and vehemently denounced Thomas Mann for rejecting the anti-Fascist cause. While the émigré movement saw his disavowal of *Die Sammlung* as a

Therese Giehse prepares for a performance of *The Peppermill.*

political betrayal, Klaus saw it as a personal betrayal—not the first but certainly the most public one in his long-troubled relationship with his father.

Klaus rarely got angry at others. Instead he turned it on himself, retreating deeper into isolation and his morphine habit. He wrote in his diary, "Long letter from the Magician, the *most* humiliating sensation: his second telegram to Fischer, his shunning of *Die Sammlung* . . . a very insulting affair. Sorrow and confusion."

Erika alone could understand how devastated Klaus was, but she was no longer fighting his battles for him as she had on the playgrounds of their childhood. Instead she helped her parents find and settle into a new home (a large three-story villa) in Küsnacht, Switzerland—the family home in Munich had been confiscated by the Nazis in late August, and Thomas finally accepted that they would not be returning to it. And Erika soon would have battles to fight of her own.

Erika and Therese Giehse, along with composer Magnus Henning and several other members of the original cast, reopened *The Peppermill* in Zurich on October 1, 1933. They needed to replace those performers still living in Germany, and fortunately discovered that a left-wing actor who had recently slipped out of Munich might be available. Igor Pahlen received a telegram in Paris from Erika inviting him to join the troupe.

He jumped at the chance to be part of *The Peppermill,* not only because the show was famous throughout Germany, but also because of Erika Mann's reputation. When he arrived in Zurich, he found that Erika was indeed, just as he had heard, "a fantastic woman." She was not only the director, lead actor, and master of ceremonies, but wrote the script, produced the show, secured the venues, hired the actors, "you know . . . she did everything."

For each run of the show, new songs were added which were increasingly explicit in their condemnation of Nazi Germany. Of all the exile cabarets, *The Peppermill* was by far the most political. In one skit, Igor Pahlen, dressed in a trench coat and sporting a Hitler mustache, sang a song called "Man of the Hour":

Na, who am I? Na, who am I?
Na, na, na, who can I be?
Am I poet? Totally cold.
Am I judge? Warmer, but still: no!

He gives various clues (he is proud, and rich, and can sleep well at night); it turns out he is the Executioner.

Beginning with the Zurich run, Erika and Therese were listed as co-directors on the program. According to Igor Pahlen, Therese Giehse never directed the actors, and the show was not collaboratively directed in any sense. Erika and Therese each had her own clearly defined area of work for which she was responsible. When pressed as to why they might call themselves co-directors, Igor Pahlen replied, "I have to say that Erika Mann and Therese Giehse were so close, they were as one, and the influence of the one on the other was so great that perhaps they did not need to collaborate. That collaboration existed without doing anything. It worked just like that."

Igor Pahlen was not a man to be intimidated or put off by strong women. In fact what he admired most about Erika and Therese was their enormous confidence. He recalled that "Erika Mann never asked anyone: 'Is what I'm doing right or do I have to use a different tone or something?' No, Erika Mann was very self-confident, and I think that was true for Giehse also."

Igor Pahlen loved the entire experience of the show, but left it after a year and a half. Ultimately he was too much of a socialist to tolerate what he called "Erika's elitism" any longer. As committed as she was to the anti-Nazi struggle, she was not an egalitarian at heart. As the stars of the show, Erika and Therese drove around in Erika's fancy car, drank expensive champagne, slept in first-class hotels, and ate in elegant restaurants (she would often march into the kitchen and demand that the chef prepare her personal recipe for steak tartare). Meanwhile, the rest of her troupe followed along on second-class train cars and did what they were told. Igor Pahlen was overwhelmed with admiration for Erika and Therese, but could not abide living in their shadow.

An enormous hit in Zurich, *The Peppermill* soon took off for a tour across Europe. In a few larger cities—Zurich, Amsterdam, Basel—the show would be booked in for a month or so; otherwise the troupe played only one-night gigs to sold-out crowds and quickly moved on. It could seem unclear from the itinerary as to whether the troupe was actually on tour or on the lam. *The Peppermill,* and Erika personally, were regularly denounced in local newspapers and at public meetings, free publicity that seemed at first only to help ticket sales. So far the attacks were verbal, not physical, but Erika sensed this was about to change.

Expecting some sort of trouble, Erika arranged to have plainclothes policemen and private security guards at the theater door when the show returned to Zurich after six months on tour. One night in November 1934, a pro-Nazi group calling itself the "Swiss Front" invaded her theater and, with a military whistle to give the signal, began shouting: "Jews Out" and "Switzerland for the Swiss." The disruptions made it impossible for the show to continue, and escalated quickly into open rioting and subsequent police arrests. As Erika recalled years later in a television interview, "Motorized police formed a ring around the theater every evening. There was an uproar every evening [for three nights]. I still remember that on November 18th—by coincidence that was my brother Klaus's birthday—the police made 32 arrests. Guns, strange knives, and brass knuckles were confiscated by the police. It was all very dangerous."

In Switzerland, the press picked up the story and placed the blame entirely on the performers. Headlines read "Public Protest against Immigrant Agitation" and editorials spoke out "Against the Jewish cabaret, Peppermill."

Erika handled the bad press and the personal threats against her with intelligence and grace. She answered the newspapers' charges with her own detailed account of the events. She did not condescend to deny the accusation that hers was a "Jewish émigré cabaret," even though only a couple of the performers were actually Jewish. Instead she proclaimed, "I know, that such a cabaret stage is almost meaningless compared to the great world stage. But even so, I also know that every artistic work must have its convictions. . . . We try, in the light manner that we have chosen, to say the difficult things that must be said today." When she learned of a rumor that she might be extradited to Germany, she still continued the theatrical run but left Zurich directly after each evening's performance, taking a bus to Küsnacht, where the local police would meet her at the station and escort her to her parents' home.

Erika always maintained that these violent incidents were provoked by the extremely wealthy, influential, and pro-Nazi family of Annemarie Schwarzenbach, in whose family home Erika was no longer welcome. Miro's mother, Renée, a possessive, overbearing parent and overt lesbian who brought her lover to live in her grand Swiss villa right under her husband's nose, had taken a jealous dislike to Erika from their first meeting anyway. Miro's father was so out of touch with who his daughter had become that he urged her to go back to Germany and help build up the new Nazi regime, which would contribute toward keeping his factories safe. Renée's brother, Commander Ulrich Wille, was a high-ranking military man who violated Switzerland's neutrality stance by paying secret visits to Adolf Hitler and his henchmen. In the typical satirical style of *The Peppermill*, Erika added a song to their repertoire that included a wordplay on his name, a mocking allusion to the publicly disgraced military man without naming him directly. It was exactly at this point in the performance that the disruptions first began, signaled by a whistle which, it turns out, was given by one of Annemarie's cousins.

Annemarie was deeply distressed by the situation, both by her family's pro-Nazi position and by Erika's anger. She was a politically engaged journalist, novelist, and travel writer by now, as well as a photographer who powerfully documented the encroaching darkness of National Socialism. And yet Annemarie was convinced her family was not responsible for the disruptions—they might be capable of it, she admitted, except she knew that such scandals would be far too embarrassing for them. But even if they did not cause the disruptions, her family still blamed Erika for the entire situation. Annemarie, lovesick and drug-addicted, somehow managed to stand up to her domineering mother and defend Erika, and also wrote letters of protest to the press: "Some towns have banned 'The Peppermill' . . . to avoid trouble with the National Front. It is difficult, indeed impossible, to protect a work of art from mindless brutality. This small, dubious success for the National Front is a symptom which demands our attention. One of the finest Swiss traditions is violated when intellectual and artistic expression is gagged by brute force." This was Miro's first radical act against her family, and she desperately wanted Erika to know she was on her side. But their relationship had deteriorated so completely because of these Swiss Front incidents that she felt incapable of writing to Erika; she wrote a desperate letter to Klaus instead:

> I can't stand this separation from Erika, I simply can't stand any separation from her. So I write to you. . . . And my brother [Klaus], the darling rabbit, who pretends to be so brave, friendly and good, intends to keep a false peace. . . .
> I force [Mother] to read the disgusting accusations [in the press against Erika], I write, I tell the police inspector . . . I write to the *Basler* [newspaper], also very loudly, I call the editors and state which side I'm on. . . . I'm only so depressed because I know how little use it is to Eri. Does she even care about my newly won courage? And then I lose my will, all my will, and I feed myself on tuna fish [heroin] until it makes me sick with throwing up, staying awake nights, paralyzing weakness. I ask, what good is it all—if it doesn't serve to . . .
> You, Klaus Heinrich, you know that one cannot live without Eri. Me too, I always knew it. . . .

Soon afterward, Klaus went to Zurich to visit Erika, and paid Miro a visit. They took heroin together, and he admitted in his diary: "Constantly under a slight heroin influence; I want to give the stuff to Erika to hide. . . . Evening: Annemarie. Atonement visit. She is beautiful, lean and dear. Very much under the power of the drugs. Together from eating this dish (until three a.m.). Life. Mysterious."

After this reunion it was clear even to Klaus that Annemarie would have to check into a sanatorium for drug withdrawal, which she eventually did, several times, without success. He decided he too had to "stop a little—also to oblige E, and Miro is a new warning," although it was a warning he didn't heed. Two weeks later, Annemarie tried to commit suicide by way of a skiing accident.

Although she ended up with only an injured leg, the attempt gave Klaus a serious jolt, and he wrote in his diary: "I THANK GOD, for her, for E and for me, that it was unsuccessful. What a wretched confusion."

Annemarie Schwarzenbach's existence could not have been more problematic had she been an émigré herself. But she was Swiss, and she had, according to Marianne Breslauer, "everything that everybody wanted." She was extremely wealthy and extremely beautiful, and, unlike most of her friends, she had a passport and a place to live. At the end of her long, complaining letter to Klaus, Annemarie wrote, in closing, "Eri told me that you're deep in trouble and that you don't have a passport." It was the first and only sentence in the letter that was not about herself. Marianne Breslauer felt that once the Nazis came to power, and the German émigrés in their circle had real problems, "nobody was ever interested in Annemarie's problems anymore. I had the same experience myself, I must say."

Given the pro-Nazi climate in Switzerland, Annemarie realized it was unsafe for her to remain alone, unmarried, in her house in Sils. She also was determined not to "impose on Eri anymore." Her solution was to marry a French diplomat, also homosexual, and travel with him to Persia (where she had worked the previous year on an archaeological excavation), although this created more problems than it solved. It was a short, unhappy liaison, during which Annemarie suffered deep depression and found herself mixed up in a complicated romance with the daughter of the Turkish ambassador in Tehran—not surprisingly, this romance also came to a swift, distressing end.

Klaus returned to Amsterdam, where he settled back in his hotel room, under the watchful eye of the Gestapo. The Gestapo had been investigating Klaus and Erika since early 1933 and knew practically everything about them. What it did not know, it made up. A 1934 Gestapo document makes the following assertion:

> From certain rumors we have learned that there exists between the siblings more than a sibling relationship. Klaus and Erika Mann are the downfall of the Mann family. Klaus's literary abilities are insignificant; he merely tries to capitalize on the name of his father.

The Nazis finally came up with more substantial grounds for wreaking havoc in Klaus's life. *Die Sammlung* and the fact that Klaus endorsed an anti-Nazi declaration protesting Germany's annexing of the Saarland were used to find him guilty of high treason and make him eligible for public "denaturalization." On November 1, 1934, his name was included on the second of Goebbel's famous four lists which publicly stripped Germany's intelligentsia of its citizenship (Heinrich Mann's name had been on the first list). Klaus became stateless.

When *The Peppermill* arrived in Amsterdam for a three-day run, Erika flew directly into the arms of her brother—still, despite their separation,

Erika and Klaus, publicity image for their book *Escape to Life*.

her closest friend and unconditional ally. Klaus heard a rumor that Erika's name was to appear on the next list; her citizenship would also be revoked. The intention of Goebbel's lists was to shame those who could not reconcile themselves with the new program, but it backfired when the excommunicated saw themselves instead as a "Legion of Honor," ironically appointed by the Nazi regime. Still, Klaus knew firsthand the daily trials of life in exile without a passport, and it was none too glamorous.

As it happened, the English author Christopher Isherwood and his German lover Heinz Neddermeyer were in Amsterdam when Erika arrived. They too were moving from country to country, trying to keep a few steps ahead of the Nazi authorities, who were looking to conscript Heinz into the army. Klaus and Isherwood had met in Berlin several years earlier and immediately became, in Isherwood's words, "intimate friends who seldom saw each other, for Klaus was always on the move."

As they always did when they met, the two authors asked each other what they were currently working on. According to Isherwood, Klaus "laughed, made a little grimace," before answering, "Oh—a pre-War novel." This exchange took place in 1935, when no one but Klaus was anticipating a war. The humor was, Isherwood observed, "so typical of him," ironic, visionary, playful, and dark, all at the same time.

Klaus took Isherwood to see Erika's show. He was struck by her "beautiful poise and courage" but was especially astonished by "the un-forgettable" Therese Giehse. He loved the scornful humor with which the cabaret defied their Fascist enemy. The image that stayed with him most strongly from that evening was "a scene in which [Therese Giehse] nursed the globe of the world on her lap like a sick child and crooned weirdly over it." Therese Giehse sang to the tune of a lullaby:

> The bullet hits
> Go to sleep, my child
> We ought not to talk about such things
> Does the sky turn red somewhere?
> Does someone shout: "Fall in!"?
> Did anyone die of hunger?
> We ought not to talk about such things
>
> After your death, it could be
> That things will change
> They will be new and light and pure
> Can you still hear
> The words I'm singing?

Klaus explained to Christopher Isherwood that Erika's life was en-dangered, that on occasion she had to sneak out of town in the middle of the night, and that as Public Enemy of the Third Reich she was about to lose her citizenship. After the show, he introduced his sister to his friend. Upon their meeting, Erika, somewhat nervously, laughed and said, "I have something rather personal to ask you: will you marry me?"

With reluctance, Isherwood turned Erika down, both because he had a "rooted horror" of marriage and, more urgently, out of concern for Heinz, who had enough trouble without becoming mixed up with the troublemaking Mann siblings. Isherwood came up with another suggestion: he cabled his friend W. H. Auden in England. "Delighted," Auden wired back.

On the morning of June 12, 1935, twenty-nine-year-old Erika Mann boarded an airplane to London and from there caught a British Rail train bound for the English Midlands. It chugged due north, the sprawling gray cityscape outside her window giving way to green rolling hills dotted with small villages that were nothing more than clusters of red brick. As she looked out at the peculiar English countryside, she must have reflected on the bizarre twists and turns her life had taken to bring her to this point.

After several short stops along the route, the train pulled into a station bearing a name that sounded familiar. She stood up, dashed out onto the platform, and spotted a handsome man standing there with a flower in his lapel. "How good of you to marry me!" she exclaimed in her best English.

Erika Mann had donned a man's tailored suit jacket and tie, incidentally the same clothes she would wear for her wedding, nearly matching those of the groom. Her short-cropped hairstyle, fashionable in Berlin since the Roaring Twenties, clearly had not reached middle England. The handsome man on the platform took one look at her and recoiled. "Not at all, madam!" he murmured as he brushed past her. In her confusion and excitement Erika had gotten off at the wrong station—Malvern Link instead of Great Malvern.

Not only did Erika Mann not know what her future husband would look like, but she also had never heard of him before, despite his rising fame as a poet. W. H. Auden, for his part, had had the sense to ask for a photograph of her in advance. Twice daily, he checked the mailroom at the Downs School, a boys' prep school in the English Midlands where he was employed as a teacher, until he was handed a large envelope. As he tore it open, out fell two theatrical pictures from Erika's anti-Nazi cabaret, *The Peppermill*, showing Erika dressed as a Pierrot, her eyes ringed with black stage makeup.

Auden now knew what his bride would look like, but not much else. A few days before she arrived, he went with a teaching colleague to the nearby sleepy town of Ledbury to obtain the marriage license. "Her name?" asked the clerk. Auden stammered, "Well, let's see, she has been married and divorced . . . I'm not sure." "Her age?" Auden looked at him blankly. He was, at least, able to answer the questions about himself, and emerged triumphant. As they started back for the Downs School, Auden commented, "He would have married me to the poker."

Husband and wife: Wystan H. Auden and Erika Mann, 1935. (Photo
courtesy of Thomas Mann Archive, Eidgenössischen Technischen
Hochschule, Zurich.)

Erika eventually arrived in Great Malvern and got acquainted with
Auden over a drink at the local village pub. Auden's teaching colleague
was there for this encounter as well, and described her as "nine-tenths a
man." The betrothed pair agreed to have no financial obligations to one
another and to request no wedding presents. The very next day, June
15, they were married at the Ledbury registry office. The witnesses consisted of the art teacher from the Downs School and a young gardener
who tended the school grounds and with whom Auden had recently
started an affair. (Rumors circulated around the school that Auden was
living in the garden shed, so often was he seen sneaking off in that direction.) Although no celebration followed, the wedding party returned to

the home of the art teacher, where some photos were taken, and Auden drove Erika back to her hotel, with flowers and cabbage leaves trailing from the back of his car. From there he returned to finish his day's teaching at the Downs School.

The wedding took place just in time. Five days later, Erika's German citizenship was revoked. When asked why he agreed to the marriage, Auden would simply shrug, "What else are buggers for?" He felt a deep sense of responsibility to helping fellow homosexuals in trouble, and he had heard Isherwood's reports on Erika's life being in danger. Afterward, he wrote to Stephen Spender, "I didn't see her till the ceremony and perhaps I shall never see her again."

Auden did see Erika again, often, and developed a relationship not only with Erika but with the entire Mann family. He dedicated a book of poems to Erika and visited the family home in Küsnacht, where he met Thomas Mann, whom he both admired and resented. The Magician, for his part, was impressed and amused by Auden, or so Erika's brother Golo thought as he witnessed the encounter, but took no interest in Auden as a poet. Auden must have sensed this; he was often heard joking, "Who's the most boring German writer? My father-in-law!"

Erika and Auden developed what Golo called a "serious friendship," although Auden seems alternately to have claimed and disowned the relationship as it served his ends. When Erika lectured in England about the dangerous events in Nazi Germany, Auden would accompany her and stand by, shaking hands as the proud husband of the anti-Fascist activist. Yet he also tried to play down their intimacy. He would recount the heroic story of Erika rescuing Thomas Mann's manuscript of *Joseph and His Brothers* from the Munich home, and invariably end it with: "I can't say we're friends, but she did us that service."

Their private correspondence gives the impression of a more substantial relationship. He would write to her about nightmares or about writer's block, admitting he hadn't "the slightest idea how to begin to write the book. . . . At present I am just amusing myself, with occasional twinges of uneasiness, like a small boy who knows he's got an exam tomorrow, for which he had done no work whatsoever." In another letter, Auden reiterated "how much I like and admire you" and bemoaned how little chance they had to see each other. He ended it by giving her advice: "Dont do too much and dont—here uncle is speaking or the cheeky gay brother don't hate too much. Much love, Wystan."

As a favor to Erika, Auden arranged a similar marriage of convenience for Therese Giehse to John Simpson, an English writer he knew through

E. M. Forster. When the wedding took place in 1936, at a registry office in Solihull, a residential suburb of Birmingham, the substantial Therese Giehse eclipsed the tiny bridegroom, and her English was so poor that Auden had to supply her answers to the registrar. Auden, dressed in striped trousers and with a carnation in his lapel, ordered a round of brandies at the local pub afterward, and announced that Thomas Mann was picking up the tab.

A British subject through marriage, Erika truly became a citizen of the world (well, of all but Germany). She admitted it was somewhat unpleasant to be found guilty of high treason and condemned to die if she stepped foot in German territory, but found it "consoling to think I can still go more places in the world with safety than [Hitler] can go!" Her oath of allegiance was to the entire world and especially to its children—for whom she wrote many children's books—because, as she often proclaimed, "who has the youth has the future."

Klaus, too, was "a German who wanted to be a European: a European who wanted to be a citizen of the world," but unlike Erika he became instead a man without a country. He saw himself as someone "striving for a true community but never finding it; disconnected, restless, wandering."

As an anti-Fascist, Klaus could not in good faith align himself with the Communists, as his literary idol André Gide did, briefly, and which perhaps would have given Klaus the sense of belonging he sought. Even if he could overlook the Soviet Union's "cult of official heroes, the nationalistic complacency, the rampant militarism," undesirable qualities he might be able to understand and excuse, he could not abide with "the shallow and erroneous doctrine of dialectic materialism." He also was disappointed by the Soviet Union's gradual move away from its earlier liberal social policies; in 1934, for example, sexual relations between consenting male adults were criminalized for the first time since the 1917 revolution. The blatantly discriminatory statute, passed by the Central Executive Committee of the Communist Party, coincided with "The Night of the Long Knives" in Germany, an anti-homosexual purge of Nazi ranks and of the general populace in December 1934 (triggered by Hitler's disposing of one of his leading henchmen, a homosexual named Ernst Röhm).

Soon after these two events took place, Klaus, feeling more of an outsider than ever before, wrote a passionate, farsighted essay titled "Homosexuality and Fascism." Published in Prague, it railed against the German Left in exile, which spoke out against human rights abuses of all kinds across the globe, except when it came to homosexuals, who were being victimized by the Right in Germany and by the Left in the Soviet Union. Klaus argued against the association of homosexuality with bourgeois decadence by Russian authors such as Maxim Gorky, and against the association of homosexuality with Fascism by German anti-Fascist writers, who almost without exception interpreted "The Night of the Long Knives" as a hypocritical act, since Fascism supposedly bred homosexuality.

To see the Soviet experiment firsthand, Klaus had gone to Moscow for two weeks in July 1934, along with Annemarie Schwarzenbach, to attend the First Congress of Soviet Writers. In the manuscript of his "Notes from Moscow" is a remark which reveals both his belief in the noble purpose of literature and his misgivings about its role in the Soviet agenda. In response to Karl Radek's speech at the Congress, Klaus posed these questions: "What does Karl Radek mean when he speaks the word *literature*? Does he mean that broad front of the spirit that affirms the future, illumines what is around it, and remains aware of its great task and responsibility in these times? Or does he mean a propaganda instrument of the Third International?" Klaus left Moscow disillusioned by the obvious answer he witnessed.

Klaus later wrote that while he had respect for the basic objectives of the Soviet regime,

> I could never embrace a gospel that promises salvation of the human race by virtue of an economic measure. I reject a philosophy which banishes and defames all metaphysical thought as a capitalistic contrivance to distract the proletarian attention from the only matter that counts, namely the class struggle. I do not believe that religion is the opium of the people (although I realize that religious ideas have been often abused to paralyze the human will to progress). To betray and slander the Mystery is no less pernicious than to sabotage Progress.

Klaus found the Communists' rejection of the metaphysical so unacceptable that he even held it partly responsible for the death of his friend and onetime lover René Crevel. Crevel, together with a number of other Communist writers, had organized the first Congress of Intellectuals in Paris in the summer of 1935, which would feature some of the most important literary spokespeople of their time. "But all the time he was writing manifestoes or organizing meetings," Klaus later recalled, "there were enigmatic flashes in his wide-open eyes, and he seemed at times to be listening to voices calling him away." The very night before the Congress began, Crevel sat in a café with the group of Communist organizers, and then went home to take an overdose of tablets—as it happens, the same drug he had used a decade earlier to kill the hero of his novel *La mort difficile*. The Communist writer Johannes R. Becher, who called Klaus with the bad news early the next morning, shortly before Klaus was scheduled to speak, reported that the night before, René Crevel "seemed entirely normal. . . . Not depressed, or anything. Only sometimes he had such a curious way of staring into space—as if looking for something. But he couldn't find it—whatever it may have been." Klaus felt Crevel was looking for this something, this "it," denied by the Communists, when he chose death.

The author Sybille Bedford, looking back on the time she spent with Erika and Klaus during the thirties, referred to their circle as a "lost generation," somewhat different from the lost generation of Hemingway, F. Scott Fitzgerald, and other, mostly American, writers in Paris in the twenties (except for René Crevel, who was on the periphery of both groups). This other lost generation of a decade later was also made up largely of émigrés, but from Germany rather than the United States, and with no central place to congregate. Extraordinarily gifted and intelligent individuals, bound together by a shared abhorrence of Fascism, they were constantly drifting, often without passports, and were drawn to star-crossed sexual liaisons, drugs, and, in many cases, suicide.

Klaus more than anyone else exemplified this lost generation. Christopher Isherwood saw him as a wanderer, "temperamentally drawn to other wanderers, the confused, the lost, the astray." Although Klaus was quick to help any and all of these people, Isherwood mused, "they could give him little in return. He found no permanent companion on his journey."

The distinguished literary critic Hans Mayer has written that "suicide was a thread running through the fabric of [Klaus Mann's] life." If so, it must have been the thread that, when pulled, unravels the entire cloth. And yet many of his closest friends were hardly aware of his strong suicidal bent. Only shortly before Klaus's death did Isherwood come to understand that "far beneath Klaus's brightness, courage, apparent freedom from self-pity, there was an obstinate drive towards self-destruction."

Klaus's dark side revealed itself only in his diary, where he wrote almost daily of his struggle with life. It was a life propelled by three fervent needs: drugs, sex, and writing, which appear as a kind of mantra throughout his diary as "genommen," "gegangen," and "getippt." Genommen:

Taken. Whatever drug he could acquire—speed, morphine, heroin—Klaus took it. "Genommen" is often followed in the diary by "again too much. Absolutely decided to stop next time round." Gegangen: Walked (or, in today's parlance, cruised). Klaus only noted this activity in his diary when someone took the bait. Sometimes it must have been sweet, but often it wasn't; in his desperate search for some tenderness, Klaus was vulnerable to any brute responding with his own agenda. One entry notes, "Regarding the boys: not much kindness, but a few pleasures." Getippt: Typed. This was Klaus's modest way of saying he wrote, without assigning what he was working on the burden of naming it "writing." Writing, above all else, was his lifeline. "Getippt" appears almost daily in his diary, regardless of what else he did, where he was, or how late into the night it became.

In 1935, Klaus wrote an especially poignant novel, *Pathetic Symphony: A Novel about Tchaikovsky,* which reveals more about the author than the composer. He dedicated it to his friend Christopher Isherwood, who somehow missed the tragic autobiographical component. Klaus's Tchaikovsky was, "for all his genius and intelligence, . . . somehow incapable of coping with the realities of life." He was homosexual, and wouldn't lie or pretend otherwise; in fact his one pretense, a short-lived marriage to avoid scandal, almost killed him. As a child he fell under the spell of a popular schoolboy, Tchaikovsky's "bad angel," who convinced him that "it's silly to love women—it's wrong for people like us. Let's leave that sort of thing to the Philistines who want to have children and lead a regular life."

Years later Klaus would claim that he wrote about Tchaikovsky because he loved his music, even while admitting he was "no Beethoven" (just as Klaus was no "Thomas Mann"). Klaus further explained his motivation: "I know all about him. Only too intimately versed in his neurasthenic fixations, I could describe his aimless wanderings, the transient bliss of his elations, the unending anguish of his solitude. . . . He was uprooted, disconnected." With his inability to find inner peace, Klaus identified completely: "I could describe all of it; none of it was alien to me." The novel draws on documentary sources and stays faithful to the historical facts of Tchaikovsky's life, except in one telling regard: at the end of the novel Klaus's character commits suicide by choosing to drink contaminated water, whereas there is no evidence suggesting that Tchaikovsky's actual death by cholera was at all deliberate.

Throughout the decade of the thirties, Klaus was himself flirting with an intense death wish; his diary reads as though death were the most seductive, irresistible lover imaginable. In late 1935, he wrote that he was alive only because "E stands between me and death." On the last day of the year, he weighed his pros and cons in a bizarre taking of accounts. On the negative side, there was "the tuna [heroin] problem, ever more disquieting and more central. The high point of 'taking' in Budapest; afterwards the deepest depression, the strongest death wish. The ill-fated Persian trip [planned with Ricki and Annemarie]. Miro's suicide attempt and continued danger. René [Crevel]'s death." On the positive side, there was only Fritz Landshoff, their friendship, and Klaus's worries about Fritz, since he was also a drug addict. "And Erika—constant. Also her circumstance. Her work, her success, her moral position. Her love."

A month later, he wondered whether even Erika was enough to stop him from caving in to his longing for death, although "it is dreadful, that I must do it to her." By August 1936 he was almost begging for death to come quickly:

I am not granted a long life. I am TOO strongly drawn to the other side—that must have its reason. But of course I should first write something that is beautiful, rending.—Also standing between me and the dark valley of promise—still always, still always, always— is my sister.

Although not moralistic, Thomas Mann had a deep, innate sense of morality and, according to Golo, he "disapproved of the 'lifestyle' of his son." Thomas was a man who could not help but take the most respectable route, whatever its personal cost. His protagonist in *The Magic Mountain* envied the freedom of the terminally ill patients at the sanatorium he was visiting; he would fantasize about "how it must feel to be finally relieved of the burden of a respectable life and made free of the infinite realms of shame." Thomas Mann himself could never be relieved of such a burden. Governed by the rules of decorum, Thomas considered Klaus's despair to be "inartistic and immoral." Although he knew about Klaus's drug addiction, he certainly did not understand, as Klaus did, that the despair was in part due to the drugs. Klaus noted in his diary that "the craving for drugs is hardly distinguishable from the desire for DEATH."

Klaus too was deeply moral, agonizingly so, although his morality pertained to political behavior rather than sex and drugs, and to be morally responsible in the increasingly immoral Europe of the thirties, where thieves and murderers were rewarded with positions of power, was often further cause for despair. Klaus not only repudiated the self-loathing that plagued most homosexuals of his generation; he made no secret of nor apology for his inclination. Instead, he sought to bring his sexual heterodoxy and his literary drive in line with his political and moral outlook, a radical position in his day which only accentuated his existential isolation. Just as Thomas Mann's bourgeois morality precluded him from seeing Klaus's life as anything but a process of carting oneself away, as Thomas Mann viewed it, Klaus's radical morality, which involved a strong sense of individual responsibility and accountability, made it impossible for him to understand his father's ambiguous political position. Relations between Thomas Mann and his eldest son were considerably strained during these years.

Meanwhile, Thomas Mann, still afraid of his books being banned in Germany, continued to maintain his uneasy balancing act and had not spoken out against the Nazi regime. Bermann Fischer's own position was also untenable, and he was considering moving his business either to Austria or Switzerland, but so far hadn't made up his mind. On January 11, 1936, Bermann Fischer was attacked in the Paris-based German-language émigré newspaper, *Neue Tage-Buch*. The newspaper contended that all the relevant German literature had "transferred abroad" and that Bermann Fischer was nothing more than a Jewish protégé of Goebbels. Thomas Mann immediately abandoned his long-standing position of keeping "absolutely mum" as Bermann Fischer had instructed. He, together with two other German writers, shot off a letter to *Neue Zürcher Zeitung* (the same Swiss newspaper that had slandered Erika when her show ran in Zurich) in defense of Bermann Fischer. For their father to finally speak out, and have it be in support of his publisher in Germany while he criticized the editor of the leading émigré journal in Paris, was more than Erika and Klaus could bear. For them, his unwillingness to align himself with the émigré cause at this late date was entirely unacceptable. It was time for a showdown. Erika wrote to her father:

> That your "protest" in the newspaper made me sad, and seemed awful to me, of course you must realize. On my part, I know that I have no right to mingle in your affairs.

Erika went on to mingle nonetheless, letting him know that his behavior was so shameful that it was now "difficult for me to look you in the eyes." She wondered what disgraceful deal Bermann was able to make with Goebbels to keep in business (she pointedly dropped the "Fischer," which Bermann himself had added to his surname to associate himself with his widely admired father-in-law, Samuel Fischer, and to emphasize his familial link with the firm).

Erika's quarrel was not limited to her father's association with someone she considered unsavory; it was also with her father directly. She disagreed that his absence from Germany was enough to demonstrate his anti-Nazi sentiment; she felt it was high time he made an explicit statement. She resorted to the one thing that she knew would make him see things her way—she made him choose between Bermann Fischer and herself. In a thinly veiled threat, she vowed to cut off her relationship with him altogether:

> You are stabbing in the back the entire émigré movement—I can put it no other way. Probably you will be very angry at me because of this letter. I am prepared for that, and I know what I'm doing. This friendly time is predestined to separate people—in how many cases has it happened already. Your relation to Dr. Bermann and his publishing house is indestructible—you seem to be ready to sacrifice everything for it. In that case if it is a sacrifice for you that I, slowly but surely, will be lost for you—then just never mind. For me it is sad, and terrible. I am your child, E.

Erika had put everything on the line for her convictions and now seemed willing, if it came to that, to sacrifice her relationship with her father. Klaus, equally passionate about the anti-Fascist cause, lacked what Klaus called Erika's "unconditionality," or what their younger sister Elisabeth called her "intellectual violence." As Elisabeth would recall, many years later,

> [Erika] threatened never to want to see him again, I mean she went as far as that in her letter. She was full of real and deep political passion, Erika was. And quite, quite uncompromising. Klaus did not ever have the same kind of intellectual violence, you know. He also had strong convictions, he also felt betrayed when he did not get the support for his journal that he had hoped he would get [from Thomas Mann]. That was a bitter disappointment for him, but he never had the aggressiveness that Erika had, never.

Klaus was incapable of taking such an uncompromising stand, but still he sent a strongly worded telegram, signed jointly with Fritz Landshoff, beseeching Thomas Mann to make a statement in solidarity with

"Erika was the stronger personality," recalled their mutual friend, the photographer Marianne Breslauer.

the émigré writers, as "this time it is really a question of life and death for us all." Klaus's telegram had a far weaker effect on Thomas despite its drastic tone; Klaus's opinion simply mattered less.

Katia tried to make her eldest daughter reconsider her threat. She reminded Erika how important she was in her father's life, and let her know how much her letter had pained him: "You are, aside from me and Medi [Elisabeth], the only person on whom Z's [The Magician's] heart really hangs, and your letter hurt deeply and made him ill." Katia had anticipated anger and trouble from Erika, but not this. "But that your . . . disapproval would go so far, that you virtually would break with him,

I really did not expect. And as for me, in so far as I am firstly his accomplice, it is also truly hard."

Two days after Katia's letter, Thomas wrote to Erika himself, asking her to be patient with him. He anticipated that "the day may come, *might* come, when I, uninhibited by raving madness, speak out myself to the world and Germany, saying: 'This is enough. Come on. Away with this rabble.' Perhaps this should not happen too soon." Despite Katia's appeal, Erika was in no mood to be patient. She responded even more sharply, if it is possible, reminding him that he'd done nothing to help her when *The Peppermill* had been viciously attacked in the Zurich newspaper— not even to cancel his subscription! She charged (somewhat unfairly) that he'd done Klaus more harm than even the Nazis had, when he dissociated himself publicly from *Die Sammlung*. After this, Katia couldn't take it anymore; she felt compelled to take action to save her family. She herself started writing a rough draft of Thomas's open letter to the newspaper, and demanded Thomas finish it. He worked on it for several days. Although it was no fiery indictment of the Nazi regime, it did defend German literature in exile as legitimately "German," and claimed that his country's rising nationalism and anti-Europeanism were an "attempt (symbolized by the withdrawal from the League of Nations) to shake off the ties of civilization, and this is threatening to create a ruinous alienation between Goethe's country and the rest of the world." Published in the *Neue Zürcher Zeitung* on February 3, 1936, the letter was Thomas Mann's first public statement against the Nazis since they had come to power three years earlier. After mailing it, Thomas Mann wrote to a friend, "*I am finally saving my soul. . . .*"

Immediately Thomas Mann was notified that his honorary doctorate degree from Bonn University was rescinded. In response to this news, he wrote "A Letter to the Dean of the Philosophical Faculty of the University of Bonn," a document which became a classic in anti-Fascist literature. He saved his soul, but the names of Thomas Mann, Katia Mann, and their four younger children appeared on the next, and last, of Goebbel's famous four lists. They finally joined the German émigrés' "Legion of Honor"—by losing their citizenship.

At this very moment, Klaus was deeply preoccupied with the question of saving or losing one's soul. He was in the midst of writing what has since come to be his best-known novel, *Mephisto,* a modern-day parable borrowing from Goethe's *Faust,* in which a man—bearing a striking resemblance to Klaus's erstwhile lover and brother-in-law Gustaf Gründgens—sells his soul to the devil.

The previous November, Klaus received a letter from a fellow émigré writer and friend, Hermann Kesten, who suggested to him that he write a book about a homosexual opportunist who rises to power in the Third Reich, in short a novel based on Gründgens. His suggestion served to crystallize a vague idea that already had been floating around Klaus's brain. Little did Kesten know how obsessed Klaus still was with the man, both in his waking hours and in his dreams. If Klaus met someone who irritated him, the person inevitably reminded him of Gustaf. When Klaus learned of "The Night of the Long Knives," the Nazi's anti-homosexual purge, he immediately worried about Gustaf and his "awkward position." Watching a Hollywood film starring Leslie Howard, he'd sigh to himself that Gustaf wished he could act like that, and would go home and listen to Gustaf's performances on his gramophone. As new émigrés arrived from Berlin, Klaus would hear endless stories about Gustaf's rising theatrical success in Germany. Gustaf Gründgens, the man Klaus couldn't help hating and loving in equal measure, just wouldn't stop haunting him as he wandered around Europe.

Determined to profit by the Nazi regime, Gründgens had managed to whitewash his objectionable past—including his flirtation with Communism and his brief marriage to Erika—and relaunch his acting career with a dazzling portrayal of Mephistopheles in Goethe's *Faust*. With, as Klaus describes it, "sparkling charm and saucy wickedness," Gründgens so convincingly embodied the evil spirit to whom Faust sold his soul in the opening night's performance that a captivated Hermann Göring sitting in the audience decided to appoint him manager of the State Theater.

Erika and Klaus were far from surprised by this turn of events. They had long come to see that "his utterly cynical ambition was the most powerful trait in his rather complicated character." Erika was only sorry to have once had that prominent surname featured on her passport.

Klaus Mann's *Mephisto,* published by Querido Verlag in 1936, portrays an opportunistic actor named Hendrik Höfgen, who buys his success in the theater world at the expense of his moral principles. Klaus was sure this was exactly what Gustaf had done, and doubted whether he had any regrets or a guilty conscience for doing so. But as much as Klaus wished to discredit Gustaf by making his character immoral, vain, and depraved, Hendrik Höfgen also comes across as charming, witty, and graceful; ultimately one feels the author admires him in spite of himself. Klaus stops short of making Höfgen homosexual, although homosexuality features in virtually all his other novels. Klaus would never use homosexuality to discredit someone, even Gustaf, but the compromising sexual life he contrives for Höfgen to put him at risk in the Third Reich—a sadomasochistic liaison with Princess Tebab, an Afro-German dominatrix—is a somewhat far-fetched displacement.

Klaus's antagonism toward Gustaf Gründgens began years before Gründgens signed on with the Nazi program, although perhaps Klaus saw something in his personality that was already heading in that direction. As early as 1931 he claimed he could "see right through him" and found himself irritated that Ricki Hallgarten could not; indeed Ricki seemed quite taken with the man. Since Klaus had already based a character on Gründgens in a previous book, *Treffpunkt im Unendlichen* (Meeting Place in Infinity), he had to wonder, Why this obsession? "Why do I think so much about him and with such agitated antipathy? He is not my adversary, if I see it clearly. Through Gregor Gregori [the first character Klaus had based on Gründgens] I should have gotten over him."

Shortly before its publication by Querido, *Mephisto* appeared in serial form in the German émigré newspaper in Paris, *Die Pariser Tageszeitung*. The editors of the paper introduced it, not without good reason, as a Schlüsselroman (a novel featuring real people under fictional names). Klaus objected strenuously to this designation in a letter to the editor, insisting that the protagonist of his novel was a character type, based on a real person's characteristics, perhaps, but not a portrait of a real person. This position was dubious—the physical attributes, personality traits, biographical details, and even signature apparel of Höfgen describe Gründgens precisely—but Klaus continued to maintain it, especially when Gründgens retaliated against the book. He might not even have known of *Mephisto,* since the novel (like all of Klaus's work) was banned in Germany throughout the Nazi years, but the first name on the long list Klaus gave to the publisher of those to receive complimentary copies, even ahead of Thomas Mann, was Gustaf Gründgens.

The debate over the fictional portrayal of Gustaf Gründgens has dominated virtually all discussion of *Mephisto,* then and now. And yet the novel is remarkable for purely literary considerations, such as its uncanny ability to put the reader so fully inside an unsympathetic character's interior mental and emotional world. Höfgen is a complex and multifaceted enough figure that when he makes his pact with the devil—he lets himself come under the powerful protection of the fat prime minister, clearly modeled on Hermann Göring—we experience his unease about whether this ultimately would turn out to be a wise move. When he finally makes a decent gesture—he pays anonymously for a Communist friend's burial when that friend was murdered by the state—we suffer with him, even knowing his decision is not so much a generous, selfless act as it is part of his "insurance policy" as he calls it, taken out as precaution against the regime's possible collapse or overthrow.

Klaus could see even more clearly into Germany's heart of darkness than he could into Höfgen's. Just as he, in 1927, more than five years before the Nazis came to power, had anticipated going into exile, in *Mephisto* he anticipated the mass murder of the concentration camps—more than five years before the Wannsee Conference made it official policy. One of his characters who witnessed the inside of a concentration camp had "seen what no human eye can look upon without clouding with despair. He had seen evil naked and uncontrolled and organized with a horrible meticulousness. He had seen absolute and total baseness, which even as it tortured helpless victims glorified itself as a patriotic enterprise." Klaus knew that this level of torture in 1936 was only the beginning; far worse crimes were to come. Into the mouth of another character, a demonic poet, he put the following prophetic words: "Up to now we have—to my knowledge—burned only books. That's nothing. But our Führer will soon hand over to us something more. I have every confidence in him. Fires blazing on the horizon; rivers of blood in all the streets; and the frenzied dancing of the survivors, of those who are still spared, around the bodies of the dead!" The novel anticipates not only the hidden violence within Germany but also the eruption of war across Europe: "This militarily organized, disciplined, well-drilled youth had only one aim— the war of revenge, the war of conquest. Alsace-Lorraine was German. Switzerland was German. Holland was German. Denmark was German. Czechoslovakia was German. The Ukraine was German. Austria was so completely German that the case did not even have to be stated."

In 1936, when *Mephisto* was written and first published, the chilling effects of Germany's Nazi government were already beginning to be felt across Europe. An actual law was passed in Switzerland, the *Lex Pfeffer-mühle*, which specifically singled out Erika's theater troupe, stating that it could no longer perform in the district of Zurich. It seemed to Erika that other countries, succumbing to the pressure of the Nazis, would soon follow suit. In Holland, where the show had its greatest success, the Dutch National Socialists protested it so vigorously that Erika was notified she would have to eliminate the political content if the performances were to continue. In Erika's words, "Finally it came to this point: Perhaps our best and most fertile hunting ground, Holland . . . bowed to the German threat. Indeed, the Dutch government indicated to me they would like us to continue to perform in their country. . . . But unfortunately from now on, we would have to give up even the most indirect political inclination."

The show was so financially successful, not only for the troupe but also for the investors who sponsored it, that the Dutch government was loath to discontinue it altogether. So they suggested instead that Erika "just continue the show as pure entertainment." Erika politely declined the offer, at which point the Dutch government withdrew its license to perform—provoking angry protests in the newspapers and even within Parliament, to no avail. Outlawed first in Switzerland and now in Holland, it became clear that "we could not stay in Europe any longer."

Erika and Klaus had fully expected civilized Europe to unite against Germany's sordid crimes against humanity. Instead, from the very first days of their exile, they encountered contempt, not because they were mistaken for Nazis when they were overheard speaking German (although this happened occasionally once they moved to the United States), but because, so uncritical of Nazi Germany was Europe in this time, they were perceived as unpatriotic and traitorous for denouncing their native land. Erika commented that "it was a heartfelt blow to experience this calm indifference, this moral impotence with which the German misdeeds were accepted everywhere in Europe." By 1936, they found, as Klaus would write, that "the air in Europe [was] becoming more sticky and more oppressive from season to season, even from month to month. . . . At bottom I sensed that my position was precarious, if not untenable. A liberal German writer had no chance in Europe, considering the present state and obvious trend of affairs."

Essentially run off the continent for stirring up anti-Nazi sentiment, the siblings considered leaving for the United States. Klaus wondered, "Would I find conditions more propitious on the other side? What was in store for me over there seemed even more uncertain than what I left behind."

On August 14, 1936, Erika staged a farewell performance of *The Peppermill,* a private show organized by her old mentor, the director Max Reinhardt, who wanted to help her get a foothold in America. He invited a number of rich Americans to his baroque castle in Salzburg, thinking they might be in a position to secure theatrical engagements in the United States. Helen Hayes and her husband were in the audience, as were Marlene Dietrich and a dozen other big stars. Instead of a theater with a wooden stage, they had to perform in a big hall with stone floors; Erika was unhappy about the acoustics. Because of all the canceled shows in the previous month, her troupe had dwindled to five performers. Nonetheless, Erika cheerfully recalled that "this soiree was really the beginning of the American tour."

Therese Giehse gave a far more disheartened account. She pronounced the entire evening "a dreadful affair." The reason Reinhardt only invited sixteen guests, she revealed, was that he was deeply in debt, and could not afford to host an event for more than that. His castle was lit by candlelight, which was quite romantic but not intentionally so: he simply hadn't paid his electricity bill.

It was not Reinhardt's financial status but rather the apathy of the American audience which depressed Therese Giehse the most:

> The guests, all rich Americans, did not want to know more than they already knew, which was actually nothing, about the political situation. Our performance must have seemed highly odd and exotic to them. But they watched very hopefully. The only one who understood us somewhat was Reinhardt. Our program and the purpose of our work meant nothing to him either, but he had an artistic appreciation of it. He was impressed with the quality of our work. . . . During our program Marlene Dietrich, one of the posh guests, received incessant phone calls: Madam, New York calling for you, Madam, San Francisco. . . . Her wonderful exits and reentries were more interesting than our performance. Hers was a very exclusive performance. . . . I knew then with absolute certainty that an American tour [of *The Peppermill*] was completely senseless. But Erika—she forced it to happen.

With no prospects to open *The Peppermill* in the United States, Erika and Klaus Mann set sail on the Dutch liner *Statendam* and crossed the Atlantic together in September 1936. According to FBI documents, Erika traveled on a British passport issued in Zurich, and Klaus, still without citizenship, had only Dutch stateless papers accompanied by a three-month visitor's visa. Klaus boarded the ship in Rotterdam with their luggage; Fritz Landshoff accompanied him from Amsterdam and saw him off. It was an emotional departure, with Klaus wondering where and when he'd ever see Fritz again. He wrote in his diary, "What comes next? Oh, life: what kind of difficult, mysterious thing it is . . . 'Genommen' [took drugs], rather strong. Probably (hopefully) for the last time—for a long while."

Erika had flown to England two days before to squeeze in a short visit with Auden. She boarded the ship one day after Klaus did, when it dropped anchor near Boulogne for several hours; a freighter had brought her over from Southampton. Three remaining members of *The Peppermill*'s troupe waited, restlessly and skeptically, back in Europe while Erika promised to line up a theater and most of all raise funds to bring the show in New York. Therese Giehse was tempted by offers of prominent roles in the Zurich theater, but she remained committed to Erika even though she had no desire to go to New York (and couldn't speak any English). Erika would send for the three *Peppermill* performers soon, although not by luxury passenger ship such as she and Klaus had taken, with swimming pool, cinema, and elegant bar—they'd follow behind on a cement freighter.

It was nine years since Erika and Klaus had made their first, far more lighthearted journey to America as "the literary Mann twins." Life in exile made them "wise and weary" according to Klaus, but they were still only twenty-nine and thirty years old.

CHAPTER 5

ESCAPE TO LIFE

UPON ARRIVAL IN NEW YORK, Erika and Klaus checked into the Hotel Bedford on East 40th Street, an upscale residential hotel housing a disproportionate number of German (predominantly German Jewish) émigrés. It was a comfortable, stylish place run by a German American couple, well-acquainted with the requirements for *Gemütlichkeit*. Blanche Knopf, wife of Thomas Mann's American publisher, had discovered the hotel and booked their reservation.

Later that day a young dancer named Michael Logan arrived to deliver greetings from Annemarie Schwarzenbach, who had recently made her first trip to the United States. Annemarie and her American friend, photographer Barbara Hamilton-Wright, had traveled together by car into the Deep South as well as to Pittsburgh's coal regions in order to document "The Other America": the massive unemployment, labor unrest, and racial discrimination that constituted the underside of the American Dream. At that moment Annemarie was recovering in Washington, D.C., from a drug overdose, her emissary reported, but would soon be on her way to meet them in New York. Klaus found Michael to be "very sympathetic, also intelligent," and in no time at all, "*Michael reste la nuit chez moi. Tendresse.*"

Michael "*reste la nuit*" on and off for the next month, until he suddenly disappears from Klaus's diary. He's replaced by Emery, an Italian boy who came in to clean the room. "A tremendous flirt. Perhaps—*perhaps* this is the beginning of a great love." The great love lasted all of eight days, after which Klaus returned to Michael Logan.

Erika too found romance in New York City—in her own hotel no less. Among the many German guests staying at the Hotel Bedford was a doctor from Berlin, Martin Gumpert. When Annemarie arrived in New York, she became his newest and most troublesome patient. Erika wrote to her mother that Miro caused Gumpert and the siblings "great annoyance throughout the height of absurdity [her drug withdrawal treatment]— what a stubborn angel of misfortune." With the stubborn angel playing an unwitting cupid, Erika and Martin soon became inseparable.

At this point in her life, for inexplicable reasons, Erika "turned toward men," as Sybille Bedford put it. "Certainly she very much loved Therese Giehse, that was a very important friendship, but I only know that once she turned, she went off women, she really became interested in men, she went off with people's husbands even." A streak of opportunism can be discerned in her choice of partners; it may well have been sheer ambition that prompted the shift. Whatever the reason, Therese Giehse was in for a big surprise.

Before the *Statendam* had even docked in Hoboken, New Jersey, Erika began courting rich patrons for the New York opening of *The Peppermill*. Through the sheer force of her personality, she was able to find several interested sponsors within just a few weeks, including the popular author Fanny Hurst (best known for *Back Street* and *Imitation of Life*), publisher Alfred A. Knopf, and the extremely wealthy banker, philanthropist, and publisher of the *Nation*, Maurice Wertheim, whom Erika called her "crazy gentleman," because (presumably for tax purposes, but also, it turns out, with romantic intentions) he was willing to invest and possibly forfeit money on her show. For a while she led him to believe that her interest in him was more than strictly monetary, although the money was never far from her mind. In her letters home she never referred to him without commenting on their considerable age difference (he was twenty years older than she was) and his enormous wealth. The New York premiere of *The Peppermill* became a certainty when the Columbia Concert Corporation agreed to produce it and secured a theater, the Chanin Auditorium, on the seventeenth floor of the Chanin Building, at the corner of 42nd Street and Lexington Avenue. It was to open for a limited engagement on January 5, 1937, with nightly performances and a Saturday matinee, followed by a cross-country tour.

At the end of October, Erika wrote to her mother: "The troupe, I think, sails on the 4th [of November 1936]. Will they have visas? And if they—oh, oh, and oh—can learn English?—Giessky [Therese Giehse] needs to, urgently." But translating the lyrics proved even trickier than securing the visas, memorizing the English lines, or raising the funds. Most songs were simply untranslatable. Erika couldn't judge in advance which ones would work, so she had them all translated. She wrote to Katia, "All the little jokes, emphases, and foolishness that make sense in one's mother tongue,—where am I supposed to get that from?—and where am I supposed to go with it?"

Erika recruited her husband to translate one song that had been a staple in the cabaret for several years, "Why Is It So Cold?" Auden's translation turned out to be an improvement on the original.

> . . . Coldly we stand and witness justice shot,—
> Our hearts are cold,—for whom shall hearts be hot,—
> For other's wrong we have no wish to burn,—
> Let it alone,—it is not our concern.
>
> O why are we so cold,—
> And this cold hurts us so?
> Why,—for we shall soon
> Be only ice and snow.
>
> No,—it is your concern, your world, your hour,—
> And yours alone,—you only have the power,
> To make a little warmth, a little light
> Shine in our cold and wicked winternight.
>
> With harms swarming and by nightmare shaken,
> Only so long, as you refuse to waken,
> Take part in it,—what ghost is there that can
> Struggle at daybreak with the living man?
>
> Cold trembles in the dark,
> But perishes in light,—
> Why? Because the day
> Always defeats the night!

Most of the translations were far poorer, some even embarrassing. Klaus had contributed a poem, "The Loreley," which worked well for countless performances in Europe but ended up in English as:

I don't know what it's supposed to mean,
Since love has come to me,
But all of the folk in the village
Look angrily at me.

My old father threatens a beating,
Mama says her heart will break,
Because the young man I am meeting
Is old Mr. Levy's son Jake.

"But you are an Aryan German,"
Exclaims all the village vermin,
Ah, how I hate those venomous
people whispering: "Jews are enemies,
Jews are enemies, Jews are enemies."

Therese Giehse, accompanied by the two remaining *Peppermill* members, composer Magnus Henning and dancer Lotte Goslar, arrived in New York just in time to join Erika, Klaus, and Martin Gumpert for a large Thanksgiving feast at the Hotel Bedford. Erika was annoyed to discover that Therese had learned no English during their separation. Therese was annoyed because the trip had been long and uncomfortable, although Erika countered that her cement freighter must certainly have been steadier through the storm it encountered midway across the Atlantic than her own luxury liner, the *Statendam,* had been in a light breeze. Therese was further unnerved by her experience coming through immigration; she gave inexact and suspicious information, which almost landed her on Ellis Island—where, the word was, one could get out only by posting $1,000. Erika claimed that had this happened, she "would have raised the sum within a few hours." In any case, Therese, having made it through the ordeal, took her own room at the Hotel Bedford, bringing with her all kinds of "trouble," as Erika put it. She was nervous about the English language and extremely jealous of Erika, who had developed many seemingly close relationships and friendships in Therese's absence. She would have been even more wild and irate had she known that the recently divorced Maurice Wertheim had proposed to Erika only days before Therese arrived. Erika (still married to W. H. Auden) postponed giving him an answer.

Therese took a look at the translations and, to the extent that she could make sense of them, decided they were terrible. She complained that nothing was prepared for the premiere, and that there was no time left for her to consider all the details carefully with Erika as she was used to doing. This time Erika was moving ahead quickly without Therese; she had too much to do, "organizationally," to worry about the translation problems, and, furthermore, Therese's jealousy and negativity were getting on her nerves.

Under a lot of stress in the weeks leading up to the opening, Erika was not all that easy to get along with. Klaus had a "somewhat fierce quarrel" with her in late December, something to do with Michael Logan not being able to attend a *Peppermill* rehearsal, in which she seemed excessively harsh about Michael and unfair to Klaus. He finally was developing a relationship independent of Erika, and sure enough it was causing strife between them. There also were some unpleasant scenes concerning his escalating drug consumption. Klaus, no fighter, simply fell into inconsolable sadness.

Ever optimistic, as anyone in show business must be, Erika had high hopes for the American premiere. The show had been a runaway success across Europe, so despite Therese's gloom, Erika felt confident. But when the cabaret opened in early January, it was an unmitigated flop. According to Erika, the producer "did the same thing to our contract as was done to the Versailles treaty," and after only one week "we closed." The *New York Times* review could find nothing in the show worth praising except Erika herself: "a winning hostess with mettlesome eyes and an alert personality." Klaus reflected on everything that went wrong:

> I suppose that "failure" is an unduly harsh word to describe what happened to Erika's show. . . . But somehow it didn't quite click. . . . Maybe Erika made a mistake when presenting her show more or less in its original shape, but not in its original language. It was too outlandish and not exotic enough. The vigorous talent of Therese Giehse was hampered by the foreign idiom as by an inflexible corset. . . .

The Peppermill didn't translate well into English, and Therese's English *was* incomprehensible (the Columbia Concert Corporation cited

that as one of the prime reasons for breaking the contract), but it wasn't only linguistic problems that plagued the New York opening. Americans had no experience with the European style of literary cabaret—it was completely unknown to them as an art form. The humor, sophisticated and witty, sailed over the heads of the audience members. But the biggest obstacle was that Americans weren't ready to hear its political message. Erika realized too late that Americans "didn't want to be what I call Hitler-conscious. They were still so involved with the New Deal and all their internal political developments and difficulties. So they really couldn't understand *The Peppermill.*"

Erika took the failure hard. She had a "hell of a time" before the show started, once it began, and, most of all, when she learned it was to be discontinued. The financial deficit it incurred was considerable, for her personally as well as for her benefactor and suitor Maurice Wertheim. Apparently he didn't really want to lose money on the show, as Erika had thought, but lose money he did, and without getting any further with his marriage proposal to Erika.

Erika's cavalier liaisons entangled her in a complicated personal drama, played out in the bedrooms and hallways of the Hotel Bedford. Therese Giehse was jealous of Martin Gumpert and Martin Gumpert was jealous of Maurice Wertheim. *The Peppermill*'s troupe charged Erika with, on the one hand, paying them terribly while she lived like a millionaire and, on the other, not spending enough time with them because she was always off "with this dirty capitalist." Erika reported on the hubbub to Klaus: "Before I left the Bedford, there were those suicide speeches and talks, part of it with Giessky [Giehse], part of it with the Old Doc [Gumpert]. . . . Annemarie on the other hand moved around from room to room, talking into a frenzy and causing a lot of damage." Gumpert lost a lot of weight through the ordeal, sixteen pounds in a single week, and "would have most certainly ended his life if I had left him," Erika claimed. The portly Therese was also suffering, although not losing weight. Both suspected Erika of selling out to the highest bidder.

Then, under considerable pressure from Thomas Mann and Martin Gumpert (Klaus was not consulted, as he noted glumly), Erika decided to turn down Wertheim's offer of marriage. He was a shade "*too* rich" for her, anyway, she realized. Erika wrote him a beautiful good-bye letter, moved "as a beggar" into the Astor Hotel, and "actually left the friendly, extremely useful, and highly interesting Maurice . . . simply because he is not going to die from it." But he did promptly become severely ill, and, though he would recover, Erika considered herself to be his "murderess."

All this, and the hardest part of the entire New York fiasco, she told her mother, was dealing with Therese's "unsound psyche."

Meanwhile, Erika received an invitation from the New School for Social Research to reopen *The Peppermill* in its theater for a two-week run. The New School was home to the recently formed "University in Exile," an institute for the displaced German intelligentsia in New York who made up much of its faculty; it seemed the perfect venue and Erika became enthusiastic all over again. She made some changes in the attempt to Americanize the show for its revival, but it was too little, too late. One day before it was scheduled to reopen, her troupe gave up in despair and sailed back to Europe. Erika didn't even try to stop them.

She realized Therese in particular had to leave; there was nothing in New York to hold her, while stardom was beckoning her from the Zurich stage. Erika, on the other hand, was convinced that her own "personal chances here are good"; she was determined to stay on in the United States and make a life for herself. But first she had to either cancel the opening night of the run or face her audience entirely alone. With typical Erika resolve, she chose the latter. She stood on the bare stage and announced:

> Ladies and Gentlemen,—I am very proud and pleased to be with all of you tonight and I only am sorry, that my European Peppermill troupe just has sailed yesterday taking most of our words and music with them. So I shall just be able . . . to read for you a little poem by Wystan Auden, called the "Dictator's Song."

It was wise of Erika to choose a new piece written for her by W. H. Auden instead of a translation from the German. "Dictator's Song" brought home how easy it was for ordinary Germans to fall prey to the seductive Nazi rhetoric. Erika recited the lines in her thick German accent,

> Are you living in the city all your dreary little life?
> In a dreary little office with a dreary little wife?
> I will give you flags and banners,
> And processions and a band.
> You shall march in step together,
> You will feel just grand!

Refrain:
For I am the simple answer to the man's and maiden's prayer.
I am the spring in the desert, I am the song in the air.
The clue to history, I am the mystery, I am the miracle man.

Despite the absence of cast, musicians, and props, the response that night was the best *The Peppermill* received in New York. The University in Exile turned out in force, and understood both the medium and the message. Erika probably could have performed the show's entire repertoire in German, without a single complaint from the audience.

The positive response from the University in Exile audience was some consolation but it was never Erika's intention to preach to the choir. In Europe she had deliberately avoided performing in non-German-speaking cities like Paris and Marseilles, where the only audiences who would understand the show were German émigrés like herself. There was no point if they already knew—all too well—the calamity that had befallen her homeland.

If she were to reach the American public, Erika realized, she'd better learn English properly and deliver that message in a form they could understand:

> The medium there, that one could really do something with, was for me the lecture circuit. I had already certain things that made it easier, as an actress and especially with so much cabaret experience, so I found direct contact with foreign audiences relatively easy. The language was for me a very difficult hurdle, naturally, as I spoke only a little school-English, and I had to really learn it.

Erika started out her new career as a lecturer with a bang. She accepted an invitation from the American Jewish Congress to give a speech in two months' time; it was to be delivered as part of a rally for peace and democracy at Madison Square Garden in New York City. Erika quickly learned proper English and shed her German accent, replacing it with a British one (from her school-English drills back in Germany) that she would retain her entire life. Also on the program that evening was New York's mayor, Fiorello La Guardia. Enormously proud of his daughter, the Magician sent her a telegram from Switzerland, stating that she was representing him on the stage as well as herself. It was the first time he expressed a willingness to be associated with the activities of either of his two eldest children.

On the occasion of your appearance before the American Jewish Congress I congratulate you heartily STOP You are speaking there as an independent person but also in a sense you are speaking in my stead as my daughter and as my intellectual disciple STOP It is a fine opportunity to bear witness in favor of the good and right of truth and humanity and against violence and lies which so often in these times seem victorious and are seductive to many STOP You are speaking to Americans, and you may tell them that the entire world is looking to the great America, the land of Lincoln, of Whitman and of Franklin Roosevelt, and believes in its mission to lead humanity forward on the path of peace and social justice into a future of which mankind need not be ashamed STOP Love

The telegram moved Erika so much that she chose to read it to the packed Madison Square Garden audience—but not until she had finished giving a speech in her own right, on a subject which was her own urgent concern: "Women in the Third Reich." She began by pointing out one essential difference between Fascist and anti-Fascist rallies: namely, that Fascist rallies perpetuate and propagate lies, whereas anti-Fascists have the advantage of truth on their side. She went on to declare an uncomfortable truth behind the Nazi rise to power: women voters had been primarily responsible for electing Hitler. And yet the ungrateful Nazis turned around and made them the first casualty: they demanded women cease studying, working outside the home, having personal ambition—in short, they demanded women transform themselves from rational individuals into baby makers for the Führer's war machine. This is a theme Erika would return to time and again: the plight of women—and its corollary, the plight of children—under the Swastika.

With adroitness Erika segued into a discussion of the Nuremberg "Race" Laws, and began reading from this bizarre document. A typical sentence reads, "Further forbidden are marriages between a German Jewish mongrel with one Jewish grandparent (one-quarter Jew) and another German Jewish mongrel with one Jewish grandparent." Another provision stipulates that "German-blooded" domestic help under the age of forty-five may not be employed in German homes that have Jewish tenants. Although Erika admitted it all sounded rather ridiculous, she assured her audience that it "is far more dangerous than it is funny." She ended her speech with a rallying cry which was also her own personal mission: "We must do all in our power, everything, with all our head and heart, *to help make mankind see,* so that it may unanimously recognize its enemy, the arch-enemy of civilization, of progress, of all human dignity—Hitler's Fascism!"

Klaus missed Erika's rousing debut. His three-month visitor's visa ran out in mid-January, and he set sail for Europe once more. Erika wasn't happy about his departure, and wrote to him soon afterward: "It was a terrible time to slip away and I knew at the time that I needed [your] presence and support in all these situations." Right before he departed, he had joined Erika and the three departing *Peppermill* performers for a night out. The relationships between Erika and the rest of the troupe, and even between Erika and Klaus, were somewhat strained. In his diary he wrote, "Erika's tears . . . Endless emotion from the troupe, tenderness, and the enduring sense of affiliation between my life and theirs . . . Genommen [took drugs], last night and today, rather a lot."

Klaus sailed to Amsterdam, where he visited Fritz Landshoff, traveled down to Paris, and eventually made his way by train to his parents' home in Küsnacht, Switzerland.

It was not a cheerful homecoming. At first no one was there to meet him at the station; his letter had arrived too late. Finally his younger sister Elisabeth showed up, but the entire family went out that night, leaving him alone.

When he did see his parents, he was "not very happy" to learn that Thomas was embarking on publishing a bimonthly literary journal for German émigrés, called *Mass und Wert* (Measure and Value), something of a successor to Klaus's recently defunct journal, *Die Sammlung*, although his father hadn't thought to inform or consult Klaus about it. An editor named Ferdinand Lion was already appointed, despite Klaus's considerable experience. Thomas Mann's newest work, *Lotte in Weimar,* would soon appear in the journal in serial form, virtually guaranteeing its success. Klaus had some initial apprehensions about Ferdinand Lion that would prove to have been valid. A year later he wrote publicly, "It must, however, be said that large sections of the exiles are, on the whole, disappointed with Herr Lion's editorship. The rather capricious exclusiveness he shows toward a large number of exiled writers has not always, many think, been to the advantage of the review."

At the time, however, Klaus's disappointment was solely with his father. He wrote in his diary, "I perceive, again, very strongly and not without bitterness, Z's [the Magician's] complete coldness to me. Whether benign, whether irritated (a very curious kind of 'embarrassment' at the existence of his son): *never* interested, *never* engaged in any real sense with me. His universal lack of interest in people is here especially intensified. Consequently, lines from his monstrous pool of superficialities—because he's uninterested, . . . forgetting me entirely in the matter of this journal."

These superficial exchanges with his father were especially exasperating to Klaus, who shunned shallow pleasantries even when meeting casual acquaintances, let alone close friends or family. He cared passionately about so many things—from the private troubles of his friends to the momentous issues of his time—and took it for granted that others would care passionately too. His personal intensity, combined with a touch of Old World quiet reserve, kept him from ever uttering the empty or frivolous phrases that have cluttered modern colloquial language. Christopher Isherwood said of him, "I don't think I ever heard him utter an insincere remark. Insincerity is a form of laziness, and he was one of the least lazy people I have ever known."

While in Switzerland Klaus had a long visit with Therese Giehse (now living in Zurich); they discussed the "complex situation: E[rika], New York, The Peppermill, Maurice [Wertheim], etc." Klaus also paid a visit to a well-known Zurich specialist, Dr. Katzenstein, to ask his advice about withdrawal cures. For the past few weeks, Klaus had written almost daily in his diary about his addiction, admitting to himself that it was taking on alarming forms; he had gone too far and did not know how to come back.

Erika, back in New York, sensed this. In early February she had written, "Don't eat too much H[eroin]. I myself had some in the last phase, but that's going to stop now." In late March she wrote again, commanding him more strongly: "Don't take any more 'tuna' [heroin]—I won't either!!! It is unhealthy! It is expensive! It is dangerous! Don't you recognize that?" She ended the letter with "I embrace you, my love—we are too far removed from one another and it gnaws at my marrow."

On March 25, the primary event that drew Klaus back to Europe occurred: he was awarded Czechoslovakian citizenship. It was granted as a personal favor to Thomas Mann by President Beneš himself, and it extended to the entire stateless Mann family, including Uncle Heinrich—all but Erika, who already had citizenship, in Britain, through her marriage to Auden. Klaus loved the democratic spirit of Prague, and the hour of informal conversation he spent with the intelligent and amiable Czech president "belongs to my most cherished memories," he later wrote in his autobiography. But best of all was the arrival of a passport, valid for five years.

From Prague Klaus traveled to Budapest, which seemed to him the Fascistic counterpart to democratic Prague. "Not quite openly, and seriously, so," Klaus explained, not quite like Germany or Italy, but Klaus bristled at Hungary's despotic tendencies at the same time he was drawn to its more rebellious sides: the garish, pleasure-seeking nightlife along the Danube and the anti-Fascist community of intellectuals, adhering to the humanitarian principles of Voltaire, that congregated privately in Budapest. Klaus stayed in the palatial mansion of one of these intellectuals, the Baron von Hatvany, who had already been exiled twice, once by the leftists for being a baron and once by the current dictator Horthy for being a liberal. His third and last period of exile would begin one year later, when Hitler's troops marched into Hungary.

Through the baron Klaus met the young American Thomas Quinn Curtiss, an aspiring filmmaker who had studied with Eisenstein. There was something about Curtiss's face which strongly recalled that of René Crevel. Despite their uncanny resemblance, however, Klaus realized immediately their differences: Curtiss was not only younger in years, but the product of a younger, less troubled civilization. He was less complicated, and he had no wish to die. Klaus briefly noted their first encounter in his diary: "In the evening, picked up the little Curtiss (cute, a little blasé and arrogant kid) at the Hungaria."

Four days later he took Thomas Curtiss to dinner. It was late May and they sat outdoors in a garden restaurant, gazing at each other across the table. They hiked up Gellert Hill to the old Citadel, to take in the grand view of the rushing Danube from up high, then sat outside on the terrace of the Hotel Gellert as the moon rose. Klaus was thirty and ready to fall in love; Thomas was twenty and looking for kicks. Klaus took him home to the mansion that night:

> Stayed with him. Happiness and mystery of a new encounter. His hysteria, sadness, intelligence, tenderness, sensuality, his laughter, his sighing; eyes, lips, gaze, voice . . .

It was not his usual drifting that had landed Klaus in Budapest. Klaus had come on the recommendation of Dr. Katzenstein in Zurich, to try a heroin cure at Siesta, a famous sanatorium. After a week at the baron's mansion, much of it spent with the young Thomas Curtiss, he checked himself into Siesta.

Klaus was escorted to a room with barred windows, which he immediately transformed into "home" by displaying his personal photographs. He then lay in bed, sweating profusely, with what he complained was only a "minuscule" drop of heroin entering his vein. A few days into the cure he wrote a letter, thanking the baron for his hospitality. His handwriting was barely legible—the demons colonizing his mind seem to be writhing across the page. One can hardly make out from the scrawl that he was commanding Hatvany and "Curtiss-dear" not to visit him. His doctor forbade it, fearing they might smuggle in some drugs.

Erika hadn't heard from Klaus directly in ages—this in itself was extremely odd. Finally, in early June, Michael Logan showed Erika a short note from Klaus which confirmed all her worst fears about his condition and gave the sanatorium as his return address. Immediately she wrote to Klaus, chastising him for causing her extreme anxiety. Not only was she worried; she was "very angry as well," so much so that "we have to invent new curse words for you and the things you did. I don't have the courage to do that right now because I imagine you're very weak." She went on in the most forceful language to beg, plead, beseech, and implore Klaus not to leave the sanatorium even one day before the doctors felt he was completely cured, not "until everyone asks, 'what do you still want from here, mister, you've made it.'"

On June 6, before Erika's letter arrived, Klaus telephoned his sister from the sanatorium. The rarity of a transatlantic telephone call in 1937 was enough to make Thomas worried—he decided to call Klaus's doctor, Robert Klopstock, directly for a firsthand report. It's not clear that Dr. Klopstock was the best man for the job; an acquaintance of Thomas's, he was more scholar than physician and seems to have been out of his depth when it came to Klaus. When Dr. Klopstock asked Klaus why he took the morphine in the first place (which led to the heroin), Klaus simply answered that it was his "urge to die."

The withdrawal cure, deemed by Klaus an evil torture, could not be called a complete success. In his diary Klaus confided his worries about how he could live without taking drugs:

> How will I be able to survive *without* this dangerous consolation. Will I be able to love the dear Thomas Curtiss enough? I pray that I will be able to love him enough.

In the summer of 1937, Klaus traveled in Europe with Curtiss, showing him some of the sites of his exile—Annemarie's house in Sils, where he had written the last chapter of his Tchaikovsky novel, *Pathetic Sym-*

phony, and had also worked on *Mephisto*, his adopted cities of Amsterdam and Paris, his parents' home in Küsnacht (he told his mother in advance that he wanted her to meet his special friend). The trip, like everything else he did, was paid for by his allowance from his parents.

In Paris Klaus had plans to visit with his uncle. Heinrich always gave Klaus his unconditional support, in stark contrast to Thomas. Yet Heinrich felt Klaus was pulling away, resisting his uncle's offers of assistance and advice. Klaus did agree to think and rethink before joining any and all émigré groups, since Heinrich convinced him that he "has his and our name to protect." After Klaus stood him up for their second meeting, Heinrich wrote to Thomas,

> You know how highly I estimated Klaus at his expressive best, in Tchaikovsky [Klaus's novel about the composer]. I find it the more painful then that he is personally inaccessible—this due not so much to severity as forgetfulness. In Paris we had arranged for a second meeting, which I thought would be more substantive than the brief get-together late in the evening. It didn't happen because of a misunderstanding, which also might ultimately have been evasion.

His austere room at the Siesta haunted Klaus throughout his travels, and somewhere between Holland and the Côte d'Azur he began writing one of his best pieces, *The Barred Window*, a melancholy novella about the tormented, eccentric gay Bavarian king, Ludwig II, held prisoner in his own castle on the shores of Lake Starnberg. In the story, his psychiatrist, Dr. von Gudden, tries to convince Ludwig that nothing is wrong, that he is still king, but the bars on his window betray the deception.

The narrative imprisons its readers as well by using only the inner musings of the lonely, mad king, a stream of consciousness written in first-person voice, to trap us in his unstable mind. His thoughts are preoccupied by mourning for his dead protégé and lover, Richard Wagner; his realization that he will never hear Wagner's music again is simply unbearable. Under the pretext of needing a walk, Ludwig finally convinces Dr. von Gudden to let him go outside. With suicide on his mind, the king walks into the lake. His doctor tries to stop him, and after a struggle they both drown.

Klaus had been fascinated since childhood by the legends surrounding this tragic, romantic figure. He dismissed much of his historical knowledge and instead reinterpreted the legends, focusing not on "the

Klaus Mann at the Hotel Bedford, his New York home.

charmed fairy-tale prince . . . but rather the marked, lost one, the victim of secret intrigues and his own hubris." He wrote in his diary, "I like the sad story. Autobiographical, here even as strongly as in Tchaikovsky [*Pathetic Symphony*]." Klaus felt an affinity with the abject king of his story, but never recognized the considerable literary achievement of the work, perhaps because it was written quickly and seemingly effortlessly. Publicly he tended to denigrate the novella as insignificant, "only a slim tale," although it is one of the most innovative and imaginative of his many books.

By September, Klaus felt obliged "to forget all about the inspired melancholia of drowned or immortal kings. Hitler was neither drowned nor immortal. He had to be done away with." So Klaus said his good-byes to Europe and set sail for New York once more, to "do my bit," as he saw it. He took Thomas Quinn Curtiss, whom he nicknamed "Tomski," with him.

Photographers and journalists greeted Klaus on his arrival, and one from the *New York Post* asked him about his love life. Klaus did not introduce Tomski, standing right next to him; instead he mentioned something vague about a romance with a Swiss girl, alluding to Annemarie Schwarzenbach. Tomski, who had been away from the States for three years, spent his days visiting family and old friends, but he spent his nights with Klaus. For the first time since Poschinger Street in Munich, Klaus felt at home—in his single room at the Hotel Bedford in New York City.

Erika also met them at the pier and announced that she would help Klaus through his withdrawal. She meanwhile continued to take recreational drugs herself, although she now stopped short of heroin. It was something of a perpetual power play between them, with Erika needing to prove she was the one in control. According to their sister Elisabeth, "Erika always was of the opinion that Klaus could not cope with the problem [drugs], whereas she could."

Klaus handed over to her his remaining stash, and tried not to take anything for several days—except for two "new, interesting tablets" (Klaus didn't even know what he was taking) given to him by Erika's doctor friend Martin Gumpert.

Erika warned "Old Doc" that she'd dump him next, but whether she'd really follow through, she wasn't completely sure. She felt that Klaus underestimated Gumpert; he "is quite strange and decent, also writes beautiful poems, and has his merits—above all if I don't relinquish too much space in my daily life for him, which I don't have to do." Klaus seems to have had more use for Gumpert than Erika had: the doctor would come to supply Klaus not only with pills but with a variety of prescribed injections. Whether he thought he was actually helping Klaus or trying to undermine Erika's efforts to help Klaus is unclear.

Erika and her managing agent, William B. Feakins, had arranged a lecture tour for Klaus. Immediately upon landing he began preparing for it, and soon was zigzagging the New World much as he had the Old, occasionally meeting up with his sister en route. Over the next few years, Erika and Klaus gave countless lectures, together and separately, across the country. The titles of these lectures ranged from contemporary political questions ("What Price Peace?" "What Does the Youth of Europe Believe in Today?" and "Children in Goosestep") to literary themes

DISTINGUISHED SON OF A NOTED FAMILY

KLAUS MANN

Novelist

Editor

Playwright

Studio Stein, Paris

offers for this season's lecture subjects

AFTER HITLER—WHAT?
A FAMILY AGAINST A DICTATORSHIP
MY FATHER AND HIS WORK
THE TWO GERMANYS
SCHOOL OF HUMANITY
(Democracy and the Youth)
GERMANY YESTERDAY—GERMANY TOMORROW

> Mr. Mann will be glad to speak on a suggested
> literary subject if notified far enough in advance

("The German Theater until 1933 and Since," "German Literature of To-day," and, reluctantly, at the demand of their agent, "Our Father and His Work"). Perhaps surprisingly, Klaus found he too had a talent for lectur-ing, and when the siblings appeared at the Congregation Children of Israel Temple in Memphis, Tennessee, the local paper noted that Klaus "succeeded in charming his large audience, and amusing them with oc-casional attempts at American slang expressions with which he is hardly familiar."

Erika was also easygoing and relaxed as a lecturer, but her style was quite different from Klaus's. Igor Pahlen recalled, "Whenever she spoke to the public, it was in the manner that a very nice, understanding teacher would address her schoolchildren, or perhaps as a nurse would talk to her patients." And she would win over her listeners because they would feel flattered that "the famous Erika Mann is speaking to us, almost as if she were one of us."

As lecturers, Erika and Klaus were forthright, informed, passionate, articulate, persuasive, and provocative—but *charming* was the word most frequently used by their audiences to describe them, whether they lectured together or alone. When Klaus spoke at the First Presbyterian Church in Buffalo, New York, the organizer admitted that the full room of listeners initially came to hear the son of a famous father, but soon was gripped by Klaus's sincerity and his rich and tolerant spirit. The director of the Ford Hall Forum, which invited Klaus to Boston, thought Klaus the best speaker they'd ever had; the packed audience was absorbed not only by his articulate, urgent message but by his charming personality. Erika's reviews were equally laudatory; thank-you letters from Lake Erie College, Pennsylvania Teachers College, and Kent State University men-tion her "personal charm" and "delightful personality." Her Kent State audience was surprised by her impeccable English, which "is superior to that of many speakers who use it as their native tongue."

Not everyone loved the lectures, however. Erika would often run into messenger boys backstage after her talks, waiting to hand her let-ters marked "Urgent" or "An American Mother" or even "Heil Hitler." These letters, invariably written in a foreigner's English, warned her that the letter writer's "patience is exhausted" concerning Erika, and that "a violent death will soon end [her] criminal, treacherous and warmonger-ing activities." Erika never considered backing down. "Well, I can take it," she told herself, "determined as I am never to let my own patience get exhausted, but to go on with my educational job, at the same time slowly but surely improving my own education. Patience, we have been told, comes from Heaven, and as long as it is coupled with militant activity I whole-heartedly agree."

Despite the death threats, the grind of being on the road, and having to get used to the peculiar flattened-out sound of their own names in the mouths of Americans, Erika and Klaus enjoyed the lecture circuit; it became "a pleasurable habit." The Pullman cars they traveled on were peculiar at first, and it was challenging to have to dress and undress behind the green curtains, but soon they realized "one gets used to everything." Often the surprises they encountered were friendly ones, such as when a troupe of children came out in pink tights and did acrobatics right before their talk. They took each engagement as a small personal challenge, not necessarily to win over the audience to their point of view, although of course this was the ultimate goal, but simply, "by means of sundry tricks," to keep them awake and entertained, which as lecturers they saw as "a matter of professional honor."

They met people in their audience they'd never have the chance to meet otherwise, "conservative club women and radical politicians, rabbis and professors, snobs and Quakers, 'misunderstood geniuses,' real young poets and false prophets, wise people and foolish, ambitious and confused, modest and clever." They felt they had meaningful things to say to all these people, and genuinely sensed there were meaningful things to be learned from them as well. Erika and Klaus soaked up everything they could learn about America, because they truly believed in America, as imperfect as it was, as the last hope for the civilized world.

Erika and Klaus both loved America and felt at ease in the New World, but they had very different relationships to the place they made their home—New York City. Erika had complete faith in the principles of American political life, and particularly admired President Roosevelt, but socially she surrounded herself with German intellectuals rather than Americans, and flitted noncommittally between New York and California. Of the entire continental United States, Klaus loved only New York, and rather than socialize with émigrés he was drawn to Americans, who seemed so innocent, optimistic, and refreshingly naïve, unburdened by the weight of history and the metaphysical quandaries which plagued him. He was particularly beguiled by young working-class men who didn't understand or share his inner turmoil. His attraction to New York and America was more than ideological; it was psychosexual.

Under Klaus's initiative, the siblings committed themselves to write two nonfiction books together about the exile experience: *The Other Ger-*

many and *Escape to Life*. Written before the outbreak of war in Europe, *The Other Germany* sees Nazism as a particularly German psychosis: "A case of collective insanity such as National Socialism has deep roots in the character and psyche of the stricken nation." The book acknowledges that the Germans are an enigmatic people, "the 'bad boy' among the nations," aggressive, condescending, both tyrannical and submissive. Yet it also makes a desperate plea for the recognition of an Other Germany, the enlightened culture that produced the world's greatest composers, philosophers, and scientists, the Germany to which Erika and Klaus, no longer German citizens, still belonged. The book sweeps through the history of Germany from the days of Martin Luther to those of Adolf Hitler, a history "rich in glory yet burdened with guilt and misery," and tries to reconcile the contradictions of the German character. As Klaus would later write, "It was a ticklish, not to say painful job to analyze, at that crucial point, the famous Two Souls which, alas, dwell together in the breast, not only of Goethe's Faust, but also of Goethe's nation."

Although *The Other Germany* would feature both of their names on the cover, Erika set off in the middle of their collaboration to accompany their parents on Thomas's first lecture tour across the United States. She took on the daunting task of trying to acclimate the exceedingly German author to the strangeness of American customs. Both her parents approached the new continent with the inquisitiveness of intelligent children, but Thomas spoke no English and misunderstood much of what he witnessed. When Erika told him something about a football game, he replied, sadly, "I don't understand very much about baseball," and Erika politely abstained from correcting him. His supply of Swiss cigarettes was exhausted, and he didn't believe he could smoke the American ones. He received letters in which he was asked to sponsor one thing or another. " 'What is a sponsor?' he asked me, with a look of despair."

While Thomas, Katia, and Erika and their fourteen suitcases shuffled in two taxis from train station to hotel to train station, Klaus was left to write most of *The Other Germany* alone. Erika's slightly patronizing, somewhat prosaic writing style is occasionally discernible in the book, interrupting Klaus's more passionate, vulnerable literary voice, but the two never fully merge into a coherent whole despite the constant use of the pronoun "we."

Escape to Life, on the other hand, was a true collaboration, and it reads as though Erika and Klaus had fun writing it, notwithstanding the rather grim subject matter. The book marks the beginning of both Erika's and

Klaus's transition to writing in English, and the early unpublished drafts reveal all their charming mistakes. Intended as a documentary portrait of German culture in exile, the book includes their own personal stories, Erika's in the form of a playful interview by her ideal interviewer, and Klaus's in a more reflective piece. Erika begins by locating the siblings in a small Midwest town, where they are waiting for a train connection. She describes their mood as somewhat sad. Klaus chimes in, "Too bad we don't know anyone here! Not a soul. It would be so nice if someone were to come just now, if we could see some friendly face. An interviewer is what we need!" Erika concurs, "An interviewer. Quite right, but not just an ordinary one—the ideal interviewer." At this point Klaus takes on the persona of the ideal stranger, and the interview ensues:

> KLAUS: Which is your favorite city?
> ERIKA: Munich. I was born and brought up there. . . . Of course you know better than I that we were inseparable from each other and from our bicycles.
> KLAUS: When did you begin to take an interest in politics?
> ERIKA: In Germany I never took any interest in politics, almost until the end. I was of the mistaken opinion that politics was the business of politicians, and that people should mind their own business. And a lot of us thought so; that's why Hitler came to power.
> KLAUS: When did you leave Germany and how and why? Did you know that you wouldn't see your country for a long, long time?
> ERIKA: When shall we ever see it again?
> KLAUS: I thought I was asking the questions here, not you.
> KLAUS: Was it a grave, a terrible decision?
> ERIKA: No, it wasn't bitter. It was bitter to see the Nazi flag. But where it waved we couldn't live.
> KLAUS: You came to America in the Autumn of 1936?
> ERIKA: I've lived here ever since. I love America.
> KLAUS: I didn't ask you about that.
> ERIKA: But I want to say it. For the first time since my flight from Germany, I almost feel at home somewhere.

Klaus's personal story starts with the announcement that he is almost thirty-two years old, and can't say whether he is in the middle of his life or already nearing its end. "It's always good to count on a sudden ending. For that matter, the circumstances we grew up in, and are living in today, have robbed us of any confidence in the stability of things." He recaps the imaginative childhood he shared with Erika, tells the story of their sudden exodus from Germany, and ends, curiously, with a meditation on whether life is worth living:

> Life, with all its struggles, its enchantments and its unendurable torments must bear its own enigmatic sense within itself. Since in this creation no energy is wasted, why should the energies of our hearts lose their way and be lost? If at the end—an archangel or the "ideal interviewer"—were to ask me: Are you glad you lived? then, still exhausted by the wear and tear of earthly life, or already refreshed by the joys no mortal can conceive, I would reply: Life on earth was a vile business. I shall be eternally grateful for having been allowed to share it.

Before Erika and Klaus even began compiling their account of the plight of other émigrés, the individual stories they could tell multiplied out of control. In March 1938, Austria fell to the Nazis with little resistance, indeed welcomed the Nazis with open arms, and a new wave of refugees flooded out of Vienna. Erika and Klaus dealt with the shock of this news by burying themselves in work, "as if it were a solution or a narcotic." Fortunately they finished the manuscript before they would be forced to add any more refugee groups—Hitler invaded Czechoslovakia that September.

Escape to Life was favorably reviewed, sold well, and went into a second printing. Klaus didn't take much pleasure in its success, however: the book could do little to help those suffering under Fascism in Europe, and furthermore, as a journalistic effort, *Escape to Life* was less dear to his heart than his novel *Der Vulkan* (The Volcano), written simultaneously (although in German) and published in Amsterdam by Querido.

> Neither effort, however, was adequate to resuscitate one of Hitler's victims; nor could my prose save anybody from the claws of the Gestapo or melt the callous heart of democratic consuls. . . . For the novelist can only immortalize the suffering of his fellow men, while the consul is in a position to shorten it by means of a stamp in a passport.

Der Vulkan was Klaus's longest, most ambitious, and probably his best work. From his prodigious output, this novel shows virtually his only serious attempt to experiment with literary form, for Klaus was, as he had written of André Gide, "daringly progressive, even revolutionary, in his social and psychological views [yet] rather conservative in his literary preferences." It is written in a modern fragmentary style influenced by André Gide's *The Counterfeiters*. Of *The Counterfeiters,* Klaus wrote, "The texture of the novel consists of a multitude of dramas, all of which are interwoven with the utmost skill and a great deal of musical tact. The reader is allowed, or required, to visualize every character as belonging in several groups simultaneously and as playing a role in several actions at one time." This contrapuntal structure is exactly what Klaus attempted in *Der Vulkan,* although "tact" is not a word that could ever be used in relation to Klaus's writing, and his frantic state of mind seemed incapable of exercising "the utmost skill." One critic wrote of him, "Is it any wonder that one who took aim so nervously and hastily should so often miss the mark? It is more surprising that he sometimes hit the bulls'-eye." While it is unduly harsh to say he so often missed the mark, he did come closest to the bull's-eye with *Der Vulkan.*

In the novel, the destinies of his many characters unfold simultaneously in Paris, Amsterdam, Zurich, and New York, all places he himself had cast his anchor. The characters can be viewed as a dramatis personae of German émigrés Klaus had known, a wide array of performers and intellectuals living in exile or fighting in the Resistance. Marion von Kammer is a German actress who travels around Europe for one-night shows and is pestered by adoring lesbian admirers; she is clearly Erika's fictional counterpart. Eventually she marries the German intellectual Professor Benjamin Abel, ostensibly based on Thomas Mann. On closer inspection, all the characters seem more autobiographical than anything else, but none of them so resembles Klaus as his protagonist Martin Korella, a frustrated author and drug addict who leaves behind his unfinished life's work about the exile experience when he dies. Klaus's descriptions of the torments of heroin withdrawal are rendered with excruciating realism:

> All of him was twitching: feet and hands jerked themselves into spasms. He threw his tortured head here and there. Never would he have thought it possible to be simultaneously so exhausted and so stirred up. He was too weak to leave his bed, but his wet, trembling body couldn't bear the same position for thirty seconds. No

other illness was nearly as terrible. Fever and a more solid, controllable pain were outright positive feelings, compared with this colossal embarrassment. "This is how a fish must feel, who has been thrown on land," thought Martin. "I am wriggling just like a fish on dry land. My God, my God, what have I done, that I must flap like a poor little fish?"

To Klaus's great disappointment, the novel sold only three hundred copies. Yet it earned him the praise he craved most of all—that of his father. Thomas admitted to Klaus that at first he "secretly had the wicked intention" of not reading it entirely, but rather "just looking into" the book. That was what he usually did, hastily flipping through Klaus's books simply to appease Katia. A few years earlier, a family friend noted that whenever a new book by Klaus appeared in the house, "Thommy is not permitted to read anything else before it. On that Katia is very strict." But this time instead of skimming he actually read the novel carefully, and urged Heinrich to read it—as "it would do him good to hear a positive word from his famous uncle." His far more famous father took the time to write a serious response:

> Well, then: fully and thoroughly read it and it touched me and made me laugh, I enjoyed it and was really satisfied and more than once I was really moved. For a long time now people didn't take you seriously, they saw you as the "son-of" (T. Mann's little boy), a spoiled brat, I couldn't change that. But now it's not to be denied that you are capable of more, more than most—therefore my satisfaction on reading, and my other emotions rightfully stem from that too. . . . In a word, I congratulate you sincerely and with fatherly pride. Sincerely, Z [Magician].

It is a crafty document which conceals more than it reveals. Thomas wrote countless congratulatory letters filled with meaningless compliments to colleagues whose work he privately scorned, using similarly empty phrases. As for those "people" who didn't take Klaus seriously, Thomas couldn't do anything about them because he himself was at the top of the list. And he never denied that Klaus was capable of more; that was the source of his disappointment. Not a lot more, just "more than most." This book proved it again for him by falling short of what Klaus was capable of.

This letter coincided with the publication of Thomas Mann's novel

Lotte in Weimar (published in German by Bermann-Fischer, now operating out of Stockholm). In it the son of the great poet Johann Wolfgang von Goethe is an unsympathetic character trapped in the role of *Dichterkind*. Although August von Goethe bears little resemblance to Klaus, once can discern in him Thomas's reworking of his troubled relationship with his own son. The character is introduced to the reader with "August is his son; and to the father's mind the boy's existence exhausted itself in that fact." Despite the unattractive qualities with which he endows August von Goethe, Thomas expresses sympathy for the impossible situation his character finds himself in: "To be the son of a great man is a high fortune, a considerable advantage. But it is likewise an oppressive burden, a permanent derogation of one's ego."

Thomas's letter to Klaus becomes heartfelt when it addresses the sections of *Der Vulkan* in which Martin Korella undergoes an unsuccessful detoxification cure for heroin addiction. Thomas found Klaus's description of this process "so extraordinary a piece of narrative that I stopped thinking about Germany and morality, politics and struggle and just read on, because I had never before read anything like it." Here he seems genuinely affected by the book, although not by Klaus's writing so much as by the new and somewhat shocking subject matter. And of course it is telling that he knew nothing about this experience even though his own son had gone through it only one year before.

Klaus was painfully aware of all of this, the bland compliments, the disappointments, the lack of interest in the crucial events of Klaus's life. Concerning his father's superficial attitude toward him, he had written in his diary, "Pleasant utterances, almost incidental, for *Journey into Freedom** or *Mephisto* NO exception. He writes to complete strangers just as pleasantly. A mixture of highest intelligence, almost charitable courtesy—and ice-coldness. This is especially accentuated when it concerns me. I am not mistaken."

Nonetheless Klaus needed to find in his father's words the approval he craved. Thomas wanted Klaus to prove himself to the world, but Klaus wanted to prove himself to his father, the only "they" Klaus really cared about who didn't take him seriously. Klaus wrote back, acknowledging his gratitude to his father for reading the book and commenting on it before revealing his awareness of his father's sleight of hand:

---

* *Journey into Freedom,* the first novel Klaus wrote while in exile, was published in German as *Flucht in den Norden* (Escape to the North) by Querido in Amsterdam in 1934, and by Knopf in New York in 1936.

Dear Magician,

. . . Your letter, which arrived early today, is such a beautiful, comforting, and fortifying gift, that I decided I must answer and thank you for it immediately. . . . You wrote that the good parts of *Der Vulkan* gave you satisfaction. And satisfaction is exactly the right word to describe my feelings when I received your epistle. For, if it is a satisfaction for the father to see his son prove himself, at least to a certain degree, to the world, then reversely *le fils* feels satisfaction to prove to "the great (all-seeing) father" that one is more than just a little "son-of" and a buffoon. And this all the more so because the father's eye has also for some time been cast somewhat full of concern and scorn.

When Klaus finished *Der Vulkan* in the summer of 1938, he and Erika left for Spain to report on the Spanish Civil War, not as objective journalists but as passionate defenders of the Loyalist cause. As usual, the siblings were prescient. They realized that "what was happening in Spain was but a bloody prologue, a sort of mortally serious rehearsal of what might be in store for the world at large." They were horrified to see the devastation inflicted by the growing German war machine, which was using the Spanish Republic to perfect its technological advances in aerial warfare. During the three weeks they spent in the war zone, they interviewed everyone from homeless children to government officials, from Catholic priests to soldiers. The endurance, passion, and heroism of the Spanish people as well as of the International Brigade moved them deeply, even though it already seemed to be a lost cause. They gave a radio broadcast from Barcelona and wired their articles to various newspapers abroad.

Erika embarked on writing several books without Klaus. Her most influential book, *School for Barbarians*, was a well-documented indictment of the Nazi education system, or more accurately, the systematic brainwashing of Germany's children. Published in New York in 1938 (and in Amsterdam by Querido the same year, under the title *Zehn Millionen Kinder* [Ten Million Children]), *School for Barbarians* makes for deeply disturbing reading. It outlines the typical day of a German child, who learns to count bombs instead of apples, studies racial superiority instead of science, and memorizes Hitler's speeches instead of Goethe's poetry—which does nothing to further the child's language skills, as Hitler "is hardly a master of the language. . . . It is beyond his power to speak a few consecutive German sentences correctly." With this curriculum in place, and each child given the opportunity to learn nothing else, the Nazi pro-

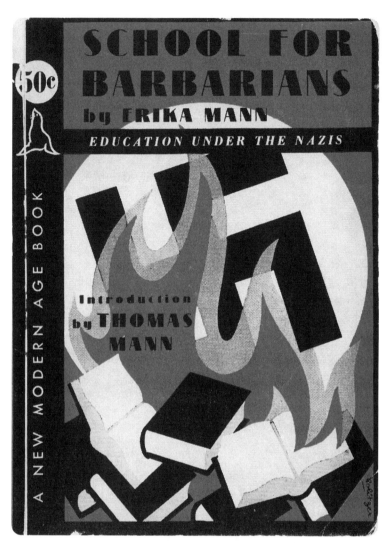

"Who has the youth has the future," wrote Erika.

gram builds the foundation for its future. There is little in the book to support Thomas Mann's claim, in his introduction to both the English- and German-language editions, that despite its repellent subject, "even its pain and anger are appealing, while the author's sense of humor, her power of seeing 'the funny side,' the gentle mockery in which she clothes her scorn, go far to make our horror dissolve." A review in *Time* magazine called Erika intrepid, angry, and emotional, her book "sensational but thoroughly documented."

It seems Erika had to harden herself to her own devastating revelations, requiring her to leave out any personal connection to her subject—with the exception of one brief lapse in the prologue. While doing the research in the border towns around Germany, she interviewed countless firsthand witnesses to the Nazi indoctrination program, including one woman, a Mrs. M., the wife of a Nazi official, who drove over the Alps for a clandestine meeting with Erika in Switzerland. Erika was surprised to find herself overwhelmed with homesickness as soon as she heard Mrs. M's voice, because she had "the southern accent that I love. And she will be able, surely, to tell me about Munich, my native city, my childhood home that I have not seen in over four years. Sometimes in dreams I wander in its streets, or float dreaming over the Marienplatz, across the old section of the town, down towards the Isar River." Erika could not allow herself to succumb to such feelings, and cut short her momentary nostalgia: "But Mrs. M. and I have things to discuss; no time for emotional excursions into dream cities."

The comment was pure Erika—she had little patience for emotional excursions, her own or Klaus's. Much as Klaus wore his heart on his sleeve, Erika distanced herself from messy human sentiments and stuck instead to moral certainties and clear plans of action. It may well have been Klaus's demanding emotional frailty that made her cut off examination of her own feelings; whatever the cause, the effect was a certain coldness and lack of sensitivity.

The book's publication in autumn 1938 turned out to be good timing, as the political climate of American isolationism was finally starting to change. Sales were also helped by Thomas Mann's introduction, and the cover, a swastika engulfed by bright red flames, was an eye-catcher. To Erika's surprise, *School for Barbarians* became a best seller (it sold 40,000 copies in the first three months), and Erika became, by her own reckoning, one of the highest paid and most requested female lecturers in the country.

When war broke out in Europe in 1939, Erika pleaded the case for American involvement in an essay, "Don't Make the Same Mistakes." It was published in 1940 in the book *Zero Hour: A Summons to the Free,* a collection of essays that grew out of conversations she had with the poet Stephen Vincent Benét about the urgent need for the United States to mobilize for war.

Erika's essay, the only one in the book by a woman and the only one by a non-American, tells the story of her becoming politicized after the poetry reading-turned-riot back in Munich in 1932. She uses the device of writing a letter to a young man she encounters on a train between Chicago and Los Angeles, who represents her younger, more innocent self. In emotional tones she impresses upon him the need to act: "Things have gone too far already. And it is America, it is your country, it is you who will have to make the decision." At this, the young man is amazed. "'I?' he exclaimed. 'I am a student, a nobody, a grain of sand on the beach.'" Erika points out that he represents the American youth, much as she had represented Germany's youth, and ends her letter to him with a desperate plea: "Act! This is your hour, it's the final hour—the zero hour!"

The book reviewer for the *Los Angeles Times* singled out Erika Mann's essay, and beseeched his readers to read it "with care." He declared that if he could, he'd "make all Americans listen" to her warning that "we are repeating so many of the errors of the now fallen countries."

In addition to her book royalties and lecture fees, Erika collected income from popular American magazines for articles she wrote on the road, often describing with humor her life as a lecturer. In one of these, titled "Lecturer's Lot," Erika complained that women's clubs, in particular, invariably scheduled a luncheon for its members, after which the lecturer is all talked out, a bit hoarse, and in need of a nap—just before the lecture is scheduled to begin. In another, "My Fatherland, the Pullman," Erika claimed that, acclimated by her many lecture tours, "I am really at home in a lower berth and nowhere else on earth"—even though smoking was not permitted in the lower berth, and Erika couldn't survive long without a cigarette. She would charm the Pullman porter who had already reprimanded her for lighting up, so that he'd stand watch to make sure she didn't set fire to the train. "Whereupon he stations himself near my berth, a faithful guardian of my slumbers, which are disturbed by jumbled dreams, dense cigarette smoke and rough bumps of the train."

Erika came off a demanding lecture tour in early 1939 and settled back into the Bedford. The *Champlain,* a ship coming into port from Southampton, England, had W. H. Auden and Christopher Isherwood on board, and Erika and Klaus wanted to be the first to greet them in their new country. Auden and Isherwood, both British, were forsaking their native shores just in the nick of time to take refuge in America. Unbeknownst to Erika and Klaus, they had decided on the deck of the *Champlain* that they were sick of the anti-Fascist struggle, sick of the united front, sick of political rhetoric. Isherwood remarked, "'I suppose they're okay, but something's wrong with me. I simply can't swallow another mouthful.' And Auden answered, 'No, neither can I.'" Isherwood described in his diary the "exquisite relief" with which "we confessed our mutual disgust at the parts we had been playing and resolved to abandon them, then and there. We had forgotten our real vocation. We would be artists again, with our own values, our own integrity, and not amateur socialist agitators, parlor reds."

In order to join a quarantine launch that was setting out to greet the ship, Erika and Klaus presented themselves as journalists eager to interview the noted writers on board. Of course Erika and Klaus knew nothing of their sudden transformation; the siblings assumed that their good friends were firmly in their political camp. Isherwood found Erika to be "nervous and ill," while Klaus was "full of gaiety and gossip." They didn't discuss politics.

Isherwood and Auden were promptly invited to Thomas and Katia's red brick house on Stockton Street in Princeton, New Jersey, which they had rented shortly after the Magician's cross-country American lecture tour in 1938. They were neighbors of fellow émigrés Bruno Walter, Max Reinhardt, and Albert Einstein. A magazine photographer showed up during Auden and Isherwood's visit to take pictures of the famous author, his wife, and his six children for an upcoming profile. Who were these other two men, he asked. Auden was easily explained: Erika's husband. And Isherwood? For his role in orchestrating Erika's marriage, Thomas quipped, "Family pimp."

Auden was evasive about his true political, or rather apolitical, position. He avoided telling Klaus outright that he was sick of political rhetoric and would not advocate for the United States entering the war. In July 1940 Klaus managed to get into a big argument with Christopher Isherwood over his and Auden's silence, which Klaus felt was being misinterpreted as a statement against U.S. involvement (which in fact it was). He pleaded with Isherwood to "make a definitive statement" in support of the Allies. Isherwood refused on pacifist grounds.

Klaus maintained that he too was a pacifist; certainly he "couldn't possibly kill anyone personally. But pacifism couldn't possibly be applied to every case: if you let the Nazis kill everyone, you allowed civilization to be destroyed." Klaus found Isherwood's view, that "no war is always better than any war," to be "merely cynical." But their deep fondness for each other took the edge off their arguments, and their relationship remained close.

Not so with Auden. Klaus had recognized in Auden "Gustaf's cold charms" but was never seduced by them. Klaus and Auden had their drug habits in common or, as Auden called it, "the chemical life." But their friendship was short-lived; it deteriorated by the early forties. Auden liked to remark, apropos Klaus: "For an author, sons are an embarrassment, as if characters in his novel had come to life." Such jibes were hurtful to Klaus, who was all too aware of this embarrassment himself.

Isherwood never saw Klaus this way; on the contrary, to him Klaus was "lovable." Isherwood

> supposed that it couldn't be easy for him, as a writer, to be his father's son. But Klaus was evidently able to accept Thomas, Nobel Prize and all; he didn't waste his life shivering enviously in that huge paternal shadow. Nor did he affect the grandeur and alienated gloom of so many European literary men. His manner was easy, lively, witty; yet he was capable of caring deeply about his friends and the causes he believed in, and of fighting on their behalf. [I] found this combination lovable.

Soon Isherwood headed for Hollywood, "the real America," as he called it. Auden decided to share a dilapidated four-story house in Brooklyn Heights with an odd assortment of other writers and artists, including the novelist Carson McCullers, the burlesque artist (and struggling novelist) Gypsy Rose Lee, the magazine editor (and struggling novelist) George Davis, the composer Benjamin Britten and his partner Peter Pears, and Auden's very young lover Chester Kallman. Six months later, when Gypsy Rose Lee moved out, the composer and soon-to-be author Paul Bowles, together with his wife, the as yet unpublished but promising novelist Jane Bowles, moved in (Erika had been the one to introduce husband and wife three years earlier). Carson McCullers drank sherry by the bottle, pined after Annemarie Schwarzenbach, and found a kindred spirit in Klaus Mann. Klaus thought the bohemian household would make for an amazing novel, and after a visit in October 1940, wrote in his diary:

> This strange house in Brooklyn, where George Davis has settled down in the middle of a chaos of furniture, papers, lamps, colors, work tools. He showed me the whole wonderful picture: the living quarters of Wystan, whom I saw, together with Chester, for a few minutes—of Carson McCullers, who arrived later from the theater with her mother. What an epic one could write about this!

George's love affair with this popular Broadway star, Gypsy?—
McCullers, consumed by her talent, her drug consumption, and
her senseless love for Miro [Annemarie Schwarzenbach]. And so:
Miro → E, E → Wystan, Wystan → Chester. What a story!

Klaus at that moment was hatching the plans for a new project, an
English-language literary journal, and the Brooklyn Heights household
seemed to promise substantial support for his endeavor. Despite their disagreements, Auden agreed to serve on the editorial board, while George
Davis advised him on marketing and design and Carson McCullers offered to assist with editing. Klaus first told Isherwood that it would be
called *Zero Hour,* but a month later he changed it to *The Crossroad.* At the
last moment he mentioned the project to the author Glenway Wescott,
who thought the name implied a somewhat undecided position for an
anti-Nazi publication. "Undecided?" Klaus repeated, "Not my magazine!
If *Crossroad* sounds undecided, why, I'll call it *Decision.*" To that he added
a subtitle: *A Review of Free Culture.*

The first issue appeared in January 1941. In it Klaus states nothing less
than his own relentless idealism, his high hopes for the future, his love
of America, and the inseparability of culture and politics which was behind all of his undertakings. The war in Europe was to him far more than
a contest between opposing political systems; the ideas and values he
cared deeply about were at stake, indeed culture itself was in danger. In
the face of such mortal peril, he asked, didn't it seem rather inconsequen-
tial to start a literary magazine? He went on to insist that it was exactly
the right time and place for such a venture:

A new forum for the creative spirit—*now,* at precisely this moment
of fatal decisions; and precisely here.
. . . Where else is the creative spirit to continue its play and
work, if not in this last haven of free thought and free expression?
Where else is the seriousness of our plight to be recognized and
discussed, if not in this country—the last bulwark of liberty, focus
of our hopes?

In the beginning Klaus could hardly believe the journal's success; he
was astonished when Sherwood Anderson actually came through with a
story, and was amazed that Decision, Inc., had managed to open a bank
account, rent an office, and even hire a secretary who "looks exactly the

way a real secretary should look . . . and apparently fails to notice that I don't look like a boss."

The poet Muriel Rukeyser signed on as associate editor, and soon became a close friend as well. So respectable had Klaus made the magazine, in order to attract public attention and financing, that he himself was dissatisfied; he felt all the big names dominated and didn't leave enough room for newcomers and more experimental approaches, something he intended to remedy once the journal became more solvent.

Decision was a highbrow collection of stories, poetry, literary and political essays, symposia, and reviews of theater, books, music, film, and art. It had the dimensions of a paperback book, ran to roughly eighty pages, and sold each month for thirty-five cents a copy, or four dollars for a yearly subscription. Display ads on the inside covers advertised both new and established authors published by New Directions and Knopf. The Bedford Hotel also agreed to take out an ad; the array of "interesting people from the far corners of the world" and the "combination of American comfort and continental charm" were the hotel's selling points. Klaus splurged on a band of color across the front cover, featuring the names of his distinguished contributors and supporters: Wystan Auden, Jean Cocteau, Janet Flanner, Horace Gregory, Christopher Isherwood, Stephen Vincent Benét, Marianne Moore, Bruno Walter, and Stefan Zweig, to name but a few.

With *Decision,* Klaus tried to reestablish in New York elements of the identity that he had assumed in Europe—as cultural spokesperson, moral intellectual, and published author. In each issue he wrote an editorial called "Issues at Stake," in which he reflected on the current world situation and expounded his ideas on art, philosophy, and politics. His position as the editor of *Decision* enabled him to meet many of the people who made up New York's cultural elite.

But Klaus's overwhelming neediness, the desperation of an addict, deterred close friendships. Glenway Wescott, an American in Paris in the twenties who now seemed to Klaus "as conspicuously European in America as he used to be conspicuously American in Europe" and whom Klaus admired for his suave and highly civilized character, privately called Klaus "that tragic twerp." Janet Flanner, who regularly published in the *New Yorker* under the name Genêt, and who contributed a piece called "Paradise Lost" to the first issue of *Decision,* found Klaus to be egotistical and pathetically dominated by Erika—whom she adored. When a New York editor paid Auden and Chester Kallman a visit, and he announced that he would soon be publishing Klaus's autobiography, Auden and

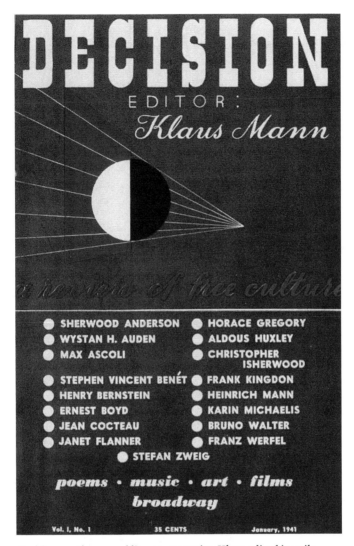

Decision was the second literary magazine Klaus edited in exile.

Chester joked and laughed. "What will you call it? The Invisible Man? The Subordinate Klaus?"

Only his closest friends saw him differently. Christopher Isherwood thought Klaus was "without vanity or self-consciousness" and that "his great charm lay in this openness, this eager, unaffected approach." Klaus had used *Decision* to help shove Isherwood out of a long period of writer's block, by insisting he write a memorial to Virginia Woolf following her suicide in 1941, and Isherwood was grateful for his thoughtfulness. It is ironic that forlorn, insecure Klaus could be taken by many for an egotist, while Erika, supremely self-confident, even cruel at times, used her consummate acting skills to charm and seduce whomever she chose.

But with Europe besieged by war, Erika lost interest in hanging about New York, charming and seducing her many admirers. In the summer of 1940, she received an invitation from Duff Cooper, British Minister for Information under Churchill, to become a correspondent for the BBC. Although the job was a dangerous one, Erika jumped at the offer. She simply couldn't stand by and watch one European country after another fall to the Nazis. England could well be next.

> After the fall of France I felt compelled to leave behind my beautiful, cosy American lifestyle and go to England. I was convinced, in spite of all the evidence, that England would resist. And my reasons for this conviction were purely moral ones.

Less than a month before her departure, Christopher Isherwood again visited Erika and Klaus at their parents' house. The family fretted about Erika's imminent plans and was distressed over the fates of Heinrich and Golo, both living in occupied France. Golo had signed on as a volunteer ambulance driver for the Red Cross, but when France fell he was promptly packed off to an internment camp in Nîmes and was in danger of being extradited back to Germany. (Thanks to Thomas's influence, Golo was soon released from the internment camp. He and Heinrich got out of France by crossing the Pyrenees in the darkness of night, up a steep mountain path "made for goats and smugglers but not for elderly novelists," Heinrich grumbled. From Franco's Spain they slipped into Portugal and by October 1940 had boarded a Greek ship destined for New York. After a quick stay in Princeton with his parents, Golo Mann would take over the attic of Auden's Brooklyn Heights household.)

In spite of Thomas Mann's trepidations that summer about Heinrich, Golo, and Erika, Isherwood recalled, the great author was as "urbane as ever. If the English saved democracy, he said, he would gladly tolerate all their faults, even the Oxford accent." Isherwood also noted that Thomas looked "wonderfully young for his age," something he could not say for Klaus. He was surprised to find Klaus looking tired, pale, nervous, somewhat fatter, and with the beginnings of a bald patch at the crown of his head. "But, as always, there is something very attractive and even stimulating about him. He isn't a despairing loafer, like so many of the others. He's always on the alert, always working. He has energy and courage."

In August 1940, Erika flew to London to take up her new position with the BBC. With "much envy and anxiety" Klaus witnessed Erika's departure. Klaus wrote that he could not make sense of the feelings that were tangled up in his heart: fear, envy, pride, sadness, and the feeling of being left behind.

CHAPTER 6

THE TURNING POINT

ERIKA'S JOB with the BBC took her to the war's battlegrounds, which is exactly where she wanted to be. It was a case of her strong sense of moral obligation synchronizing with her craving for adventure, which hadn't diminished an iota from her car-racing and world-traveling days. In one of her BBC broadcasts, which was also published in *Liberty* magazine (a popular American weekly, offering national and international news commentary), she tells of how she managed to put herself right in the line of danger by boarding a rescue boat in the Strait of Dover.

The rescue boats were standing by, ready to fish out any airmen who had to make parachute landings in the rough, cold English Channel. It was a rainy, foggy morning, and Erika had had no dinner on the train down from London, no rationed breakfast at the understocked hotel, and only a few cigarettes she was able to grub that were made of "heaven knows what stuff." In one pocket Erika had her "nice neat Air Ministry permit," which entitled her to board a rescue boat, and in the other a small bottle of brandy to keep her warm at sea, though she couldn't quite picture herself opening it in front of the British naval officers. They resolutely refused to let her to board a rescue boat anyway, and she was almost ready to cave in and accept their verdict—until she discovered the real reason for the resistance:

I realised that the whole thing was not a question of civilians, of reporters, not being admitted, but of women being refused. "There's nothing for females out there—and we've never taken one." That was what I couldn't possibly stand.

Erika, who had never been held back from anything on account of her gender, recoiled at such paternalism. She put up a huge fight and didn't back down until she won. She didn't have much time to savor her victory, however. She took off on a naval boat with a twenty-two-year-old college student at the command when suddenly, "out of the Calais air, the Messerschmitts [WWII fighter planes] leaped at us. There were two of them. Their crosses and swastikas could be easily distinguished." The gunner on the rescue boat, a young man named George, sat behind his huge machine gun, held his breath, and took aim as the planes dived, climbed, and circled. He was just about to shoot when, as Erika recalled, the twenty-two-year-old captain shouted:

> "You are not to open fire." The captain's voice was hoarse. "Do you hear me? This is an order!" Then—the devil knows where they came from—suddenly there they were: two more Messerschmitts at our back, at George's back, rushing toward us, the air full of that buzzing crescendo which the screen has made so familiar to all of us.

After the four fighter planes departed and everyone breathed a huge sigh of relief, the young captain explained that this was a "good old decoy performance." Rescue boats were supposed to be off-limits as targets; they could not be attacked without provocation. The Nazis wanted the boat to shoot at the first two planes, so that the second two could justify opening fire. Then, the captain explained, the second set of Messerschmitts "'would have finished us up from the rear like that.' He snapped his fingers."

With Erika's new position at the BBC, she found she had even less time for Klaus back in New York. Her cables to him were infrequent and brief—one read only "safe so far"—which did little to quell either his loneliness or his incessant anxiety about her, as she was stationed in London during the Blitz. Klaus tried to talk her out of her heroic deeds and into returning to America, partly out of genuine worry and partly out of a sense of abandonment. He wrote, somewhat dejectedly, "You were always very strict when others put themselves in danger—be it traveling into unfriendly terrain, be it eating tuna [heroin], whatever, and now you do these follies. Maybe right now there's more to do here, and you could go back to Europe when things are clearer." He was incapable of being angry with her, however, and just wanted to hear directly instead of getting secondhand news: "Please tell me everything, honestly and right away; I can forgive everything even if there are sandbags and gas masks in your room already."

In London Erika did nine broadcasts over the BBC World Service in German for German listeners. In the middle of broadcasting one of them, a bomb hit a nearby building. She and the radio technician hit the floor as the explosion went out over the airwaves. Undeterred, they jumped right up again and Erika resumed her address. The loud blast only underscored the message she was conveying in her broadcast: "Mr. Hitler was very much mistaken if he thought that he could actually frighten London to death. He couldn't frighten London at all."

Erika appealed to her German listeners, asking them to imagine what might happen if Germany did win the war, as dismal a prospect as that seemed. The picture she painted of the world under Nazi domination was not a pretty one. "Most German men would be stationed in foreign countries, in a futile effort to keep foreign peoples down, there would be a constant period of fighting and neither peace nor wealth would return." She pointed out that the German people would be hated and despised all over the world; how great would that feel? She went on to describe another, more likely, scenario, that Germany would be defeated with Hitler still in power, which would be even worse for the Germans. Erika ended her broadcast proposing the only positive course of action that was still within the reach of the German people: she tried to persuade her listeners that they should end the war themselves, that they should "get rid of Mr. Hitler before this war is lost to Germany."

When Erika prepared to return to London the following year (she spent summers working for the BBC and winters on lecture tours across the United States), Klaus again despaired of losing her. Her return to England was not a decision Erika took lightly; she agonized over the pros and cons, but Klaus was not factored in on either side of the balance. Ultimately, she decided that "it is my profession to accept this trip, and also several times I explained to Duff C. [Duff Cooper, British Minister for Information] my wish to work in England, because it is the right place for me, that is where I feel 'okay.' . . . And that's how it is destined from God's counsel."

Just slightly lower than God in Erika's book was Franklin Delano

Roosevelt, whom Erika met in January 1941 when she and her parents were invited to the White House for two days as guests of the president and his wife. Roosevelt took a liking to the Manns, and privately served cocktails to them in his workroom while his other guests were waiting downstairs for dinner. Erika *had* to take up the front-line assignment—as Roosevelt "has asked me himself to write something in *Liberty*—no joke!"

It was nonetheless with some ambivalence that she came to her decision to return to England. She wrote to her father, who worried about her safety, "The most terrible thing is the understanding of how much disturbance and sorrow I bring to you." Thomas realized that it would be futile to try and prevent her from going. He also must have realized the shift, from Klaus to himself, taking place in Erika's personal allegiances. He wrote to Klaus about Erika's decision, and with a sensitivity atypical of him, tried to present the outcome as being dependent on the entire family's approval, Klaus's included, even though this was not the case:

> It seems certain that [Erika] is going to England. Who should stop her? She insisted it be dependent on our approval, but what is consent in a matter like this? She must go her own way, and take responsibility for her spiritual and mental condition. If we try to hinder her, we cannot take that on. Naturally it is a time of anxiety, and one can only hope, that her trust in her guiding star will prove justified.

Klaus's unhappiness about Erika's departure was compounded by his own assortment of troubles. In March 1941, he did a series of radio broadcasts, including one with Auden on "The Function of the Writer in the Political Crisis." Klaus made a passionate plea for activism among artists, whereas Auden insisted that poets and writers should avoid all political involvement—a convenient position, some have said, to justify his avoidance of military service. This public argument was one of the final blows to their friendship and marked the end of Klaus's visits to the bohemian Brooklyn Heights household (which fell apart nine months later, when the United States entered the war).

Even more disturbing for Klaus, the initial success of *Decision* was short-lived and the financing became an unbearable struggle. He kept courting wealthy patrons who would not deliver on their promises— "How cruel and capricious are the rich!" he wrote in his diary—and with each issue the magazine went deeper and deeper into the hole.

There was no equivalent in New York of Klaus's Amsterdam publishing house, Querido, to publish the journal, and Klaus felt he had little support. This time around his father was willing to lend his name (and contribute $1,500 in cash, a large sum for 1941), but he too had some misgivings about the venture, as Klaus clearly did not have enough financial backing to pull it off. Klaus found it demeaning to be asked to list his father's name instead of his own as the journal's editor (a compromise was reached, whereby Thomas Mann became "Editorial Advisor" without actually doing anything) in order to please a financier who then still did not come through with the funds.

Personally Klaus was as destitute as his magazine. His rent to the Hotel Bedford was at least $500 in arrears. In May 1941 he wrote to his mother, "The other drop of bitterness is that I—it really can't be helped, it is very distressing to me—must ask for some money: two hundred dollars, I can't manage with less." He was now thirty-four years old and still unable to support himself.

And there were other small, daily humiliations, which dragged Klaus's spirits down. When the Library of Congress wrote a very encouraging letter to the journal, it was addressed to the associate editor Muriel Rukeyser, and made reference to the journal's many prominent authors, but never acknowledged Klaus himself, who was its driving force. Klaus felt he was a victim of anti-German sentiment in America, a by-product of the anti-Nazi sentiment he himself had tried so hard to stir up. But it was more apathy than hostility that cursed his little magazine. And on the personal front, he felt abandoned by most of his friends.

I suppose this is the most lonely summer I've ever experienced. The city seems to be deserted by everybody I know. Erika is in England. . . . The only person I see is Muriel Rukeyser, who recently joined the staff of the magazine. She is a great help in these trying days. . . . But even she, the only comrade in this arid solitude, escapes to the country from Saturday until Monday: while I have to stay—paralyzed, as it were, by the demon of this fierce and relentless summer. At times I actually fear suffocation in the stifling hole that's my room. The only comfort on those painful Sundays are the calls from Savannah [Georgia, where "Tomski"— Thomas Quinn Curtiss, the aspiring young filmmaker he had met in Budapest—was stationed in the National Guard].

According to Erika, Klaus fought for the journal's survival "like two mother lions," but she believed that the sooner the journal folded, the better for all concerned, especially Klaus. Her patience with Klaus's depressed state of mind was wearing thin. From London she wrote to Annemarie Schwarzenbach:

> That nut Klaus has run out of ideas and the end is in sight. But before he falls, several things will have to change on our part. And after his fall, several things are still going to be wrong. Sooner or later we will enjoy the chance to experience his fall and the end of this terrible situation. . . . But of course the desperation continues and no one knows how he's going to carry on.

Erika apparently didn't realize that Annemarie's mental state was no better than Klaus's. After two suicide attempts, followed by incarcerations in psychiatric clinics (she escaped from one of them), Annemarie convinced her family to let her return to Switzerland with a nurse as her escort. Her subsequent letters to Erika and Klaus sound relatively stable after her escapades in New York; she began work on a new novel, and reported to Klaus that Therese Giehse visited her in Sils for almost five weeks.

In September 1942, Annemarie had a serious bicycle accident which was probably no accident at all—but rather another halfhearted attempt at suicide. This time, though, she fell into a coma and lingered on in a semiconscious condition in a hospital in Sils for two months until, mercifully, she died. She was only thirty-four years old, and left behind a prolific, deeply arresting body of written and photographic work.

Erika was in San Francisco on a strenuous lecture tour to fifty American cities when she received the news; she was heading next to Lewiston, Idaho. She said nothing at all except "sweet Jesus why?"—in reference to Idaho, not Annemarie. Klaus also kept his feelings to himself, and didn't even note the date in his diary.

Yet Annemarie's death, following that of Ricki Hallgarten and René Crevel, could only have served to make suicide more appealing to Klaus. He once wrote, apropos of Ricki, that "Death, which used to seem so alien to me, has become more familiar since so intimate a friend of my earthly life voluntarily entrusted himself to it. One feels rather at home visiting a place where a friend is living, before going there oneself." Klaus was contemplating such a move himself—when at the last minute Tomski called and Klaus "was saved by 'sheer accident,'" according to Erika—although she didn't learn of his intended suicide until years later, so far apart had the siblings drifted.

In the autumn of 1942, Klaus wrote about this incident in his diary,

Tomski called and asked how things were going. I told him, miserably, that I had nothing to eat and no money for a haircut and just absolutely nothing. He replied it was awful, and why didn't we eat together? He had arranged to have a few drinks at six o'clock with someone from Camp Stewart, but . . . promised to call me at seven. So I said okay, and postponed the suicide.

But two days later, Klaus did make an unsuccessful attempt at suicide. This time he had typed an explanatory farewell document, and, typical of Klaus, he introduced it with a stab at humor:

Son of famous novelist commits suicide as magazine fails. . . . This is not so very much a sensation. Less startling, I suppose, than some story on Barbara Hutton's divorce.
   Nobel Prize Winner's eldest son takes own life, disappointed with success of literary review. . . . Not so hot. No news value. . . .

There is a disturbing paradox in this joking about his own demise; he defines himself, twice, by his relationship to his father, when in fact what kept him going on with life despite his longing for death was his unwillingness to die as simply the son of Thomas Mann. Although he yearned for death, his diary attests to his overriding need to make his own individual mark on the world, to write something beautiful and meaningful before he died. His suicide note goes on to reveal how demoralized he had become in a short time with the promise of America, turned sour for him because of the hypocrisy he encountered in trying to sustain his magazine.

I am going to tell you the inside story of this dreary case. . . . The son of the noted novelist—and, incidentally, a fairly gifted writer himself—wished and decided to die, *not* because of the failure of his magazine. . . . I had to drop the magazine, and I want to die, because I was—I *am* unable to face and to endure the exorbitant mass of mediocrity and malice, of ambitious ignorance and selfish laziness that rules the world and this country.
   Why do I write down these complaints? Why do I spoil my last evening with the formulation of my bitterness? . . . There are countless other things in my mind—some of them so sad that

they might have killed me years before; others so sweet and beautiful that they could almost prevent me from killing myself, even now. . . .

It was Muriel Rukeyser who sustained Klaus through that dark period when Erika was no longer able to. She felt endless compassion for Klaus, "whose youth and birth tore at him," she once commented, referring both to his family name and his German heritage, "whose advantages and disasters were at almost any moment interchangeable." Erika acknowledged, years later, the crucial role Muriel Rukeyser played in this stage of his life: "Thinking back on Klaus's life before he went into the army, I keep remembering that—apart from 'Tomski'—you were his one true friend and pillar in those fateful times which left their mark on him forever."

Even the deep affinity he felt with Muriel Rukeyser was not without turbulence. At one point he thought their friendship was over, because of "some gossip or misconception—that makes you turn against me, all of a sudden," although he couldn't fathom what it might be. But Klaus was imagining things; Muriel remained a loyal friend.

While publishing *Decision*, Klaus decided to write his autobiography, *The Turning Point*, as a way of using his own life as a vehicle for discussing the world around him. Doubting the importance of his own life story, he wrote in his diary, "Every testimony counts. Why should mine be worthless?" Yet despite the doubts the words fell out of him and onto the page like an avalanche. Muriel Rukeyser described the process: "And he would write. The work would pour, spilling into notebooks."

Klaus had planned to begin *The Turning Point* with a prologue, in the form of a letter addressed to Tomski (which he didn't finish and ended up not including), to justify why his life was a worthy enough subject for an autobiography. In a scratched-out handwritten draft written on *Decision* stationery, Klaus wrote:

Dear T.

It's only because I want you to understand me a little better. I don't mean *me,* as an individual, with my personal troubles and complications. You know me only to[o] well, and besides, I have learned to be skeptical and resigned as to the possibility of understanding each other—one another's individual enigma and intrinsic mystery.

At this point, the letter's coherency and legibility become borderline; clearly whatever drugs he had consumed were now kicking in. The handwriting is erratic, with often only a couple of words scrawled loosely across each page. Yet one sentence is unmistakable: "I dedicate this book to you out of my guilty conscience." Settled in America, Klaus wrestled for the first time with his share in the collective guilt of his native Germany. The sense of guilt hit him all at once when he laid eyes on the young, gentle Thomas Curtiss about to depart for basic training, looking completely wrong in his National Guard uniform. It nearly broke Klaus's heart to see Tomski like this, shelving his youthful dreams and plans, perhaps forever, all because of his own wretched compatriots— even though they disowned him, wasn't he also a German? He tried to elaborate, "I don't want to excuse myself—quite the contrary, I want to stress my own share of guilt and responsibility. . . . *Whose* fault?— Ours . . ." The sentences break into fragments, and the letter ends with "May I wish . . . Cruel times . . ."

Klaus wrote in English with the same frenzy that used to characterize his writing in German, but privately worried he was losing all grip on language: "Am I not already half estranged from German? Perhaps it will lead to my unlearning my mother tongue, without ever becoming fully conversant in the new language. But if I no longer had any language, what is left for me?" His personal diary he now wrote in English, and he was even unwilling to read fellow anti-Fascist authors if they wrote in the language that "Hitler has polluted." He discussed his linguistic metamorphosis, as he called it, with Muriel Rukeyser, trying to sort out how it worked both for and against him as an author. She recalled, "When we talked of the traps of crossing-over in language, I marveled at the crossing he had made, which I cannot imagine—he would refer to that fluency of his, knowing where it might be a virtue and where a flaw, where it might be absorbed in a writer's life."

Klaus's autobiography is part personal history, part family mythology, and part reflection on his restless, misguided homeland as it was falling prey to the Nazis. His father plays only a small role in the book, but when he appears, the sketch is primarily an affectionate one. As Erika and Klaus entered adulthood, they noticed that their father addressed them with "a sort of cordial vagueness": "he never seemed to remember exactly with whom I lived, which book I was working on, or where I had been spending the time since he had seen me last." One scene that Klaus remembered his entire life, a scene he found to be "insignificant in itself but strangely moving," took place during Klaus's many arrivals and departures from the family home in Munich. As he walks out the front door carrying his luggage, headed for some unknown destination, he sees his father at the upstairs window, about to close the blinds for his afternoon siesta. The Magician suddenly notices Klaus and calls down to him with "a sort of solemn jocularity": "Good luck, my son! And come home when you are wretched and forlorn."

In June 1942, less than a year after he started it, Klaus finished writing *The Turning Point.* In August he mailed his parents a copy. To his mother, to whom the book was dedicated (along with Erika), he wrote an elaborate apology, which he had originally planned to include in the introduction of the book—but, like the prologue to Tomski, this too was eventually excised. The apology was for the "thousand mistakes I have made, and above all, for my mistake Nr. Thousand-and-one, which is: that I failed to tell more about you" in the autobiography. He justified the omission, rather disingenuously—or why write an autobiography at all?—by claiming that "the most essential things are the unspeakable ones.—Everything I might have tried to say with regard to you would have turned out to be inadequate and clumsy." He wasn't really concerned about her forgiveness; her love was always unconditional and boundless. She immediately responded with a telegram:

> Whole family reading frantically. Dad deeply captivated. Mielein [Katia] confused and touched by splendid monument which should bring creator as much glory as it brings her honor. E greatly surprised moved and affected. Everyone wishing luck and sending love. Your Dear Ones.

Muriel Rukeyser vividly evoked "the stony heat and the despair of that summer. Despairs of war, despairs of writing and of love." She recalled a lot of waiting, which Klaus found unbearable: waiting for money to come in, for friends to call, for news from Erika. He waited, frantically, for a letter from his father in response to the book. Muriel Rukeyser was with Klaus at the *Decision* office when the letter finally arrived: Klaus tore it open and read it "in a moving, suspended moment of all the mixed feeling that can be found in the autobiography itself." The long-anticipated letter from the Magician describes one chapter in particular, titled "Olympus," as the "pièce de résistance" of the book in terms of its "critical achievement." It is the one chapter that pays tribute to Klaus's intellectual and literary gods—Plato, Nietzsche, Whitman, Novalis—rather than focus on Klaus's own story. The letter also questions the "wretched and forlorn" comment he supposedly made to Klaus from the window—he had absolutely no memory of ever saying that. Yet presumably it pleased him to be depicted as such; he ended the letter by saying, "I can only repeat, what I said at the window."

Klaus was indeed "wretched and forlorn" throughout the early 1940s. His desperate condition, a fusion of many factors—including but not limited to his sustained drug habit, his failing magazine, his need for his father's (unforthcoming) approval, and Erika's growing estrangement—was further compounded by external forces about which he knew very little. Though he suspected, correctly, that the FBI was investigating him, he couldn't be sure, and would never know the reasons behind the investigation. Nor did he link his personal difficulties to the FBI probe, or realize the extent of the surveillance and interference in his life. Yet hundreds of FBI documents released through the Freedom of Information Act reveal that his increasing paranoia was wholly legitimate. By considering these government documents in relation to Klaus's own private documents, it is possible to rewrite his personal history in a way that he himself, the author of three autobiographies and copious diaries, never was able to.

The FBI was tipped off to the actions of both Erika and Klaus by an anonymous letter charging the siblings with being "very active agents of the Comintern. . . . Klaus Mann was an active agent of Stalin in Paris, for many years. We hear that he is now editing an English publication, 'Decision,' in the United States." The source of this unsigned letter seems to be someone who personally had known Erika and Klaus during the twenties—back when they were involved in the avant-garde theater and wild gay nightlife of Weimar Berlin, and had virtually no interest in politics. The information was offered in exchange for some visas from the State Department for several German friends residing in southern France. It is very likely that the same person wrote letters to the Gestapo, since similar false accusations appear in the Gestapo files.

While Fascism swept across Europe, the FBI expended considerable time and resources harassing two of the strongest and most dedicated advocates for liberal democracy, both of whom had great respect for the government of the United States. The FBI surveillance of German émigrés was hardly an outgrowth of an anti-Nazi stance; it was rather an expression of American xenophobia toward all foreigners, and part of the well-documented campaign against liberalism and socialism. The FBI was not a renegade operation in this regard, out of step with the rest of government policy. The House Un-American Activities Committee, for instance, was founded in 1934 to investigate both Communists and Fascists but, incredibly, in 1938—as Fascism spilled out across Europe—the committee seemed to lose interest in Fascists altogether and focused instead on the Left as the more dangerous threat.

Though unable to link either Erika or Klaus to the Communist Party, the FBI continued to treat them as dangerous suspects because of their "premature" anti-Fascism, as well as their candid admission of homosexuality. In the FBI's convoluted moral code, "premature anti-Fascists"—those who opposed Fascism in Germany, Italy, and Spain before the onset of World War II officially established these countries to be the enemy—had less credibility than patriotic Nazis during the early and mid-thirties, and homosexuals had no credibility at all—an ironic twist given what we now know about J. Edgar Hoover.

Soon after the FBI opened its dossier on Erika and Klaus, a statement regarding their "more than sibling relationship" appeared in an undated report originating from the Bureau:

> Confidential Informant [name blacked out] . . . stated that people are horribly shocked over the sexual perversions of a group of four: KLAUS MANN, his sister ERICA [*sic*] MANN, and the latter's husband, the Englishman AUDAN [*sic*], and his collaborator, CHRISTOPHER ISHERWOOD. [Blacked out] stated that KLAUS and ERICA MANN were having affairs together; that there was reference to it in one of the books of their father, THOMAS MANN. . . . Informant further stated that KLAUS MANN is willingly and knowingly a tool of the [Communist] Party. . . .

The FBI was apparently unbothered by the contradiction between the homosexuality of Erika and Klaus Mann and the charge that they had a sexual relationship; both were evidence of their perversion and immorality. To the bureau, Erika's depravity was polymorphically perverse: bisexual, married to Auden, in love with Klaus, she occasionally invited another man to spend the night, a doctor [Gumpert] whose office, the FBI file tells us, was on the corner of Park Avenue and 86th Street. The FBI's "Confidential Informant T5" informed his superiors that, "to all who knew him [Klaus], it is general knowledge that the subject is a sexual pervert." Erika's marriage to Auden was also under suspicion; even evaluating Auden's poetry was not thought to be overstepping the FBI's mission:

Marriage of ERICA [sic] MANN to Englishman AUDEN was one of convenience and... neither KLAUS nor ERICA believe in marriage.... Informant advised that he did not think AUDEN was a Communist, but advised that he is an excellent poet, although very eccentric....

The political motivation behind Klaus's literary journal, *Decision*, was also of concern to the FBI. Klaus established *Decision* to support "independent creative work and intellectual liberty," as it stated in its initial subscription drive; he claimed from the beginning that *Decision* "is not subservient to any political group nor limited by any particular ideology." But the FBI saw it differently:

This periodical is presented as a neutral anti-Nazi publication and belongs to the specific camouflaged Communist propaganda-instruments known as the "Innocents' Clubs." The first thing these Soviet propagandists do, is to secure highly unsuspected international personalities, who sign their appeals and declarations....

Confidential informant T5 was sent to report on an early financial meeting for Decision, Inc. According to an undated FBI document, the meeting

turned out to be nothing more than a drinking party. Informant stated that at this meeting were VINCENT SHEEAN and his wife, MORRIS SAMUELS and his daughter, STRELSIN and ERICA [sic] MANN and KLAUS MANN. Informant stated that VINCENT SHEEAN seems to be pre-occupied sexually and that there was little doubt in his mind but that ERICA MANN and VINCENT SHEEAN had separated themselves from the group that night to indulge in sexual pastimes.

After such extensive investigations the only criminal act the FBI could find was that Klaus edited the journal in violation of the employment restrictions on his INS entry visa. The FBI turned its attention back to the "decadent culture behind the magazine which was obvious from its contents." Klaus's lifestyle, more than the actual contents, served to confirm the magazine's decadence. Then "Confidential Informant T4" informed the FBI that *Decision* had suddenly folded (the last issue was dated January/ February 1942), which he learned by getting stiffed for four dollars:

> Informant T4 . . . further advised that the account at X bank maintained by the Decision magazine has been closed because KLAUS MANN had made out a check on this account for $4. payable to the informant and the check bounced because the account had been formerly closed. . . .

Klaus wrote to Muriel Rukeyser about the magazine's demise: "rien à faire: I am through. Or rather, 'Decision' is. . . . I am worn out and sad. I give up." In closing he thanked her for her help and asked her whether or not it had been worthwhile.

The FBI turned its attention to Klaus's personal life. His file reports that Klaus was "frequently in arrears in his rent" and that "many queer looking people" could be seen going into his Hotel Bedford room, which was specified in the file: room 1403, facing the front of the building, fifth window in from the east side. According to "Confidential Informant T5," Klaus became very intimate with a rich man (possibly a member of the Coast Guard) whom Klaus had coerced into contributing to Decision, Inc. T5's assessment of Klaus was that he was "a psychopathic case," "no business man," and someone whose "education must have been neglected."

In the early forties, Klaus wrote the novella *Speed,* a convincing portrait of paranoia and despair which was an all too accurate description of Klaus's own state of mind—although in Klaus's case the paranoia turned out to be grounded in reality. *Speed* was Klaus's first piece of fiction written in English. He sent it to Christopher Isherwood, who corrected it and praised it as his best work. The novella tells the story of a hustler named Speed who betrays a desperate man, a foreigner in New York with a precarious legal status who is unable to resist the danger and allure of illicit sex and drugs.

Klaus himself was drawn rather indiscriminately to the "very gratifying young proletarian types. . . . I fancy almost all of them, porters, waiters, liftboys, and so on, white or black. Almost all are agreeable to me. I could sleep with all of them." Sybille Bedford recalled that actually at this time "what attracted Klaus were the professional louts, I mean truck drivers and rough trade, as he would say, the 'quick and dangerous.' That was when he began to speak English in America. He used to come back beaten up by them and so on."

65-8483

numbers will be set out in a subsequent report when such information is
made available to this office.

On May 29, 1942, Confidential Informant T5 advised that

██
██ This informant
stated that he thought KLAUS MANN was a psychopathic case and that to all
who knew him, it is general knowledge that the subject is a sexual pervert.
Informant stated that a man by the name of ██████ whose first name he thinks
is ██████ who was a very rich individual and had put money into the organization, had been very intimate with KLAUS MANN and that he is thought to be
in the Coast Guard some place at this time.

Informant stated that to the best of his knowledge, ████████
was the first person to put any money into the corporation.

██
████████████████████████████████ Informant stated that personally
MANN is no business man and that he thinks his education must have been
neglected.

Informant advised that in his opinion the magazine was in
no way Communistic, but that once when a question of editorial policies had
arisen, KLAUS MANN had told him that he, MANN, had thought at one time that
he could collaborate with the Communists, but that he was no longer of this
opinion. Informant advised that he is not thoroughly convinced that MANN
is not still a Communist.

Informant further advised that KLAUS MANN had told him
at one time that ████████████ had been forbidden by his party supervisors

- 11 -

The FBI hounded Klaus for more than five years.

Fritz Landshoff confirmed this: "Homosexuality, which he never perceived as deviance, confronted him with a problem, that with the years grew greater and greater: all too often his preferences were for much younger, non-homosexual men who—with very different intentions from his—would make him pay or exploit him financially, causing him deep disappointment and suffering."

Not all his encounters were violent or humiliating: Ury Cabell was a big blond Russian truck driver from New Jersey with the mind of a poet and a face like Nijinsky, who, according to Klaus, was "heaven in bed." Glenway Wescott had a fling with Ury soon afterward and confirmed Klaus's opinion: "It was like going to bed with sweet butter and toast." Ury later married and had lots of children, while Klaus continued to pursue more dangerous encounters, not only because of his inclination toward promiscuity, but also because, Sybille Bedford insisted, "he only really liked rough trade. It was not possible, except I suppose with Tomski, for him to fall in love with anyone in his own world of manners."

Klaus's poor condition was also due at least in part to the distance he felt from Erika. It seems that what he wanted or needed from her was more than she could give, and he felt her pulling away. He wrote in his diary,

> Sadness, without end. Deathwish as physical desire. The feeling of loneliness like frost. Everything dissolves and goes to pieces. . . . Erika distracted by her successes, travels, activities, and her relationship with G [Martin Gumpert]. How long ago is *Anja and Esther* [their first play, from the twenties]—how she has grown. Never totally estranged, but still, step by step, she is receding— Often I think I'm Pygmalion: what would she be without me— what am I without her?

Although as a "couple" Erika and Klaus had started to drift apart as early as 1933, when they first went separately into exile, the rift between them widened considerably when they moved to New York, their joint lecture tours and book projects notwithstanding. Prior to 1936, whatever else bound Erika and Klaus together, first and foremost was their problematic relationship with their father. Erika's feelings for the Magician were always less complicated and more reciprocal than Klaus's were, and despite their disagreements she was always quick to act in his behalf, even more as an equal than as a daughter. Still, her strong moral compass pulled her away from him and directly to Klaus. In 1936, with Thomas

Mann's public denouncement of Nazi Germany and his subsequent de-naturalization, Erika eased into a more normalized relationship with her father. Klaus's estrangement from the Magician did not ameliorate with the reconciliation of their political differences; it was always about something deeper. The sacred bond the siblings shared since childhood, forged in resistance to Thomas Mann and all he represented, no longer could sustain itself with the same passionate intensity.

The Japanese attack on the U.S. Navy base at Pearl Harbor on December 7, 1941, in which over 2,400 soldiers, sailors, and civilians were killed, finally forced the United States into the war. Erika became accredited by two American newspapers as a war correspondent, and traveled with the Ninth U.S. Army to Egypt, Persia, and Palestine—which she prophetically pronounced a "powder keg" when she learned that Jews and Arabs were secretly arming themselves for a showdown. As the Cairo correspondent for *Liberty,* she interviewed General Brereton, the U.S. commander in the Middle East, something she was told would be impossible.

General Brereton, whose Ninth U.S. Air Force had just led a historic raid on Rome, did not have much time for interviews. Erika settled in her hotel room to wait for him, refusing all invitations for tea or camel rides lest she miss his call. In the meantime she did her research and learned his entire personal and military biography. When at long last she met the man, he told her the real reason for her wait—under no circumstances would he speak to women; he believed they should be at home in their kitchens and not interfering in a war zone. But she spoke to him as the informed, astute reporter she was, and he responded in kind. She couldn't help liking him, despite his cavalier dismissal of women in uniform, and he seemed to quickly forget that she was one herself.

While stationed in Cairo, most likely while waiting in her hotel room for the phone call, Erika too embarked on writing an autobiography. The words didn't pour out of her as they did from Klaus; she never got very far with it. Titled "I, of All People" (she wrote it in English), the manuscript attempts to depict her impressions and activities of the past ten years (1933–1943) and explain how she, of all people, became drawn into politics, got herself in trouble, "stirred up riots and arguments [when] all I tried to do was, to say—candidly and plainly—what I thought right and true."

This is exactly what she does in the autobiography, which is why it doesn't make for compelling reading. She claims her approach will be "not dogmatic but human," although in the very next paragraph she em-

WAITING FOR
THE GENERAL

Major General Lewis H. Brereton, U. S. Commander in the Middle East, gets plenty off his chest in a remarkably frank interview with our Cairo correspondent

BY ERIKA  MANN

Radioed from Cairo.

HAD I known then what I know now, I might not have had the nerve even to apply for an interview with the general. And if by some puckish coincidence I had chosen to put my last question first, it might have remained my last. Upon receiving his answer, I might have departed in a rush.

But this is no way to tell a story. I'd better start with the beginning and recall how, shortly after the historic raid on Rome, I determined to go and see Major General Lewis H. Brereton, Commanding General of the U. S. Army Forces in the Middle East.

I knew that the general, whose Ninth U. S. Air Force had just helped destroy Mussolini's Littorio marshaling yards, would be exceedingly busy, and that two or three days might pass before he'd be able to receive me. While waiting for orders from his headquarters I did not dare to leave Cairo. Whoever called me for tea, show me the Pyramids, or take me for a camel ride was invariably told that I was waiting for the general and consequently unable to accept any social engagements. As time went by and one week spent in expectation was followed by a second, my friends and colleagues started shaking their experienced heads over me.

"You'll never make it, my dear," they said cheerfully.

Momentous events occurred while I was waiting. Il Duce fell. Orel fell, Catania fell, and Badoglio was in the process of falling.

Our own theater of operations, however, was not in the center of events. Colonel Parham, the public relations officer in charge, rightly assumed a distinct Santa Claus attitude as one fine day he disclosed that something big was cooking in the Middle East. Our excitement was considerable and much hard guesswork was being done. The more ambitious among us were seen to prepare any number of speculative cables, at least one of which, they figured, was bound to hit the nail squarely on the head. The NBC and CBS men arranged for special bookings and everybody got ready to dispatch the news with the utmost velocity.

But the handouts we were given when the great moment had finally come contained no news whatever. Instead, we read a tiresome description of the city of Ploesti and its famous refineries. The actual story, we were told, would break at 8 P. M. Not a thing broke at eight, nor had anything broken at nine thirty, for which time Winston Burdett's radio show had been scheduled. I walked over with him to Radio House and listened to London conversing with Cairo, New York talking to London, and everybody awaiting our news. Winston, unable even to say that the real thing wasn't out yet, spoke briefly on the Italo-German tension in Greece, and we both suffered a little under the thought of how crazy he must seem to Columbia, who'd taken somebody else off the air to make place for his momentous announcement.

At ten the first official communiqué of the spectacular raid on the Ploesti refineries was finally released, and while the success of the enterprise could not yet have been determined, it became clear that the dash and

Major General Lewis H. Brereton.

braces the moral certainties of children, who "know what's black and what's white; they differentiate between good and evil" far better than adults do. Her rigid moral agenda, accompanied at times by a smug attitude of self-righteousness, weighs down the manuscript, rendering the potentially fascinating stories she tells predictable and lifeless.

Already a published children's author from the early thirties, Erika now wrote her first children's book in English, geared toward adolescent readers. *A Gang of Ten* (published in 1942) is an adventure story set in a small California town, where an international group of schoolchildren, some of them refugees from the war, are on the trail to uncover a plot to sabotage the local war munitions factory. Although this book too has a somewhat polemical tone, given its wartime urgency, it is an action-packed page-turner for the preteen set. The boys and girls of Erika's story are independent thinkers, well informed about current events, courageous and able to exercise sound judgment. The novel's first-person narrator, nicknamed "News," is a female journalist on assignment who invites the children to her hotel room for tea and tries to keep up with their mischievous activities, all performed in secret on behalf of the war effort. She bears an uncanny resemblance to the book's author, up until the last page, when she gives up her career to get married, something Erika of course would never do.

As a British citizen (through her marriage to Auden), Erika did not require American citizenship for her assignments and therefore was in a very different position from Klaus, who still had only a temporary visitor's visa in his Czech passport. He longed to enlist in the United States Army, driven by his genuine desire to fight the Nazis in every way possible but also by his desperate need to be part of something. "I *want* to go into the Army. I *want* to wear the same uniform as the others. I don't want to be an outsider or an exception any longer. Finally I'm allowed for once to feel in solidarity with the majority."

If the army agreed to accept him, Klaus could have been admitted as a regular soldier without American citizenship. But he knew he wasn't cut out for combat, and was hoping for a post in counterintelligence or propaganda, where his German background and his polyglot talents best could be utilized. For such a sensitive job, American citizenship was required. He applied for it, but it was just one more thing on which he seemed to be forever waiting. Finally he could bear it no longer, and asked that he been allowed to enlist without citizenship. Reflecting on his lifelong dread of isolation, bearing the stamp of his childhood with its twin-like pairing with Erika, he wrote in his diary,

The obsession that haunted me when I was a child—the paralyzing fear of moral and physical isolation—never ceased to perturb
me. . . . To be an outsider is the one unbearable humiliation. . . .
And so I conclude my reply to the Selective Service Board with
these words: I want to notify you of my willingness, indeed, my
eagerness to join the U.S. forces, even before my naturalization
has actually taken place.

The U.S. Army as well as the FBI had doubts about Klaus. The FBI
stepped up its surveillance when "The Special Agent in Charge" received
a letter from the director of the FBI himself, J. Edgar Hoover. Hoover
called the New York and Philadelphia FBI offices "delinquent" in the case
of Klaus Mann, and demanded "this matter be given prompt attention."
The New York office started to tail Klaus around the clock, and recorded
such mundane activities as his eating pastry and buying stationery.

KLAUS MANN entered [blacked out] Street at 12:32 p.m. at which
time he was wearing a gray suit, no hat, horn-rimmed glasses and
brown shoes. He left the doctor's office at 12:47 and took a Lexington Avenue subway to 86th Street. At this point, he left the
subway and walked over to Geiger's Restaurant at 206 East 86th
Street and made a purchase of some pastry. It was 1:06 p.m. at this
time. He thereafter returned to the Lexington Avenue subway and
took an express train to Grand Central Station. Leaving Grand
Central Station, he stopped and made a purchase at "Filing Equip-
ment and Office Supplies," on the south side of 42nd Street off
Lexington Avenue. He thereafter returned directly to the Hotel
Bedford at 1:30 p.m.

The doorman of the Hotel Bedford moonlighted as one of the main
FBI informants in Klaus's case (Erika suspected as much and tried, unsuccessfully, to have him fired from the hotel). He reported that a soldier
spent two or three nights each week in Klaus's room, despite Klaus only
having a single bed.

Informant T3 . . . further stated that unquestionably KLAUS MANN
is a sexual pervert and that two or three times a week, a soldier
by the name of [blacked out] from Governor's Island spends the
night with MANN in his room. . . . Informant further stated that the
soldier, known as [blacked out], is a large 6 foot heavy set individ-

ual with fair complexion and dirty-blond hair. He advised that . . . the only suitable sleeping place in MANN's room is a single bed.

Klaus's first physical exam revealed (according to the FBI report) a "syphilitic condition" and "13 arsenical and 39 heavy metal injections," likely injections of chelators used to treat heavy-metal poisoning, to which he could not possibly have been exposed. Klaus's diary indicates he received forty-eight injections from Dr. Gumpert, thirty-six of bismuth (a metal once used to treat stomach ulcers, before it was deemed too dangerous) and twelve of Salvarsan (for syphilis). Results from his first physical led Klaus to be classified by the U.S. Army as 4-F. The FBI informant's report stated that

> now that "Decision" had folded up he had staked everything, "including his self-respect" on joining the American Army. [Klaus believed] that the Army had rejected him "because the F.B.I. had told them that I was a homo-sexual." KLAUS MANN alleged that he admitted to the Army people that he was a homo-sexual "because that is nothing to be ashamed of."

Utterly unashamed of his homosexuality, Klaus *was* ashamed of the 4-F classification, which, he complained, put him in the same grouping as criminals and insane men. But when the army interviewed him at length after the physical exam, Klaus backtracked on his avowal of his homosexuality. He insisted that the syphilis test result was "a dubious plus-minus reaction," not a clear positive. And even if it were positive, he would have contracted it "from a prostitute in New York" rather than from "any form of perversion." Clearly he had no indication that his admissions to the U.S. Army had been passed on to the FBI.

Apparently intrigued by Klaus Mann's lack of embarrassment or guilt over his sexuality, the FBI wanted to dig deeper. An agent interviewed Tomski, and mostly wanted to know whether Klaus did in fact "entertain a lot of soldiers in his room." Unable to get anywhere with this line of questioning, they asked Tomski whether he really and truly had "no indication whatsoever that he is a homosexual?" Klaus's lover of almost five years had no inkling.

In April 1942, Klaus wrote to Erika that his "life weariness and poverty" had brought him to think of one more solution, admittedly a somewhat desperate one, to his military problem. At a concert at Carnegie Hall he met a young woman, a Miss Wagner. She reminded him somewhat of Pamela Wedekind, and made it known to Klaus that she fancied him. It crossed Klaus's mind to marry her, if only he could care *something* for "the gentler sex." Well, he finally admitted, he simply couldn't.

When Klaus was called back for another army examination on June 4, his syphilis had been cured but the military doctor was again dissatisfied with him: "Provisional Rejection" was the verdict. Klaus proposed yet another exam and retreated to his room in the Bedford, where he lived increasingly like a hermit. On September 7, after standing naked all day in a line with other recruits, he was rejected once more. His disappointment was immeasurable.

Klaus spent the next few months in a deep depression. Daily he wrote in his diary that he wished to die, nothing else. In these dark times, many were experiencing far worse fates than Klaus, and he knew it. But the awareness of his privileged condition could do little to release Klaus from the clutches of his death wish, something rarely amenable to rational thought. *The Turning Point* was published to overwhelmingly favorable reviews in the *Sunday Times,* the *Herald Tribune,* and elsewhere, but his depression didn't lift until December 14, when he took a boat to Governors Island once more for his physical exam.

This time, several friends had given him "lessons" on how to appear heterosexual—not that he really needed them. The U.S. Army was so eager for able-bodied men at this point that the military doctor was willing to overlook his homosexuality, as well as the huge scar which remained from his six childhood appendicitis operations. The army psychiatrist merely asked him if he had a girlfriend (he answered he had several), and pointed to a woman out the window, commenting, "She must have a nice bosom!" According to Curt Riess, one of the friends who gave Klaus the lessons in "normality," "Klaus, who never in his whole life was interested in any woman's breasts, nodded enthusiastically: 'Yes! Nice bosom!' And with that he passed the test and was in the American army."

Klaus was instructed to report for active duty at Fort Dix, New Jersey, two weeks later, more than a year after he had first tried to enlist. The following day, the FBI was notified, and his case was marked "closed."

On December 29, 1942 [blacked out] Clerk, Local Board 15, 570 Lexington Avenue, New York City, advised that the subject had been inducted into the United States Army on December 28, 1942. . . .
In view of the subject's induction into the United States Army as noted above the investigation in this matter is being discontinued and this case is being closed. CLOSED

From Fort Dix, Klaus was shipped off for eight weeks of basic training at Camp Robinson in Arkansas, and then transferred to Camp Ritchie in Maryland. At the age of thirty-six, he was for the first time financially independent of his parents, he was a soldier in the United States Army, and his father finally had reason to be proud of him. The congratulatory letter Thomas sent him had a double edge, celebrating the triumph of his innate masculine strength over his unhealthy writings and his unhealthy sexuality: "Obviously, neither writing nor loving could touch the health of your basic self; instead you've proven yourself to be upright and brave like a man." Katia's letters were less enthusiastic about his new undertaking. She let him know she had ambivalence about his going to war, writing, "For a mother it is a hard fate." She hoped at least that he'd be in less danger from drug consumption while under the command of the army, and in this she was completely right.

Despite Klaus's deepest wish to "belong," he remained an outsider in the army—certainly it wasn't the job he was born for. Lying in his barracks, he wrote in his diary, "So far removed from everything. Far removed from *what?* There is no place, no group, no person to whom I belong. I feel more detached, uprooted, isolated than ever before."

His fellow soldiers in basic training had little in common with him. He was a good fifteen years older than they were, obviously homosexual, physically weak from over a decade of drug abuse, exceptionally poor at sports and other physical activity, and to make matters worse, probably spoke better English than they did, but with a thick German accent—and wasn't Germany the enemy? The ostracism was such that he finally wrote to Lotte Walter, his childhood friend from Munich:

> I am sending you my portrait, 1.) as token of thanks [for sending a package of baked goods]; 2.) as a calculated move—namely, because I would like to have yours. There are two further reasons for this: a) I would really like to have it, b.) I would like to impress my comrades with a beautiful girlfriend. Send me therefore a truly seductive one, with naked shoulders, bedroom eyes and all. . . . It is very peculiar to be a soldier, and very difficult to explain it. I don't know whether I like it or not. . . .

Lotte Walter sent the photo, but it is not likely that it fooled or impressed anyone. Perhaps for the first time ever, Klaus felt sorry for himself. In a typed draft of a story Klaus wrote in 1943 but never published, titled "The Monk," Klaus described how he must have appeared to others:

The whole company called him "The Monk," because he had no girl friend in town and seemed always embarrassed when the boys discussed their ~~sex experiences~~ romances. . . . What was wrong with the Monk? Some of his room-mates suggested that he was secretly married and faithful to his ~~beloved~~ wife, although he claimed to be single. Others suspected that there were religious reasons for his prudery; but he was not a church-goer. . . . Or was it simply his high age which prevented him from having any fun?

He was indeed pretty elderly, at least 35 if not older—at any rate, by far the oldest man in the unit, which consisted mostly of youngsters. His face appeared strangely shrivelled—dried out, yellow and brittle, as if parched by a merciless tropical sun. There was something slightly Mephistophelian about his physiognomy. . . . But he had also features of a melancholy clown, with his long, pointed nose and the absurd gravity of his gestures. His eyes were pensive and near-sighted. . . . The uniform he wore—the outfit of a private in the U.S. Armed Forces—was always sadly crumpled and much too wide for his meager body. He cut a sorry looking figure. . . .

The story endows an archetypal outsider with many of Klaus's unmistakable autobiographical traits. Not only do his age, sexual identity, and foreign accent set him off from the other soldiers, but his intellectual and artistic attributes and his physical ineptitude further widen the gap. The story reaches its grotesque, ironic climax when a drunken prostitute attaches herself to "The Monk" and, unsure of what to do with her, he brings her into his barracks, thereby inadvertently earning the respect and admiration of the other men. He protests, futilely, against their unfounded assumptions. In order to prove that he did not take sexual advantage of the prostitute, he cuts out a silhouetted image of himself and the woman. This strange image shows a man and woman standing facing each other, separated by a cross and an open grave—an image devoid of sexual connotation but infused with the symbolism of religion and death.

When his unit was shipped off to Europe in the spring of 1943, Klaus was left behind—his citizenship, which finally was to be granted the very day before departure, was held up at the last minute. Klaus did not know the reason, but suspected, correctly, that it had to do with either his left-wing political views or his homosexuality. The FBI document that marked his case "CLOSED" at the end of 1942 was not the last page in

Klaus's large dossier. A memorandum to the FBI director, dated May 31, 1943, states that the judge considering Klaus's naturalization had wanted to peruse the file and "think the case over," in light of the "two charges against Mann, one of sexual perversion and the other of Communistic activities." Stuck in boot camp, Klaus wrote a seven-page, single-spaced letter to Attorney General Francis Biddle:

> Memorandum to the Attorney General, Washington D.C.:
> Of course, I am not in a position to know the exact contents of the adverse information [collected by the FBI]. Yet I am eager to contribute whatever I can to the speedy clarification of my pending case. In doing so, I take it for granted that the suspicions against me are of a primarily political nature. . . . I am aware of certain rumours according to which my political views are extremely "left"—practically those of a so-called "fellow traveler" of the Communist Party. These rumours—spread against me by ignorant or malignant people (maybe by Nazi sympathizers or by jealous fellow-refugees)—are entirely untrue.

Only a man at the end of his rope would write to the U.S. government to defend himself without knowing what the charges were. It would seem an exercise in futility, though he could have hardly done otherwise. He was desperate to be sent overseas as a member of the United States Armed Forces. He had devoted the past ten years to railing against the Nazi regime when few were prepared to listen; now he yearned to be part of the Allied fight against tyranny and Fascism in his former homeland.

After denying his affiliation with the Communist Party he moved on to defend himself against the other probable cause, his sexuality:

> It may be, however, that the adverse "special information" in question includes also rumours or denouncements of a very different kind. . . . Since I do not know what has been said against me, I take the liberty to state . . . nobody has yet dared to doubt or to deny into my face: that my character and "sex moral" are "excellent."

Klaus stagnated in Camp Crowder, Missouri, where he had been assigned to the 825th Signal Repair Service Company, "clearly a mistake, as I am not a technician and can not be of any use in a repair service unit." To do something constructive and keep himself busy, he took over editing the army camp newsletter, the *Camp Crowder Message*. He put the final touches on a massive anthology he had edited the previous year with his old friend Hermann Kesten, called *Heart of Europe: The Best of Modern European Literature*. In its preface he wrote, "As this book goes to press, I am on the point of leaving with my unit for an 'unknown destination.'" But he was not going anywhere for the time being, and wrote to Fritz Landshoff that he was a U.S. prisoner rather than a U.S. citizen. All he could do, he told Muriel Rukeyser, was "to send urgent cables and to depend on God and the War Department—two capricious giants." Finally he humbled himself to appeal to his father. Thomas, disturbed by Klaus's anxious mental condition, intervened on his son's behalf and wrote a letter to the U.S. government vouching for Klaus's integrity.

On June 4, 1943, the FBI showed up to interview Thomas and Katia at their new home—the previous year they had moved into a brand-new villa in Pacific Palisades overlooking the ocean and Catalina Island. Asked about his eldest son, Thomas insisted that he and Klaus had few if any disagreements, about politics or anything else. Both were moderate and pro-democratic in their political views. Katia (called Mrs. Catherine Mann by the FBI), in an interview conducted two days later, confirmed that Klaus was "quite like his father."

It is not clear whether the testimony from his parents was the deciding factor in turning his case around, but on August 30, Klaus faced one final interrogation, this time by a special agent for military intelligence, and his report was most favorable: "Subject is highly intelligent and possesses a wonderful command of the English language. . . . This Agent is of the opinion that Subject would be very useful in combat propaganda and . . . citizenship should be allowed Subject." In September 1943, nine months after he was admitted into the army, Klaus was finally approved for citizenship. His naturalization took place immediately.

While waiting for his transatlantic assignment, which would enable him to catch up with his original unit, Klaus wrote a letter to the chaplain at Camp Crowder, requesting an interview. He stated that he was considering joining the Catholic Church, and wanted the advice of the chaplain "as to whether my desire to do so is sincere and profound enough to make me acceptable." The miserable ordeal he had been through made him crave the guidance and comfort of the Catholic Church. He admitted that the Lutheran Church he was brought up in never meant much to him; it was Catholicism, with its grandeur and its ritual, which expressed and revealed the "ultimate metaphysical truth." Even in writing to the chaplain, Klaus admitted he had doubts—"philosophic, moral, and political"—about the Catholic Church, but thought they might be overlooked given the imminence of his departure. But these doubts—qualms and scruples he called them—proved to be too large after all; he didn't go through with it, and then his transatlantic assignment came through.

In a supreme gesture, Erika and his parents made the trip from California to Kansas City to see him off. He had little time to say everything he wanted to say to Erika, and as her train pulled out of the station (several hours before Klaus's own departure) he called to her through the window: "Well, maybe I'll see you once again *on the other side*," referring to after the war, not across the ocean. Of his parents, Klaus wrote in his diary: "At our farewell, Z. [the Magician] embraced me, something that had never happened before. Mielein's [Katia's] eyes, full of tears."

Klaus shipped out on an overcrowded transport carrying eight thousand men. Eventually it reached Casablanca, and after stops in Algiers and Tunis he crossed the Mediterranean to meet his former comrades from Camp Ritchie in Naples, where he became part of the Psychological Warfare Branch of the United States Army. Within two days of his arrival, the very street he was traveling down was bombarded, not far from his jeep. It was not the only time he would come under enemy fire. Yet Erika commented that when Klaus finally joined up with his unit overseas, it was the only time in his life, since their childhood, that he was "almost happy."

Klaus described his elation: "We German refugees, the first victims and most inexorable enemies of Nazism, were eager to contribute our bit to the fight against the Brown Plague. I was happy and proud therefore, to join the army of my new country, the United States of America, and to be sent overseas—first to North Africa, then to Italy, where I served with General Clark's Fifth Army." But despite his uniform and the military ideology behind it, Klaus remained an intellectual pacifist throughout, whose goal was to end the war as quickly as possible.

Klaus's high-security-clearance job involved producing propaganda leaflets to be dropped from airplanes over the Nazi-occupied territories, in an attempt to demoralize the German soldiers and convince them to go AWOL. His leaflets, in German, spouted such slogans as "Does SS mean Senseless Suicide?" and "To Be or Not to Be" (meaning, to die for Hitler, or to give yourself up). Even on active duty Klaus was musing on Shakespeare and suicide.

Klaus was subsequently transferred to the editorial staff of the *Stars and Stripes*, the American military newspaper. He worked as a soldier-correspondent, critic, commentator, and editor, and during his tenure the newspaper's literary and journalistic standards were remarkably

Klaus writes anti-Nazi leaflets to drop over Germany.

high. He wrote prolifically, as he always had—as if his life depended on it, which in a sense it did. Not only did he write the copy for his military job, but he filled notebooks with his diary entries and penned book reviews and literary essays, never failing to mention the irony of reading his favorite European classics, not in the language in which he first learned them, but in new English translations, from the relative comfort of his army bunk (while his barracks-mates discussed rifle cleaning). He mailed these reviews back to the States for publication in the *Saturday Review of Literature* and the *Chicago Sun Book Week*.

Now that they were both stationed in Europe as journalists, Erika and Klaus exchanged many letters, all written in English to pass through military censorship. Klaus complained, "You don't seem to have much use for me right now . . . ," which Erika brushed off as "perfectly preposterous!" although she did admit that her long silences were "an inexplicable disgrace." She tried to make up for it by saying "*Why* I never write to anyone, God only knows. . . . It makes me *quite* unhappy to think that you are hurt—believe me, dearest face, I am thinking of you a great and tender deal and there is nothing I want to do less than grieve you. See?"

From then on they gave each other regular updates—bits of news from old friends and relatives, reports on the sorry state of their respective war-zone locations. Perhaps because of Klaus's improved state of mind (his drug consumption was limited to whatever pills he could con out of the military infirmary), or perhaps because his accusations made Erika feel guilty—a very likely scenario, as in one letter she actually told him she would correspond more often, "NOT 'out of a sense of duty'— but out of sheer, unmitigated, and faithful LOVE!"—she attempted to recapture in her letters the close, easy camaraderie they had shared in their youth.

At times her efforts seem somewhat forced. In one letter, Erika wrote from Paris that she was "brooding, wondering and pondering, about the mysteries of time, life and fortune," although she probably never did this in her entire lifetime; contemplating the cosmos was Klaus's burden, which Erika, in a gesture of friendship, tried to present as a shared one. Ironically, it almost reads instead as a measure of the distance between them. Klaus had to have seen in her letters how hard she tried; did he feel sadness that their relationship had come to that? She continued, "I am longing for you . . . ," but their paths never crossed until the war was over, as Klaus was stationed in Rome, where the Mediterranean edition of the *Stars and Stripes* was published, while Erika reported mostly from France, Belgium, and Holland. She also made forays into German border towns, serving as an interpreter for advancing Allied troops. Her letter to Klaus closed with "oceans, clouds and thunderstorms of tenderness."

There was another reason for Erika's attempts to repair the rift that had been widening between the siblings: Erika needed someone with whom she could share her deepest, darkest secret, and Klaus was the natural choice for that role. She confided to Klaus that she was passionately in love with the conductor Bruno Walter, whom she had already known over a quarter century—and who was now approaching the age

"Klaus became a soldier. For the first time since our childhood he was almost happy" (Erika Mann in a 1952 radio interview).

of seventy. How could it be? Bruno Walter was the father of Gretel and Lotte Walter, two of the siblings' closest childhood friends from Munich. Bruno Walter was part of Thomas Mann's inner circle. And Bruno Walter was married to Else, a woman Erika and Klaus had adored since childhood as Gretel and Lotte's mother.

None of these minor details stopped Erika from pursuing an affair with the great conductor, but they did impress upon her the need to keep the affair secret. Their clandestine trysts in countless hotel rooms were fast and furtive, stolen moments when Erika's lecture tours and

Bruno Walter's concert tours could be orchestrated to intersect. This was never enough for Erika, the less ambivalent partner in the couple, and she tormented herself over the impossibility of the situation in which she found herself. According to Sybille Bedford's recollections (and according to Klaus's FBI file, if it can be believed), Erika already had several affairs with married men, the author Vincent Sheean among them, and presumably in these she had been looking for something other than an enduring relationship. This time, however, despite choosing the wrong person for such a partnership, she thought that building a life together was exactly what she wanted.

If anyone knew from experience that passion is impervious to reason, Klaus did. From his long, often painful affair with Tomski, in which Klaus's ardor was always by far the stronger, to his endless one-night stands and rent boys, Klaus was proficient in what today would be called "inappropriate relationships." Yet when Erika told him of her "mental illness," as she dubbed it, he seems to have felt little sympathy for her situation, and tried to dissuade her from indulging in it. Perhaps the most obvious interpretation of her infatuation—Bruno Walter as father figure—was all too uncomfortable for him to contemplate, not because of any squeamishness about sexual taboos but because of his own past and present problems: his realization that he was losing Erika to their father, and his vague awareness of the role that he himself had played in their father's sexual fantasies. Klaus did what Erika never would have suspected of him: he told their mother.

Fueled by Erika's false hopes, the affair between Erika and Bruno Walter dragged on intermittently through most of the forties, causing almost as much distress to Katia as it did to Erika. Unable or unwilling to tell her husband (although even the oblivious great author must have eventually noticed that something was awry), Katia wrote about her vexation to Klaus, calling her dear old friend Bruno that "unsuitable object" on whom Erika "has hung her heart." The obvious interpretation of Erika's infatuation immediately occurred to Katia too, and she told Klaus that such an affair seemed to her "to be just as big a mistake as when a daughter marries her own father"—no happiness could come of it in the long run. She already had a son-in-law of her own generation (Elisabeth's husband G. A. Borgese was a year older than Katia), and absolutely refused to have any more, although there was no indication that marriage between Erika and the conductor would ever be in the offing, even after Else Walter died in 1945.

While stationed in France in early 1944, and nursing her wounds after a ceasefire in the relationship with Bruno Walter, Erika began an affair with an American reporter who worked for the *London Daily Express* and the *Evening Standard*. She described the reporter to Klaus as "gentille comme tout, if exceedingly crazy and endangered. My 'Tomski,' as it were. We came over together by chance and accident and have been sharing cots, jeeps and cars ever since."

Erika's "Tomski" was a thirty-eight-year-old woman named Betty Knox from Salina, Kansas. Growing up, Betty Knox (née Alice Peden) had been an exceptionally charming girl, daughter of a shop owner, who took part in amateur theatricals and quit school at age fourteen to dance in chorus lines. At seventeen she ran away, donning overalls and passing as a boy.

Betty fled to Omaha, Nebraska, where she married a young mechanic named Donald Knox. Their daughter Patricia (Patsy) was born the following year, not long before Betty and Donald divorced. Still a teenager, she made her way to Broadway, where, some sources claim, she performed with Jack Benny. Betty teamed up with the burlesque performers Wilson and Keppel in 1928, and they went to Britain in 1932.

Wilson, Keppel and Betty performed a parody of a classical dance while dressed in pseudo-Egyptian costumes. Their famous "sand dance" quickly became as popular at the Winter Garden in Berlin, the Olympia in Paris, and the Palladium in London as it had been on Broadway. The trio happened to be in Munich in September 1938 when France and Britain signed their shameful Munich pact with Hitler, accepting his occupation of the Sudetenland (in Czechoslovakia) in exchange for a promise to cease further expansion. Hitler and his cronies took time out to see the performance. Goebbels apparently found the act immoral, but Mussolini loved it.

When war was declared one year later, Betty Knox kept dancing on London stages, even while the bombs rained down. It was almost an accident that she moved on to journalism. A profile on Betty in 1944 in her local Kansas paper tells the story:

> One night sitting with Frank Owen [editor of the *Evening Standard*] after her performance she said she wished she had been a journalist. Owen agreed she might have been a success. "Then why don't you give me a job?" she asked him. "How much are you earning?" "Fifty pounds a week." "Well," replied the editor, "I'd give you a lot *less* than that." She snapped back at him. "Give me two weeks to break my daughter into the act and I'll take it."

Soon eighteen-year-old Patsy took over as "Betty" in the act of Wilson, Keppel and Betty, and Betty, with no education or training, became a journalist for a leading British newspaper. She was clever and diligent, and quickly proved herself.

Erika must have been caught off guard by "the wild American" as she called Betty—by then Erika was certainly more heterosexual than homosexual, unless she was only trying to persuade herself that she was. Along with her demanding reportage work, Erika was juggling a complicated personal life: Bruno Walter notwithstanding, she was thinking about marrying her old flame Martin Gumpert, but couldn't reach a decision. Then, inexplicably, there was Betty Knox. Erika's war correspondent work made her feel useful and important, but when she fell in love with her jeep-mate, she found herself at a high point personally as well as professionally.

The long-awaited Allied invasion of Europe finally occurred in the early hours of June 6, 1944, when 160,000 British and American troops under the supreme command of General Dwight D. Eisenhower landed along a fifty-mile stretch of the Normandy coastline. By the time it was over, more than 4,000 of these men were dead (boys really; most were under twenty), and at least 10,000 were wounded, but the tide of Nazi domination of Europe finally had started to turn. Erika covered the historic events of D-day, giving a personalized slant to the drama:

> But for all this activity, there's a strange quiet. Anxiously both British and U.S. medical personnel look toward the approaching boat which carries an American flag but may be carrying casualties of practically any nationality. . . . Motionless under their heavy blankets, the wounded men make you feel utterly ashamed of your own onlooker's position and there is something inexplicably moving about their little belongings, their shoes and hats which they can't use now. . . .

In the summer of 1944, Erika and Betty each reported on front-line events as they unfolded in Europe. The *London Evening Standard* was a daily tabloid, and Betty's initial reports for it read like straightforward news items: the arrival of American ships carrying entire trains, which were unloaded directly onto French railway lines; the Allies' supply of "as much butter as you want" in Cherbourg, where "thin underclad children line the dusty roads"; the driving of vehicles right up to the battlefields in order to aid the wounded. Although she was not given nearly the col-

Erika relaxes with Betty Knox in California, late 1944.

umn inches Erika, in her freelance capacity, was afforded, Betty increasingly inserted a personal touch into her reports that was more typical of, and most likely influenced by, Erika's feature stories. In one report, Betty Knox interviewed young German soldiers in the tent of an American Evacuation Hospital in France. There she met one young boy who was "handsome and might well have been the model for the Hitler Youth posters. . . . His eyes glittered as he talked of his leader." Unfortunately, she found that only his good looks were exceptional; in other respects he was typical of the "fanatics for Hitler," as she called them, just another captured German soldier ready to die for the Nazi regime.

When Erika returned to the United States for her winter 1944–45 lecture tour, she wrote to Klaus that "my Tomski has come along—hadn't been here for 6 years." Over New Year's Eve, Betty accompanied Erika to the Mann family home in Pacific Palisades, where Betty behaved less than reverently toward the great author in his hallowed abode. To top things off, Erika brought Betty to a very small, intimate birthday celebration at Bruno Walter's house (virtually next door)—most likely trying to rile the old man—knowing full well it was, as Katia told Klaus, "rather inappropriate" to do so.

After this mismatched yuletide gathering, Erika played down the relationship, commenting to Klaus that Betty was "a strange acquisition—infinitely *uesis*,* quite endangered, rather worrying and—once again—not *precisely* what the doctor ordered. People are always getting so frighteningly serious as soon as they are with your sis." Erika was fairly serious about the relationship herself; even her parents' irritation with the wild American couldn't put Erika off.

Despite the fleeting tension caused by her relationship with Betty, Erika had slowly but surely grown closer to her aging parents, and especially to her father, than ever before. Over the past decade, she had become accustomed to spending far more time with them than she did with her brother. When she finally did see Klaus, shortly after the war ended—it was their first meeting in almost two years—she seems to have done it primarily to appease her mother. She wrote to Katia, stressing the personal effort it took: "Tomorrow I'll fly all the way [from Munich] to Berlin just to see K. (and you cannot possibly know how difficult it is to obtain the necessary orders)."

Erika had begun accompanying her parents on Thomas's European lecture tours back before the war broke out in 1939. On the fateful day that war was declared, the three of them had sent Klaus a cable from Stockholm: "Looking forward to witnessing together with you the twilight of the false gods" (the phrase was borrowed from Nietzsche). Now that the long-awaited twilight had arrived, her steadfastness to her father resumed with a vengeance. This realignment of the family dynamic would forever alter the relationship between Erika and Klaus. One could even say its consequences were fatal.

---

*An uncertain code word from their childhood, one of many coined by the siblings, that derived originally from "putzig" (quaint and funny) and combined elements of awkward, touching, eager to please, wide-eyed, and amusing.

CHAPTER 7

THE LAST DAY

NO MATTER HOW HARD Klaus tried not to be "an outsider or an exception any longer," he was forever out of step with the popular zeitgeist. He had been a pacifist throughout the war, even while serving in the armed forces. Once Germany surrendered on May 8, 1945, and Japan on August 14, Klaus found himself unhappy with the peace.

Amid the widespread victory jubilation, Klaus's disillusionment began to set in. He had held such high hopes and expectations for the world once the reign of tyranny and barbarism was defeated, once the forces of humanity, culture, and justice triumphed over those of iniquity. But this optimism was slowly eroded during the war, a war he felt only served to "stultify and brutalize" people, and was finally betrayed completely on the sixth of August 1945. The United States, in whose army he served, dropped the atomic bomb on Hiroshima, Japan—an action which called into doubt his previous fervent "belief, not only in the desirability but also in the feasibility of a New World—a Free World, to come. . . ."

To his friend Hermann Kesten he wrote,

> Yes, and the atomic bomb . . . To tell you the truth, I have been feeling kind of glum and apprehensive, ever since I heard about that rather alarming invention. Quite seriously, I cannot help the

feeling that this uncanny novelty may turn out to be the beginning of the end—I don't mean just the end of our civilization but the end of this globe, in a very literal sense. They won't stop fooling around with devastating gadgets before they'll have blown up our whole little universe. . . . Not that I think it would be a major loss if our earth went to pieces!

Despite his hard-won American citizenship, Klaus felt himself once more to be a man without a country. Long alienated from his former homeland, he now felt that his adopted homeland was falling far short of its promise. The death of Franklin D. Roosevelt, a month before the war ended in Europe and four months before it ended in Asia, marked as well the death of liberalism on the home front and seemed to signal the end of an epoch—the collapse of a democratic humanism in which Erika and Klaus so fervently believed. Golo recalled the gloomy discussions he would have with Klaus after the war, "political conversations as in the 1930s, but now completely without hope. There you had it, Klaus said. They, the Americans, would kill us all; all 'intellectuals,' everyone who had been for President Roosevelt and against Hitler. *That* was the war's true fruit."

Postwar America, turned virtually overnight into the world's new superpower, was, Klaus wrote, "endowed with material wealth and military power, but lacking [in] wisdom, refinement, and cultural tradition." The polarization of the globe caused by the escalating Cold War, the carving up of Europe into spoils for the victors, the no-win struggle between American capitalism and Soviet totalitarianism, "does not leave any room in the world for intellectual integrity or independence." If America was corrupted to its core by capitalist greed—was it possible to reclaim Germany?

Erika and Klaus had always imagined that one day they'd return to live in Germany—not the Germany of the Nazis, of course, but the "better Germany," as Klaus called it, the honorable, civilized Germany of Goethe and Schiller, which surely would rise again like a phoenix from the ashes of the glorious defeat. Klaus had believed that "when the Dictator has vanished—and only then, will it again be possible . . . to live in Germany, without fear and without shame."

Throughout Klaus's adult life, his geographic restlessness and his escapism through drugs expressed a pining to run away from himself, to forsake his present situation and take refuge in someplace more comforting. That someplace was invariably the faraway, idyllic realm of his childhood. The chance to unite this emotional yearning with his physical circumstances presented itself on May 9, only one day after Germany's historic surrender, when Klaus traveled over the Brenner Pass through the Alps by army jeep as a reporter for the *Stars and Stripes*. Arriving in Bavaria, Klaus headed directly for his childhood home on Poschinger Street. The journey through bombed-out Munich, now barely recognizable to Klaus, to the Herzog Park villa in which he grew up on the banks of the Isar River was a homecoming pilgrimage over ruins and rubble by Germany's dispossessed, itinerant offspring.

Klaus was horrified by what he saw—not so much by Germany's extensive physical damage after the Allied bombings, but by its complete moral and intellectual erosion during twelve years of barbarism. Although he recognized that "it will take years or decades to reconstruct these cities," the country's "spiritual rehabilitation" was the far bigger challenge. He found his former homeland a "deplorable, terrible nation" which was "morally mutilated, crippled," and Klaus was sure it would remain so "for generations to come."

There was no chance of repatriating to Germany. Klaus realized that he and his family had merely "indulged in illusions" when they entertained fantasies of ever doing so. He wrote to his father, warning him not to be tempted by any offers to return—anticipating by several months a series of letters in the German press proclaiming that it was Thomas Mann's duty to move back to Germany. Klaus wrote to him,

> It would be a very grave mistake on your part to return to this country and play any kind of political role here. Not that I believe you were harbouring any projects or aspirations of this kind. But just in case that any tempting proposition should ever be made to you. . . . Conditions here are too sad. All your efforts to improve them would be hopelessly wasted. In the end you would be blamed for the country's well-deserved, inevitable misery. More likely than not, you would be assassinated.

Of course, as Klaus knew even before he arrived, you can't go home again. This title of a Thomas Wolfe novel, one of Klaus's favorite books, never had more resonance than that May afternoon when Klaus drove up to his childhood home, the locus of his most cherished memories. He found its roof and interior walls gone, destroyed when Munich was hit by such heavy Allied aerial bombing in September 1942 that the explosions could be heard over the border in Switzerland. The attacks had been aimed

As an American soldier, Klaus visited his destroyed childhood home.

at the city's commercial and industrial centers, with the intention of sparing most of the outlying residential areas, but the Mann family home was an unlucky casualty and suffered far worse than the neighboring houses in Herzog Park. Only the empty shell of the building still stood—an apposite metaphor for Klaus's own predicament of homelessness, as well as for the collapse of the world he knew and trusted as a child.

The once-grand family residence had been confiscated by the Nazis soon after the Manns went into exile—this he already knew—but now he learned the especially repulsive use to which the Nazis eventually had put it. What he discovered was more devastating than witnessing its sorry physical condition:

> Standing there in the garden, contemplating somewhat nostalgically what used to be the happy home of my youth, I discovered,

not without surprise, that the place was not quite deserted, after all! There was a girl on the balcony just in front of my former room on the second floor. She was watching me suspiciously.

Speaking somewhat awkwardly in his discarded native tongue, Klaus struck up a conversation with the young woman, one of the many homeless people in Munich who had survived but lost their families and houses in the Allied bombings. She invited him to come up to her make-shift shelter by means of a handmade ladder she had strung together. He climbed up to his old bedroom balcony and asked her nonchalantly if she knew whose house it used to be.

I suppose it belonged to some writer, she explained, rather indif-ferently. One of those who didn't get along with the Nazis—so of course, he couldn't keep the house. Then the SS took it over; they had a *Lebensborn* established here.

Could it be the language too had changed in his absence? He couldn't figure out the meaning of that German word, although it sounded some-what romantic to his ears. The girl was surprised when he requested an explanation, but not as surprised as he was when she provided it: "A *Leb-ensborn* was a place where racially qualified young men and equally well-bred young women collaborated in the interest of the German nation." Its noble purpose was "the propagation of our Nordic race. Many fine babies were begotten and born in this house."

After this sickening discovery, Klaus felt like leaving Germany for good. But as he had been sent as a reporter for the *Stars and Stripes,* he felt obligated to stay a little longer and dig a little deeper. He visited the movie actor Emil Jannings, star of the film version of Heinrich Mann's *The Blue Angel* a decade and a half earlier, and a close friend of the family in those halcyon days. Klaus and Erika had visited him in Hollywood dur-ing their first trip around the world in 1928, when he was at the height of his celebrity, but he had since returned to Germany, where he lived through the war. Klaus was somewhat skeptical about Jannings, as he was about everyone who remained in Nazi Germany, but was nonethe-less charmed by him and found it "somehow touching to see the jolly old fellow again."

After his profile of Jannings appeared in the *Stars and Stripes,* Klaus was inundated with letters documenting Jannings's expressions of fawn-ing gratitude toward the Nazis. Klaus was devastated, not by the truth about his former friend, which he should have suspected, but by the thought of having shared a friendly chat and a bottle of wine with such a miscreant. "I decided to be more careful, from now on," he wrote— *"Beware of old friends!"*

His next stop was the master composer Richard Strauss, who welcomed the chance to speak with an American reporter (Klaus did not reveal his true identity) and sing the praises of Governor-General Hans Frank of Poland, the high Nazi official in charge of the Auschwitz gas chambers—because Frank "really appreciated my music." Hitler, on the other hand, Strauss had little respect for, from a musical point of view. "His musical tastes were deplorably one-sided. Wagner, and Wagner again! Hardly ever did he go to hear any of my operas."

Klaus also managed to track down some of his unfortunate relatives. His aunt Mimi (previously married to his uncle Heinrich) and their daughter Goschi were still alive, but just barely. Mimi had spent four years in a concentration camp in Czechoslovakia, and emerged considerably aged, stick-thin, and paralyzed on one side. Klaus's cousin Goschi had been thrown in jail, partly for being a "racial Mischling" (translates literally as "mongrel"—i.e., half Jewish), as Klaus reported to Heinrich, but also for being, "which is worse, your daughter." Mother and daughter survived by selling everything they had except for Heinrich's books and papers, which they managed to preserve. Klaus gave them some cash to tide them over, and asked his resourceful mother to send them packages of food and clothing.

Klaus was dumbfounded to see how totally the Nazi poison had taken effect among his former countrymen. He wrote an article for the *Stars and Stripes* titled "The Job Ahead in Germany," arguing that military victory, as difficult as that had been, was only the first step in the supremely difficult challenge of turning that wretched country around. He refuted "ordinary" Germans' claims of not knowing about the concentration camps, countering that such alleged ignorance was very convenient for them. He wrote another article for the *Stars and Stripes* exposing the sinister truth behind Terezín, the "model" concentration camp outside of Prague on which the Nazis had put a false front and allowed visitors to inspect. Klaus included the harrowing story of his aunt Mimi, who had recently been one of its prisoners. He wrote a detailed letter to his father about his observations and experiences in Germany at the moment of its release from Nazi domination, and then revised the letter into an essay he called "An American Soldier Revisiting His Former Homeland." He read various versions of the essay over several radio stations during his travels through Europe, and invariably ended the broadcasts with a declaration of his estrangement: "What a strange country this was, where even the creative artists, even the geniuses seemed to have forgotten the language of humanity! I felt a stranger in my former fatherland. There was an abyss separating me from those who used to be my countrymen. Wherever I went in Germany, the melancholy tune and nostalgic leitmotiv followed me: You can't go home again."

The detailed letter to his father that formed the basis for this essay was written on the occasion of his father's seventieth birthday on June 6, 1945. This cultural event was celebrated in the newly resurrected German-language journal *Die Neue Rundschau* (the New Review), now based in Stockholm, which published several moving tributes to Thomas Mann by Erika, Heinrich, W. H. Auden, Bruno Walter, and other illustrious close friends and family. In *Aufbau* (Reconstruction), a German Jewish weekly based in New York (but circulated across the United States, Canada, New Zealand, and Australia), Erika published a second homage to her father which he regarded as a "love letter." She wrote that his face seemed unchanging to her throughout the years, and his voice did too: "You only need to read aloud, sitting under the lamp near the desk in the darkened study . . . you only need to read like that, dearest, to make time and place fade into reverie."

Erika returned to Germany four months after Klaus did. She too arrived in the uniform of the American military, but unlike Klaus she was prepared for what she found. She had studied firsthand accounts of the Nazi "education program" for her book *School for Barbarians,* and after that nothing could surprise her anymore. Instead of incredulity, her reaction was one of hostility. She referred to the Germans as "vile, wretched people"; for the rest of her life she would never forgive them. To Klaus, she wrote, "The Germans, as you know, are hopeless. In their hearts, self-deception and dishonesty, arrogance and docility, shrewdness and stupidity are repulsively mingled and combined." Sybille Bedford said of her, "Erika could hate, and she hated the Germans. You see, Erika was a fairly violent character. At one point during the war, she propagated that every German should be castrated. And vengeance—Klaus wasn't like that at all. Erika was very unforgiving."

Erika also stopped in Munich, but spent no time whatsoever contemplating, as Klaus had, "the happy home" of their childhood—indeed, she had already, before her visit, accepted that the house in Poschinger Street was "lost to us long before." Still, ever practical, she registered the property with the claim authorities, who put an "off-limits" sign on it and took it into custody for the family—something her wistful brother would never think to do.

There was only one reason Erika had returned to German soil—and that was to witness Judgment Day in Nuremberg for those most responsible for the intellectual, moral, and physical obliteration of her homeland. It was "an adventure for which I'd been prepared for more than twelve years," she declared in print, while to her mother she confided, "No spookier adventure could be imagined."

Although there were quite a few accredited female reporters covering the Nuremberg war trials, among them Betty Knox and Janet Flanner (Genêt of the *New Yorker,* with whom Erika allegedly had a brief affair), Erika was the only one permitted inside the makeshift high-security prison, formerly the Palace Hotel in Mondorf-les-Bains, a charming spa in Luxembourg which fifty-two of the war criminals "had turned into a veritable insane asylum" as they awaited trial. She observed them in a living room, most of them scribbling nervously in preparation for their day in court, but didn't speak to any of them—interviews and press conferences had been suspended as the war criminals proved all too eager to plead their cases to the press.

The reports Erika cabled back to London and New York reveal her wicked sense of humor. She clearly enjoyed watching the reversal of these men's fortunes, even though the reversal was not total—the prisoners were especially well looked after. "They'll be needed to answer questions and serve as witnesses and must be kept in good shape," she was told. "Thus when a slight thunderstorm had frightened Göring into an equally slight heart attack, the creator of the Blitz (German for lightning) was given a mattress for his cot, and breakfast in bed."

Erika pointed out that Göring was never in better shape than at his trial. "A morphine addict at 23 . . . he switched to the milder paracodeine when morphine threatened his political future"—milder perhaps, but not at his normal dosage level of two hundred pills a day. Since his capture, the U.S. Army physician gradually diminished his drug use so that "Göring faces his trial a sober and healthy man—physically at least."

Other strange transformations were taking place among the criminals. Governor-General Hans Frank, the Strauss admirer charged with the murder of millions of Jews and Poles at Auschwitz,

arrived at Mondorf dying of four major wounds, all self-inflicted. Facing arrest at Tegernsee, Bavaria, he cut his throat, opened the veins in his left arm, sliced his left wrist, and rammed a knife into his stomach. Army doctors saved his life. . . .

Saved by doctors—or was it God?—the governor-general, immediately upon his recovery, had a religious conversion. He admitted his guilt, not for the wholesale murders he committed during the war but for the crime against himself which he committed by attempting suicide. He would atone by keeping suicide watch over the other prisoners:

> Having become allergic to suicides, he kept watching the others and finally decided that Ribbentrop was a candidate. The authorities agreed. For the good influence he might have on the problem child, the convert was allowed to move in with the suspect. When I visited them, the Butcher of Poland was reading the Bible to the ex-champagne salesman.

Erika let the war criminals know her identity, certain that it would disturb them considerably. Streicher lamented, "Du Lieber Gott and to think that that woman has been in my room!" Göring, who had personally requisitioned Thomas and Katia Mann's country house in Nidden, Germany (bought in 1930, when Erika and Klaus were already adults; they never had spent much time there), and flamboyantly decorated and furnished it beyond recognition, wanted the opportunity to explain to her that, "had he been in charge of the 'Mann case,' he would have handled it differently. . . . Surely a German of the stature of Thomas Mann could have been adapted to the Third Reich."

Having fought single-mindedly against Nazism for so many years, Erika and Klaus took little satisfaction in its ultimate defeat. Their firsthand experiences in Germany right after the war forced them into the sad realization that there hadn't been two Germanys after all, "only one, in which the best qualities had been corrupted with diabolical cunning into evil," as Thomas Mann also had to admit. That one Germany had allowed and implemented the most unimaginable horrors—horrors that were now coming to light. Erika and Klaus were unequivocal about Germany's guilt, and felt Germany deserved anything the Allies meted out, but the siblings could feel no joy in the retribution. Nationalism, anti-Semitism, and Fascism were still in vogue in Germany, without any encouragement from a Hitler, Goebbels, or Göring.

The end of the war caused Erika and Klaus considerable personal ambivalence. Their fight against Nazism had taken on the force of a mission. It had so sustained and even defined them for the past twelve years that they now felt left in a kind of limbo, unsure of their purpose in life. Erika, one of the foremost lecturers in America, was suddenly bereft of a lecture topic, and bereft of a calling. Klaus's literary output had focused so purposefully on his anti-Fascist agenda and his personal experience of exile that writing itself, for its own sake, felt odd to him, even though it had always been his lifeline. During the war he had written to his father, "As for my own lyre, it is getting rusty. In fact, I don't even know what kind of book I shall write, if and when I am free again to indulge in such luxurious occupations as the writing of books."

Still stationed in Italy with General Clark's Fifth Army, Klaus tried to line up some work for his return to civilian life. He couldn't bear the thought of resuming either his pre-army life of penury or the financial dependence on his parents that had sustained him through most of his adulthood. Klaus no longer saw himself as German, nor fully American either; he now considered himself primarily European. Rather than be shipped out with the rest of his unit, he hoped to stay in Europe but worried about how he would make a living. When his comrades returned to the United States at the end of August 1945, Klaus still had no firm work commitment but decided to remain behind anyway. He noted his impending honorable discharge in his diary with a sense of dread, "Dismissal. Uncertainty. Uprootedness. Nausea." The next day he asked himself, "Am I making a mistake?"

Privately Klaus was apprehensive about leaving the army and insecure about what would come next in his life, but in his letters home and in his autobiography he put on a brave face and even appeared impatient to get out. "If only I could get out of the Army before long!" he wrote to a friend. "What I try to arrange is, to get myself demobilized over here and then to stay for some more months in Europe, as a correspondent. That's not impossible, in principle. But you know how Mother Army is."

Klaus was torn between the urgency to earn money and the overwhelming need to find meaning in what he did. Even writing seemed to lack a purpose now. To the same friend he wrote,

I am disturbingly busy with all kinds of things of questionable importance—mostly article writing. . . . Also, I may do some work on an Italo-American film (G.I.s in Italy), which promises to bring some CASH and to be an interesting experience.

Rod Geiger, an American soldier stationed in Rome with Klaus, had been a film agent in civilian life, and Klaus talked to him about possible employment. Klaus initially liked the man, whom he described as "an entertaining, young non-Aryan." Geiger had bought the American rights to Roberto Rossellini's groundbreaking film *Roma, città aperta* (*Rome, Open City*), an inventive hybrid of documentary and fiction techniques that told the story of Rome's underground resistance movement, and hired Klaus to write some publicity texts for it. In one press release, Klaus wrote, "The film you are going to see is based on events that have actually taken place. . . . The film, ROME, OPEN CITY, has the accuracy and freshness of such a firsthand account. It's a factual report—enacted by people who have witnessed, or participated in, the real drama."

Klaus didn't mind "a *bit* being a civilian again—even though it is a COSTLY pleasure," he told his mother when he wrote to thank her for a package of clothes and cigarettes. "My meals, in the Black-Market restaurant, are at times delicious but always shockingly expensive—an average of about seven Dollars per meal! But I don't worry—as yet. The film job is well paid-for."

Together with another young American, Robert Lawrence, Geiger formed a production company, Foreign Films, Inc., with offices in Rome and New York, and signed Klaus on as screenwriter for his first Italian production. It seemed Klaus's gamble of staying in Europe after being demobbed was paying off; soon he was chatting with Luchino Visconti and having lunch with Anna Magnani.

The screenplay, which eventually became the film *Paisà* (*Paisan*), was slated to be directed by Rossellini, whom Klaus had already met through his publicity work on *Rome, Open City*. Klaus recorded in his diary that he and Rossellini were having dinner, attending the opera, or spending the afternoon together at the beach virtually every day in August 1945; they attended a "victory ball" together three days after he signed his screenwriting contract and two days after Japan surrendered. The next month he noted several meetings about the screenplay with Geiger, Rossellini, and Marcello Pagliero, Klaus's co-writer (and a close friend of Rossellini's), always over drinks or dessert in charming Italian cafés.

Klaus found these business meetings to be somewhat fierce at first, but eventually "more satisfactory" as the differences between the co-authors were hammered out. For the first half of September he worked daily on the synopses for at least three separate sections or "episodes" of the film, until September 15, when he was suddenly called away to Berlin by the Office of War Information (OWI), with whom he had become accredited as a correspondent.

Getting to Berlin, in the Russian zone, was not as easy as one might think, even with government accreditation. Klaus traveled by way of Paris, and spent much of the night cruising along the Seine before returning to the airport in the morning. There he learned that his name had been stricken accidentally from the passenger list; he was forced to wait hours at the airport for another flight before giving up and returning to Paris, where he squeezed in a visit to Jean Cocteau and a dinner with Janet Flanner. Having given up his hotel room that morning, and unable to find another suitable one, he spent the night in a "horrid little whorehouse" on the rue du Bac. He departed the following morning for Berlin, this time by way of a long layover in Frankfurt. But only one day after his arrival in Berlin he received a sudden "dismissal order" recalling him to Italy, and was forced to retrace his steps back to Rome and then on to Naples to receive new orders. It doesn't appear that he wrote anything for OWI after all this shuffling about. He was dismissed again on the twenty-eighth and returned to Rome once more.

During the fortnight that Klaus was out of town, Rossellini installed a second close friend, Sergio Amidei, as a third writer on the screenplay. Klaus's diary records that as of October 1, 1945, two days after his return, his dinners with Geiger, Rossellini, and Pagliero started to include Amidei as well. Klaus watched his role in the project shrink as these new writers were brought on and each was given a separate episode to write. He tried to suspend judgment for a while, but six weeks later had "unpleasant scenes" with Amidei. By this time it became clear to him that he was only going to be responsible for one episode of the screenplay (which may well have been the plan all along). He considered Amidei to be a "quarrelsome and megalomaniac lunatic" whom Klaus would be happy, "even before the conclusion of our collaboration, never to see again."

It was good timing for a surprise overnight visit from Erika, who flew into Rome on October 10. They had dinner together, and Klaus invited Robert Lawrence, Geiger's partner in Foreign Films, Inc., to join them. Lawrence, who was only twenty-four at the time, recalled the evening almost sixty years later: "I just sat there like a kid in a candy store, and listened to those two great minds."

Unable to resolve the problems with Amidei directly, Klaus felt compelled to write a personal memorandum to Lawrence, and pay him a visit as well. Lawrence had no solution either. The personality clash between Amidei and Klaus seemed irreconcilable, and it looked like one of them would have to go. Klaus quickly decided that he should be the one, and wrote Rossellini a "farewell letter," but the ordeal wasn't yet over. Two weeks later Klaus and Rossellini had a "cool reconciliation" and Klaus was back on the project, his relationship with Rossellini vacillating between "new tension" one day and "new reconciliation" the next.

As the end of the year approached, Klaus yearned to spend time with Erika. Not wishing to repeat the fiasco of the previous New Year's Eve, Erika had decided for once not to return to her parents' home for the holidays. Instead she remained in Zurich, where she and Betty were living together in the Hotel Urban. Klaus arrived in Zurich on Christmas Eve and quickly discovered that Therese Giehse, who had been living in Zurich since she left New York in 1937, was spending so much time with Erika and Betty that they were virtually a threesome. Klaus had what was probably the best holiday season of his life with the three women, despite the fact that Erika had contracted a liver disorder in Nuremberg that landed her in the hospital soon after they rang in the New Year. Klaus also reconnected with an old friend, Swiss newspaper editor Manuel Gasser, with whom he explored Zurich's burgeoning gay bar scene.

When Klaus returned to Rome in mid-January, he tried to resume his role on *Paisà*, but discovered that extensive portions of his dialogue were constantly being thrown out or revised. In the end he learned that his entire episode would not be used at all. He now started having problems with Geiger, who turned out to be a slippery character. Even Geiger's partner Lawrence didn't trust the man; he has called him "a brilliant manipulator of the facts. Geiger is incapable of veracity. He wouldn't be able to even spell the word truth." It seems the cash Klaus was expecting from Geiger was not going to materialize, since the episode Klaus wrote wasn't included in the film. Although Lawrence claimed that Geiger was the obstacle, Klaus believed that the source of the problem was Rossellini. According to Lawrence, "Klaus was very professional but he was treated poorly in the whole thing. . . . I was caught up in the whole mess and I resented the way Geiger handled it."

Upon its release, *Paisà*, which intercut fictional scenes against the documentary footage of the war, as *Rome, Open City* had done, was hailed as a masterpiece in Italian neorealist cinema. Almost two years later, when Klaus finally brought himself to see "his old brain-child" in a cinema in Paris where it was running very successfully, he noted that five authors were all given a screen credit, but his own name was not among them— despite a very clearly worded contractual obligation. He told Erika that "these uncles are going to regret that impertinence." Klaus took Rossel-lini to court and eventually won, but the credits were never changed.

The negative experience of *Paisà* did not put Klaus off the movie business. He hoped Geiger and Lawrence would finance a screenplay he proposed to write with Erika, about the life of Mozart and featur-ing their great conductor friend Bruno Walter. It was an idea that was bound to catch Erika's interest: she had resumed her hot-and-cold affair with Bruno Walter despite all indications that it could only end badly. "It's a good film idea, too. Why shouldn't we both make some *real* cash, for a change?" Klaus wrote to their father. In Zurich he had discussed it with Erika, and then he wrote to Bruno Walter, who somewhat reticently agreed in principle to the plan. Klaus told Walter that he and Geiger in-tended to go to Vienna to meet with possible actors and financiers, and Klaus did eventually make a trip to Vienna (without Geiger). Lawrence recalled,

> Klaus and I were going to do some films together [after the pro-duction of *Paisà*]. Klaus was—let's say he was a restless man. He had so many ideas and so much energy. . . . I don't think he could sit still for two minutes. He had a cigarette in his mouth perpetu-ally and was in constant movement. You could feel the vibrations of his energy.

But his energy alone was not enough to make it happen. Like so many of Klaus's ideas during these postwar years, the project fizzled out into nothing.

Klaus then pitched a collaborative book idea to Erika, intended as something of a sequel to their earlier collaboration, *The Other Germany*. Recounting their personal and political experiences in postwar Europe, it was to be part travel book, part journalism, and part dual autobiography. Erika was amenable in principle to all of Klaus's suggestions, but Klaus felt she had little time for his various schemes. This time they only got as far as a title, *Sphinx without Secret,* before they abandoned it entirely.

He tried yet again to launch a monthly journal, to be published in four languages, which he proposed to call "Synthesis: A Monthly Review of International Culture and Politics." He found a potential publisher based in The Hague, printed up some stationery, and wrote a prospectus outlining his ambitious plans for it, but was never able to garner suffi-cient financial support to get it off the ground.

As if all these setbacks weren't enough, Klaus learned that his nemesis Gustaf Gründgens was back in top form as the leading man in a play by Carl Sternheim in Berlin's grand Deutsche Theater. The onetime darling of Hermann Göring was as popular as he ever had been. Tickets for the sold-out performances could only be bought on the black market, and when Klaus managed to secure one, he was speechless to discover that Gründgens, stepping onto the stage during the first act, received a show-stopping standing ovation.

Klaus wrote a satire, "Art and Politics," in which he marveled at Gründgens's flair for personal transformation whenever the times demanded it. "Not that I have anything against Gründgens: an exceptionally gifted comedian, who incidentally was at one time my brother-in-law; personally I am inclined to be in favor of him," he declared disingenuously. "But to me it appears that these bosom buddies of Göring's shouldn't be in such a hurry. If Gründgens is stage-worthy—then why not Emmy Sonnemann?" Emmy Sonnemann had been a gifted theater actress in the twenties who, somewhat incredulously, had married the repulsive Hermann Göring. When she did so, Klaus had written one of his most influential anti-Fascist essays, "Open Letter to Emmy Sonnemann," which was printed in an anthology in 1935 and smuggled into and around Nazi Germany under the guise of a textbook titled "Deutsch für Deutsche" (German for the Germans). In it he mourned the loss of moral principles by artists in Germany who, as artists, had a special responsibility to uphold them. Now Klaus went on to question whether there were any limits at all to what former Nazis could get away with. Still pondering the possible revival of Emmy Sonnemann-Göring's career, he suggested that "perhaps someone gassed in Auschwitz left behind some stage piece in which the esteemed woman could make her second debut. The good woman surely knew nothing about Auschwitz—and besides, what does art have to do with politics?"

Meanwhile, Klaus realized that his collaborative relationship with Erika was pretty much over (she was spending ever more time with their parents and not responding quickly enough to his letters), and that his expectations of Geiger, whom he now called "the brisk little boss," were coming to naught. Feeling at loose ends, he thought it best that in May or June 1946 he go "home" to his parents' house for an extended visit. However, his timing could not have been more inopportune.

Thomas Mann, who would turn seventy-one in June 1946, had just been diagnosed with lung cancer. He was taken to a specialist in Chicago, where he was instantly admitted to the hospital and given a pneumothorax (in which nitrogen is injected to neutralize the cancer, coincidently the same treatment he had described in great detail in *The Magic Mountain*), followed by a blood transfusion, followed by an operation removing one and a half lobes of his right lung and one of his ribs. Erika flew from Nuremberg to Chicago to be by his side.

This trip marked a defining moment in Erika's relationship with her father from which she never turned back. Although Katia slept in a chair beside her husband the night before the operation, it was Erika who took on the essential tasks and subtly restructured the family dynamic. Her professional life had already made the shift when she filled the vacuum in her own career, created by the end of the war, with an increasing commitment to her father's work, but now her emotional life concluded its slow transference as well. Despite her numerous wild affairs, by midlife she had failed to establish a committed long-term relationship. Her liaison with Bruno Walter caused more pain than pleasure, yet still she didn't have the resolve to call it quits, even though she did feel compelled to pull away from Klaus, as much as she adored him—he had proven, his stint in the army notwithstanding, to be an incurable drug addict whose emotional dependency on her was bottomless. She never described the process of their estrangement in these terms (in fact she would never admit of any estrangement at all), but her actions speak clearly for her. Faced with disappointment and heartbreak, she transferred her effusive devotion to her father, and slowly but surely it became absolute.

In his weakened state Thomas Mann allowed himself to become extremely dependent upon his daughter, especially as so many flowers, gifts, and visitors arrived from around the world that Thomas worried his illness must be far more serious than the "minor lung condition" the doctors and Katia had told him about. When Erika sensed that he seemed eager to resume work, she launched into a detailed discussion of his unfinished manuscript of *Doctor Faustus* and was surprised to find the Magician's eyes filled with tears. She apologized to him for being insensitive. Thomas explained she wasn't insensitive—he was crying from gratitude.

Klaus only learned from *Time* magazine that his father was "resting comfortably" and from Fritz Landshoff (who learned from Bermann Fischer) that his "condition was excellent" after the operation. Klaus didn't write to his father directly, although he felt he probably should. He wasn't sure how accurate his information was; he didn't know exactly what to say or to what degree his father was aware of his own condition.

He wrote instead to his mother, asking jokingly whether his sprightly elder sister had control of the situation, and whether a son's visit would be too noisy, and disturb the convalescing gentleman's peace and quiet. He didn't know how long he would stay with them: he was inclined to stay for a long time, as he had a lot to write (or so he claimed) and the West Coast was "so quiet and peaceful" for writing, but on the other hand, he had concerns about contracting a "confinement psychosis" by remaining too long in this "children's home." He still hadn't learned to drive a car, a critical skill in Southern California.

Then Klaus hit upon a solution, which sounded in theory like it might just work. He proposed finding a little bachelor cottage in the neighborhood of his parents, and also thought he might "pick up an old Ford and a young driver. . . . The driver must also be able to cook a bit and have a pleasant appearance." He wanted his mother to keep an eye out for such a cottage and inquire about the price (it went without saying that whatever the price, she would be the one to pay it). He was sure he'd like this arrangement enough to stay about six months, especially if he could get some good meals with his parents and not wash up afterward. Clearly Klaus hoped to hide his melancholic state of mind with lighthearted banter.

Klaus ended his letter by admonishing Erika (via their mother) not to drink and smoke so much; when he last saw her, in the hospital in Zurich, she coughed incessantly and was far too thin. The liver condition that put her there was surely related to alcohol consumption, but Klaus was in no position to pass judgment on this.

Katia answered at once, telling him he was welcome to come in June or July, for a longer than usual stay without any danger of "confinement psychosis." As for his proposal, he had no idea how outrageous it was. "A house to rent and a car and driver who can cook, who also was attractive! With a *lot* of luck, one can get a *room* from upwards of one hundred dollars. . . . This is democracy!"

When Thomas was discharged from the hospital, Erika accompanied him from Chicago back home to Pacific Palisades. They arrived on May 28, 1946. Klaus flew to New York, gave his father several weeks to regain his strength, and then traveled by train to California at the end of July. It turned out to be his usual family visit: no bachelor cottage, no attractive driver, no six-month stay. He was back in New York by early autumn.

It turned out not to be the usual family visit for Erika. Her relationship with Thomas had developed to the point where it seemed inevitable and natural that after the hospital ordeal she would move in permanently to her parents' sprawling villa, surrounded by palm trees and eucalyptus plants, exquisite gardens and sloping hills that led down to the incomparable Pacific Ocean, sparkling incessantly in the distance.

Because of all the German émigrés who had made it their home, Southern California of late had been nicknamed "Weimar on the Pacific." It was the new capital of German literature, and Thomas Mann's opulent residence was the capital of the capital. The famed author, after a party in his home, wrote in a self-satisfied vein: "Neither Paris nor turn-of-the-century Munich could have offered a more companionable, lively and amusing evening of art."

Erika was forty-one years old, and by the sheer force of her character this cultural nucleus quickly became as much her home as her parents. She hoped to spend the rest of her days in that glorious paradise. (Not coincidently, it was almost next door to the Walter residence.) Father and daughter became virtually inseparable. At first Katia was relieved by Erika's presence, especially as she managed to keep the irascible Thomas in good cheer, but before long even Katia began to feel displaced.

Elisabeth Mann recalled, "Erika was a very powerful personality, a very dominant domineering personality, and I must say that this role that she played in the latter part of her life as the manager of my father was not always quite easy to take for my mother, because she had been used to doing all of that." Erika was not one to do things halfway. She made herself invaluable, indispensable even, to her father, and just as she intended, Thomas Mann became exceedingly dependent on her, even though he was experiencing a remarkable recovery from cancer. In his diary he referred to her as his "secretary, biographer, nurse, daughter-adjutant."

How Klaus felt about this shift, we can only imagine. Golo insisted that Erika's desertion was brutal to Klaus, that "they no longer did anything together" precisely because she now "concentrated all her attention on her father." Sybille Bedford maintained that "Klaus would never have had a jealous thought, not at all. Also, it was the right thing for Erika to be doing then. I certainly don't think Klaus would have enjoyed that role."

All sources corroborate that Klaus was not jealous by nature. But the tinge of disappointment underlying his letters to Erika lets slip that he did feel, if not jealous of her relationship with their father, betrayed by her abandonment of him. Klaus admitted, in 1948, "It is only the parts of my life in which she [Erika] shares that have substance and reality for me." By the time he wrote that sentence, those parts of his life had shrunk considerably.

The one and only time Thomas asked for his son's rather than his daughter's assistance, on an English-language anthology of Goethe, Klaus readily acquiesced—although initially it was presented to him as a genuine collaboration. His parents and sister were en route to England for a lecture tour across Europe when Klaus received a telegram. "Good news from the 'Queen Elizabeth'!" As Klaus reported in his diary, "Z. offered [me] co-editorship of the Goethe anthology." Klaus cabled back his acceptance the very same day. His enthusiasm may have been due to his lack of other firm job offers, or to the belated acknowledgment of his editorial and bilingual abilities by his father (or both)—but the co-editorship never came about. Klaus's involvement was restricted to selecting which existing translations should be included and which poems required new translations, actually a crucial role in editing an anthology, especially when one's "co-editor" didn't read English well enough to make such judgments. But the sole surviving letter from father to son regarding the project addresses Klaus as though he were in the subordinate position of part-time research assistant, and the published volume, *The Permanent Goethe,* is "Edited, Selected, and with an Introduction by Thomas Mann."

It seems strange, perhaps, that the woman who won a trans-European race car championship and dared to perform an anti-Nazi cabaret right under Hitler's nose would eagerly take on a subservient role to Thomas Mann. She was never one to take second place to anyone, or to play the role of dutiful daughter. And yet Erika after the war was as lost, in her own way, as was Klaus. "She returned home, because she had exhausted her career, and so devoted herself to the work of her father" is how Elisabeth Mann matter-of-factly described it. Financially she was broke, her bank account nearly depleted. The female lecturer most in demand during the late thirties and early forties was not in demand at all after the war ended, and her agent, for whom she had once been "the best horse in his stable," reluctantly had to let her go.

In the face of all this, working with Thomas Mann held the promise of an antidote; it made her feel wanted and needed, and she achieved a certain stature in the world as well, if only by her proximity to him. Intellectually the work she did for him challenged her and personally she enjoyed it. Her "job" consisted primarily of editing Thomas Mann's essays and lectures and serving as his all-round adviser and organizer. He already had a secretary, agent, and translator, but at times she took on aspects of these tasks as well, signing letters, as Thomas would write, "under the secretarial name of Homer Smith. Frequently callers on the telephone ask for this *gentleman*. At which times he just happens to be on vacation."

As Thomas Mann's trust in his daughter's editorial judgment grew, eventually she began editing his novels, which he knew were often over-written, with too much exposition on intellectual themes. Thomas himself, and most of his biographers and critics, agreed that her revisions benefited his novel *Doctor Faustus*, which she cut down by about forty pages.

Erika accompanied her father on his lecture tours, serving as his translator and lecture coach. She described her collaboration on his lectures as a form of cabaret, in which the unwitting American public was led to believe that Thomas Mann really could speak English.

> He wrote his lectures in German, they were translated, I worked on them and made them phonetic for him, and then we practiced, he and I. . . . Then, as he was also an ape [as I was], he gave the lecture as though he were speaking freely, and was so surprised when people were sure he hadn't read it.

After the lectures were over, Thomas Mann invariably would be asked questions by the audience. Erika felt that these question-and-answer sessions so beloved by Americans were simply "dreadful," because of the idiotic line of questioning. And that, as far as hiding Thomas Mann's linguistic chicanery went, was when "the difficulties began." He never realized that American audiences all tend to ask the same questions, and that he could have just memorized the answers. Instead, "he could hardly understand the questions and in no way answer them fluently. And so then we made our big cabaret, he and I . . . , it was another Peppermill." Erika would come up to the podium in the guise of offering translation help, whisper something to him, and then just provide her own answer to the question. "It was a lot of fun, and we enjoyed it," Erika later recalled.

Erika continued to court controversy after the war. In articles and interviews she stated unpopular opinions about the Cold War as it was being fought out over Berlin, a city deep within the Soviet zone (which would later become East Germany). Germany was jointly controlled by the four major Allied victors—the United States, the Soviet Union, Britain, and France—until, in 1948, with the escalation of the Cold War, the three Western powers decided to establish their own separate government in Bonn. This move was interpreted by the Soviet Union as a breach of the Four Power Agreement on Germany. The Soviet position (which

Erika found to be not entirely unreasonable) was that if the Americans pulled out of Berlin and set up their own government elsewhere, there was no justification for them to be in Berlin at all. In retaliation against the move, the Soviets harassed and ultimately blocked all Western ground traffic to Berlin. The West, in turn, interpreted *this* act as a breach of the Four Power Agreement.

The cordoning off of Berlin precipitated the first major standoff in the Cold War. Shortages of food and fuel began to plague the non-Soviet quarters of the city, which either had to be surrendered to Soviet forces, or rescued by Western forces, very quickly, lest supplies become entirely depleted. Since roads to Berlin were closed at the Soviet border, food and fuel were flown into the city from western Germany in an operation known as the Berlin Airlift.

Erika appeared on a radio station in California in August 1948, as part of a discussion program called "Town Hall on the Air," in which she delineated the three options facing the United States: "Either leave Berlin and risk that we, the Americans, will lose a great deal of prestige, or make war because of Berlin, and turn the entire world into endless misery, or third, stay in Berlin for a reasonable price, over which we have to negotiate with Moscow. I hope with all my heart, that this third way will be chosen." In the Cold War climate of the late forties, advocating this position of negotiation was inevitably interpreted as a form of pro-Stalinist propaganda. When someone from the audience asked her about the option of going to war over Berlin, to resist Soviet aggression, and to protect those Germans in Berlin who believed in democracy, Erika's reply was provocative: "How can we save Germans who accept democracy when we do not know any crowd of Germans who are actually doing any such thing? I do not think there should be war over Berlin, because . . . I don't think there are enough German democrats in Berlin to be worthy to fight over, actually."

This last statement found its way into a newspaper article back in her former hometown of Munich, which denounced Erika in the most hyperbolic terms as "nothing other than a Stalinist agent"—Stalin's fifth column at work. The article went on to malign Klaus as well, for having visited Berlin as a guest of "Communist" writers there as well as for having visited Prague, a city for which he long felt a deep affinity, which was now behind the Iron Curtain. Klaus sent in an immediate response to the newspaper, defending his sister (it is revealing that this time Erika did not defend him) and clarifying why he went to Berlin—he had been invited to give two lectures, one on American literature and one on André

Gide—but the original author of the article only proceeded to discredit the siblings further, for everything from the "arrogance" of Klaus's letter to the long-resented privileges of their childhood.

The demand for Klaus as a lecturer after the war had diminished considerably, as it had for Erika, although he continued to give occasional talks in Europe, mostly on such dispassionate subjects as "American Literature," and "Is There Cultural Life in Germany?" When his lecture tour brought him to Berlin, the East German press covered his visit with far less antagonism than the Munich press had. One paper simply reported that "the son of Thomas Mann is forty-one years old and looks tired."

It was no wonder. Klaus's body was self-destructing from his resumed heroin use, which escalated shortly after he was discharged from the army. From Berlin he gave a radio interview in which he was asked about such matters as his reaction to being back in Berlin after so many years, his thoughts on the role of Berlin in the Cold War, and his current literary projects. His answers were articulate and intelligent, but his delivery betrayed the fact that something was deeply amiss. He spoke unnaturally fast, almost agitatedly, as if he couldn't get his mouth to keep up with his frantic thoughts. His voice fluctuated occasionally out of its normal range. His diary shows that after a "crisis"—an overdose of Phanodorm—he checked into the Jewish Hospital in Amsterdam for a nine-day detox cure, but resumed his daily injections of heroin, morphine, opium, or Demerol (or whatever else he had to hand) immediately upon his release, and flew directly to Berlin for the radio interview.

Klaus mentioned during the broadcast that he was going to begin a new novel, set partly in Berlin during the Cold War, but only after he finished a German version of his autobiography, *The Turning Point*. His ordinarily boundless literary output was reduced at this point to translating his own English works into German: his autobiography for Querido, which was based once more in Amsterdam, and his monograph *André Gide and the Crisis of Modern Thought* for a Swiss publisher. This translation business was, he wrote to an old friend, "a droll pursuit" but privately he cursed it. Sybille Bedford remarked, sadly, that he translated his own books into the detestable language of German because "he simply needed the money and was unable to write a new novel."

Klaus's inability to write weighed heavily on him. To an army friend he wrote, "I find it increasingly difficult to work and to live (which means almost a pleonasm as the two terms, *life* and *work*, are practically tantamount to me). There are moments when I feel almost incapable of facing the world mess and my personal mess any longer. . . . But let's not go into such dreary problems." Having written very little fiction since before he joined the army, having no pressing themes to write about, and having switched languages in middle age, he was having trouble finding himself on paper for the first time in his life. Aside from the paid work of translation, Klaus was deeply committed to writing in English, yet he had trepidations about his total command of the language. His English was excellent, and he had written essays, short stories, and articles in English for the past decade, but he didn't yet dare to attempt a novel with it.

For the one piece of fiction he did accomplish in the postwar period, a three-act play called *The Seventh Angel*, Klaus reverted to German and then translated it himself into English. *The Seventh Angel* is a carefully conceived fantasy drama with a metaphysical bent, combining autobiographical elements with Christian religious symbolism. It takes a considerable departure from the anti-Fascist and exile themes that dominated his writing for so long, but it too has the ring of an apocalyptic political warning. Critics have since interpreted the play as "an allegory of the post-war world in crisis," but at the time it served as a warning to no one. Despite Klaus's dogged attempts to have it produced in Vienna, it was never published or performed in his lifetime.

Klaus hoped to write an openly gay novel, in English, to be called "Windy Night, Rainy Morrow," about two lovers whose political viewpoints drive them apart (one is drawn to Fascism; the other goes over to Communism), but he never got further than a simple outline. Even essays and articles for American magazines were proving difficult for him, although this difficulty seems more a consequence of his debilitating drug habit than a question of his command of the foreign idiom.

Klaus reverted to his prewar itinerary: he flitted between New York, Paris, Zurich, Vienna, and Amsterdam—to which he now added Southern California. He traveled around Europe with several temporary press passes and travel permits in his pocket. One pass was from the Press Club of Berlin, which listed him as being accredited with the *Rome Daily American;* another was from the Italian ministry, which had him accredited with *Town and Country.* He wrote to an acquaintance by way of explanation, "I improvise. Besides, overall I find life quite problematic."

In the fall of 1947, Klaus wrote to Erika that he was financially optimistic but "in the darkest pessimism as far as the world—and general situation of mankind—is concerned." He went on to clarify that his "financial optimism does not refer to an actuality but has more the character of a desperate caprice, considering that my cash consists of exactly 48 Dutch Guilder plus $15 in my New York account." He was hoping

"'La difficulté d'être' weighs on me, every hour, every moment. Often I find it intolerable, almost unbearable. The temptation to free myself from this enormous burden is always there" (Klaus Mann, in a letter dated August 12, 1948).

to get some more cash from the lawsuit against Rossellini, from some upcoming lectures that winter in Copenhagen and Switzerland, from Swedish royalties that were due on the publication of his autobiography, and from his play *The Seventh Angel,* which Cocteau was possibly going to translate for publication in France. Klaus hoped to nudge Cocteau in that direction, using his father's (genuine) interest in translating a Cocteau play, *La machine infernale,* into German as an additional incentive. Thomas Mann was somewhat uncomfortable with the appearance of lobbying on behalf of his son, and neither translation came about.

On May 23, 1948, Klaus took an overnight flight to Los Angeles. Erika and Katia set out that morning to meet him at the airport, but the flight was so delayed that they finally returned home without him. Erika returned to the airport in late afternoon when he finally landed, and drove him to their parents' home in Pacific Palisades. In contrast to the time when she greeted him at the ship and insisted he hand over his stash of heroin to her, at this reunion, more than a decade later, she presented him with some injections of the analgesic drug Demerol. He noted the gift in his diary without comment.

Surprisingly it was with the Magician that Klaus had the most meaningful conversations in the first few weeks of his arrival: Thomas recorded in his diary several significant talks with Klaus about such dilemmas as the Cold War situation in Berlin, the personal problems of "poor Monika" (the middle sister), the dangers of the Mundt-Nixon bill (a piece of Red Scare legislation against which Thomas Mann sent a telegram to Washington), Klaus's proposed nonfiction "epoch book," the pessimistic outlook for Germany's future, the unfortunate American "character," and Klaus's worries about his current *amour*, Harold, who had just lost his job and called Klaus with his one phone call permitted from the local prison— Harold was "in difficulties" although Klaus didn't specify which ones.

The previous year Klaus had met Harold, a working-class lad and former sailor from San Francisco, and now they were spending almost every night together. Thomas had no problem with Harold; he found him to be, unlike Erika's Betty, "good natured and silent." It was Thomas who paid Harold's $500 bail, which Klaus was sure Harold forfeited when he failed to show up in court. It turns out he couldn't show up; he had been arrested again the night before under the rather absurd charge, Klaus felt, of "suspicion of burglary."

Klaus discussed the Harold situation with his father. More surprisingly, he also raised the subject of his strained relationship with Erika. The Magician found this a peculiar admission; he had no inkling anything was awry. Klaus talking to his father was a rare enough event in itself—but about a problem he had with his sister? Klaus must have felt the rift was irreparable.

Settling in this time for the long-promised extended visit, Klaus attempted to write at least something each day. Klaus and Erika had one more collaboration in the planning stages that they intended to work on during Klaus's visit: ironically, what brought them together after everything else had failed was their father's famous novel, *The Magic Moun-*

tain, which they planned to adapt for the cinema. The Austrian producer Georg Marton now came to meet with them in California as a representative of the well-known British producer Sir Alexander Korda, who had paid $10,000 for the film rights to the book two years before.

Motivated by the meeting, Klaus "began reading *The Magic Mountain* anew (with screenplay in head)." He read the first volume in fifteen days, then began on volume two, although there is no indication that he ever finished it. If Klaus initiated the collaboration thinking it would bring them closer together, he was mistaken. Erika and Klaus never even began writing the script adaptation. (After dragging on as an idea for several years, the project died.)

Klaus's writing at this point was limited to translating his autobiography *The Turning Point* into German and completing an article he had been commissioned for by *Vogue,* on "Lecturing in Europe on American Literature," which gave him considerable trouble. He wrote daily in his diary about his lack of progress: "Why can't I write anymore? What's wrong with me???" And a few days later he panicked, "Am I at the End? Can I no longer write???"

A month into Klaus's visit, his parents asked him to leave the palatial family home. Thomas felt that with the presence of Katia's twin brother, Klaus Pringsheim, and his son (also named Klaus) and the arrival of Thomas and Katia's middle daughter, Monika, the household was "nearly overfilled with children and nephews." Soon, with the imminent visit of their youngest son, Michael, and his family, it would be an "unpleasant invasion"—even though the house was so big that while it was being built Thomas Mann felt he had insisted on too many bedrooms.

Perhaps recalling his fantasy of a bachelor cottage two years earlier, Klaus set out to find his own accommodations, his first attempt at domesticity after so many years of hotels and pensions. Erika helped find a place for him (and Harold) that was "not entirely satisfactory, but also not altogether bad (perhaps)." The first night in the new house was "rather dramatic—in a disagreeable kind of way"—Harold stayed out all night. When he returned at 5 a.m., he was not alone.

Six days later, Klaus "tried it again . . . ," as he put it in his diary. "It" was a combination of slit wrists, sleeping pills, and a gas oven, according to the police (having taken the sleeping pills, he tried the gas, then slit his wrists in a overflowing bathtub). He was rushed to a hospital in nearby Santa Monica just in time. To Klaus's great embarrassment, the incident was picked up by the news wires and reported around the world. The

New York Times ran a brief mention credited to the Associated Press, titled "Mann's Son Said to Slash Wrists": "Klaus Mann, a writer, 41 years old, the eldest son of Thomas Mann, the novelist, was taken to a hospital here after police said he slashed his wrists at the home of friends." Despite his speedy recovery, the second and final sentence would prove to be inaccurate: "His condition was not serious."

Letters came in from friends and associates. One of them was from Upton Sinclair, who begged, "Don't do it! You have written fine books & you can do a most important job in helping interpret Europe to Americans, & vice versa." Klaus thanked him for the letter, and admitted he was "ashamed of my weakness, disgusted with the indiscretion of a 'free' but irresponsible press which cruelly publicizes one's most intimate, painful failures." Ludwig Marcuse, a noted German émigré philosopher and critic, also wrote, reminding Klaus that he was not alone, that he was part of a brotherhood of loners, to which Marcuse also belonged.

The letters meant a great deal to Klaus, but the Magician did not visit his son in the hospital, and that would have meant far more. Thomas was angry at Klaus, he admitted to a friend, for "doing that" to Katia, whose steadfast understanding over the years had "spoiled him." Thomas apparently wrote a "condolence letter" (which no longer exists), with Erika acting as his secretary, two days after the fact.

Thomas Mann blamed Klaus's suicidal tendencies on his genetic makeup—which makes his anger at Klaus rather illogical. He wrote to a friend: "My two sisters committed suicide, and Klaus has much of the elder sister in him. The impulse is present in him, and all the circumstances favor it—the one exception being that he has a parental home on which he can always rely." (Obviously he overlooked the fact that he had just asked Klaus to move out.)

Katia did show up at the hospital, right away, even though it was one o'clock in the morning, and hired a nurse on the spot, but privately even she was not all that sympathetic to the dangerous ploys of her favorite son. When she received the call, she allegedly snapped, "If he wanted to kill himself, why didn't he do it properly?" Harold supposedly wept, but Erika was losing patience. She and Harold moved Klaus's things out of the new home—thus ending Klaus's one brief attempt at domesticity—but despite her helpfulness she was irritated with him. To a friend she wrote, "As you may have read, Klaus—my closest brother—tried to do away with himself which was not only a nasty shock but also involved a great deal of time devouring trouble."

Erika brought Klaus to Bruno Walter's home for a couple of nights for rest and recovery (where Erika herself had moved for a few nights, ostensibly to make room for more visitors in her own home), and Thomas Mann did pay his son an hour-long visit there; they sat around the Walters' outdoor pool and Klaus went for a swim. Over the next few days, Klaus underwent a series of psychiatric appointments and Rorschach tests. The psychiatrist predicted Klaus would try it again in nine months, and released him from his care.

Erika dropped off Klaus and Harold at the train station; they were headed north for a short visit with Golo in Palo Alto. For the remainder of his stay in California, Klaus lived in a hotel room with Harold in Santa Monica, where their relationship deteriorated into ugly words and subsequent tears. His old friend Christopher Isherwood, now living in Santa Monica, unstintingly provided a shoulder to cry on—or so it appears from his diary. Golo maintained instead that Isherwood, Klaus's only close friend in Southern California, had forsaken him now that Isherwood found success in Hollywood: "He no longer invited Klaus; he neglected him. Klaus noticed this and suffered from it; suffered so terribly because he suspected the cause—his own decline." Whichever version one believes, Isherwood was not called upon when Harold came home after 3 a.m. with another sailor; Klaus left the house and wandered the streets alone.

Fritz Landshoff sent a telegram inviting Klaus to Amsterdam, where Landshoff had reestablished his German-language publishing imprint Querido at the end of the war (he had moved it temporarily to New York in 1942 and merged with S. Fischer). At first Klaus was undecided, but one week later he flew to New York, where he visited Tomski (with whom he had settled into an affectionate friendship) and gave himself daily injections of morphine, and then on to Amsterdam, where he talked to Landshoff about publishing the German version of his autobiography. Soon after his arrival he received a telegram from Erika, reporting the shocking news that Harold was sentenced to six months in prison and three years of probation. Klaus remained in Amsterdam. He wrote regularly from his hotel room to Harold in prison and spent most of his nights socializing with Fritz Landshoff and his wife, Rini.

By the end of the year, Klaus was back in California. In his absence Bruno Walter had finally extracted himself from the sorry mess with Erika, telling her he wished their relationship to return to its "natural, that is, fatherly, basis." The reason: the septuagenarian had taken up with someone else, a singer named Delia Reinhardt. Erika, full of despair, chose to break off all contact with him. She retreated even further into the first circle of her affections, her parental home. As Bruno Walter was her immediate neighbor, the retreat was physical as well as emotional.

It fell to Katia to pick up the pieces. "My God, how can one be so hell-bent on the unfaithful old man? . . . It should have stayed platonic after all," she lamented to Klaus. The double misery of brother and sister did not manage to turn the tide that was pulling them apart. Erika had already latched on to her own life raft, and Klaus was left to drift on his own.

On January 1, 1949, Klaus jotted in his diary: "I am not going to continue these notes. I do not wish to survive this year." He couldn't keep himself from continuing to write occasional comments in the diary, but for the most part they are too fragmentary to reveal much about his state of mind. He does mention that on March 18 he finished writing a lengthy essay, "The Ordeal of the European Intellectuals," for an American magazine called *Tomorrow*. In this essay, Klaus recounts his experiences traveling around postwar Europe, talking to prominent writers and thinkers who were too baffled, insecure, and full of despair to provide the intellectual leadership needed in the polarized Cold War climate, a climate which had effectively shut down any genuine exchange of ideas. His writing demonstrates his thoughtful command of European history, literature, and philosophy. He mourns the "false credos, contradictory arguments, violent accusations" that now seemed to dominate European intellectual discourse. But he veers away from rational thought when, on the last page of the essay, he calls for "a suicide wave of the most outstanding, the most celebrated minds." He believed this radical form of protest "would shake the peoples out of their lethargy, bring home to them the deadly seriousness of the plague that man has brought upon himself by his stupidity and selfishness."

On March 20, 1949, Klaus left California for New York, and on the twenty-third he flew to Europe, stopping first in Amsterdam and then in Paris, where he met the young American author James Baldwin and also picked up a new supply of morphine. On April 2 he traveled by train down to Marseilles, and two days later arrived in Cannes.

Why Cannes? His destinations never had a clear motive, although the south of France seemed to him as good a place as any to try to write. Perhaps it had something to do with the fact that Richard Darmstaedter, the protagonist in his novel *Meeting Place in Infinity* (1932), had chosen Cannes as the setting for his suicide. Klaus checked into a room in the

"Pavillon Madrid" in Cannes, a four-story white stucco guesthouse with small balconies shaded by striped awnings. It would turn out to be the very last of his 1,200 hotel rooms.

After the war, when previously banned books sprung up in Germany like crocuses after a long frost, Klaus had good reason to hope that his novel *Mephisto* would be picked up by Georg Jacobi, a new publisher based in Berlin. But shortly after Klaus's arrival in Cannes, these hopes were dashed by a letter from Jacobi informing him that publication was impossible—"because Mr. Gründgens plays a very important role here," the publisher apologetically explained. Klaus wrote back a sharply worded reply, instructing Jacobi to have no further contact with him. He was sure his letter was not one that Jacobi would stick into the corner of his mirror. Klaus could neither see his finished books into print nor manage to write new ones.

In the Pavillon Madrid Klaus began working in earnest on a novel, his first in ten years. He intended to call it *The Last Day*. Set against the political tensions of the Cold War, *The Last Day* was conceived as two parallel plots, one concerning a cosmopolitan New Yorker named Julian Butler, who felt his "land of the free" was more a police state, the other concerning a writer in East Berlin named Albert Fuchs, who renounces the Communist Party. The inner thoughts of the two men are contrasted, rather clumsily, as the story shifts from one to the other at virtually every paragraph break. Julian and Albert, both in despair over the lack of humanist ideals on their respective sides of the Cold War, die on the same day: Julian kills himself, and Albert is killed by a Russian officer.

Only a few pages exist from his unfinished novel, but they serve as an unadorned, candid record of Klaus's suicidal state of mind. Ostensibly about Julian, he wrote,

> And suddenly he knew that he had to die. He knew that he wanted to die. How simple it was! . . . This sudden certainty—that he wanted to die—filled him . . . moved him . . . like a wave of joy, a triumph. He felt strong. . . . Absolute despair—he realized—had tremendous power, a dynamic impact. It could be organized, exploited, could be made an argument of irresistible persuasiveness. . . . A man who has given up hope becomes invincible.

Klaus told a friend that he would "deal with the issue of suicide" in his novel. Writing about it, he believed, would be "more tedious and more painful but somehow more honorable than actually doing it."

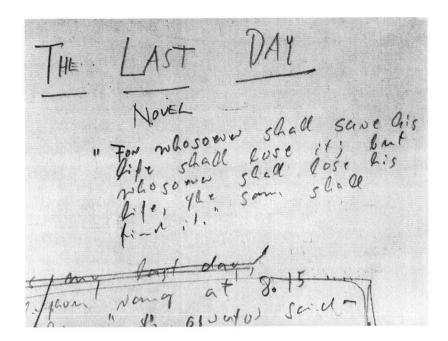

Tedious and painful indeed. Klaus was deeply dissatisfied with what he had written and had intended to start over, but he, like his character Julian, was running out of time. One fragment of the novel resurrects Klaus's idea of a Suicide Club for the desperate intellectual elite—but Julian worries that establishing such a club "would take too long. . . . No time left. . . . So how do I make the most of my personal tragedy . . . ?"

Klaus kept track of his progress on the novel, or lack of it, in his diary. On April 13, he wrote late into the night, "with help from 'stuff.'" By April 16 his work on the novel was "extremely exciting," and by April 17, he was "euphoric." The next week he was filled with despair, until April 24, when he began the first three pages of the novel over again "in all seriousness." That was his last day of actual writing. From April 25 to April 30 he descended rapidly, from "struggled" with writing to "not good, must begin all over" to "I feel bad, bad, bad. . . ."

Klaus resolved to try yet another detox treatment for his drug addiction, checking himself into the Clinique St. Luc in Nice on May 5. After ten torturous days of "cold turkey," he returned to his hotel room in Cannes feeling "decidedly better."

Following the cure Klaus seems to have returned to his gregarious self. He went out to dinner with an old friend, Doris von Schönthan, and her husband, Bruno van Salomon. The next night he went cruising in a local gay club, Zanzibar, where he met a young man named Louis. Louis came home with Klaus and spent the night. The next morning (according to the hotel bill), *petit déjeuner* for two was delivered to his room.

On May 17 Klaus had "a minor relapse" as he called it: he noted "inj" (heroin injection) in his diary and promised himself he'd send to his old friend Mopsa Sternheim "what remains of 'the stuff'—or most of it" to prevent further relapses." On the evening of the nineteenth, he attended a Chopin recital; on the evening of the twentieth, he met Louis at Zanzibar once more.

On the morning of May 20, Klaus had written a joint letter to Erika and Katia, full of forced cheer and genuine gratitude that they took the time to write to "a sickly [female] hermit and neurotic mouse." He reported that the weather in Cannes was miserable: "Still raining here most the time. For a change it hails, it storms, it thunderstorms. A May like this has never been seen before. People are not amused." Klaus's spirits were dampened by the weather, but far more by the fact that Gustaf Gründgens now seemed to be responsible for stopping the publication of *The Turning Point* as well as *Mephisto* in Germany. He asked Erika, who was en route from London to Stockholm with their parents for Thomas Mann's European lecture tour, to call Fritz Landshoff in Amsterdam. Landshoff was "in the worst condition" now that Querido had merged with the revitalized S. Fischer publishing firm. Bermann Fischer did not want to make waves for the distinguished theater director Gründgens by publishing Klaus's autobiography, even though Landshoff had committed Querido to bringing out the book and an announcement of its imminent publication had already been circulated.

As usual Klaus wrote of his money problems—he was flat broke and the regular check he expected from his mother hadn't yet arrived. He ended the letter by asking Erika and Katia when and where they'd be in Austria; he was considering meeting them there in about a month's time. A decade earlier he had written to his father, "I have been lucky with my family. One cannot be entirely lonely if one belongs to something and is part of it." The undertone of this letter to Katia and Erika suggests the distance he had traveled in that decade, from belonging to exclusion. Whether it was more forced levity or an expression of his loneliness, he also proposed to Erika that they make a side trip by car to Prague with Betty Knox. (After the Nuremberg trials, Betty had settled permanently in Düsseldorf, Germany.)

Klaus's letter crossed with one that Erika had sent him five days before. She somehow had anticipated his downward spiral of drugs and

Klaus Mann's final hotel bill, including ambulance charge, May 1949.

writer's block, writer's block and drugs. The siblings may have drifted apart, but she knew exactly what he was going through, even down to which drugs he was taking:

I don't want to say much in respect to your, for me, so sad illness. Only that, I . . . pray to *all* kinds of available gods, that you would stop this cruel game, and stay stable. . . . Were you at any point at all, . . . a little bit lucky with your work? Oh, probably you were chewing those sleeping pills without interruption. Now, of course, you are reduced and sulky and if the writing is not popping out, as though out of a pistol, you tell yourself it's not working at all anymore, and that reduces you many times over. If only I couldn't picture this so precisely. . . .

Erika was dead right in her description of his predicament. She had already arrived in Sweden, only a two- or three-hour airplane flight away, and yet she chose to remain with their parents. She had watched Klaus destroying himself little by little over the course of his entire adult life, and finally understood that there was nothing she could do about it—except refuse to watch.

Sometime after midnight, Klaus once more "tried it again." The next day the cleaning staff found him lying unconscious in his hotel room, the names of the two people he had loved absolutely—his sister and his mother—scrawled on a scrap of paper lying next to him. He was rushed by ambulance to a nearby hospital, but it was too late: an overdose of sleeping pills had transported him into an eternal slumber. Early in the evening of May 21, 1949, Klaus Heinrich Thomas Mann, forty-two years old, finally satisfied his most ardent longing.

CHAPTER 8

RAINY NIGHT, WINDY MORROW

"UPON ARRIVAL AT THE HOTEL, the worst shock," Thomas Mann wrote in his diary. A telegram was waiting for him at the front desk of the Grand Hotel in Stockholm on the evening of May 21, economically stating that Klaus was hovering between life and death in a Cannes clinic. Soon after he read it, Klaus's friend Doris von Schönthan telephoned to declare death the winner. Thomas, Katia, and Erika sat around the luxurious hotel together in "bitter sorrow," feeling powerless against "the long hand of [Klaus's] irresistible, impelling death-impulse," as Thomas Mann saw it.

In consideration of Erika, Thomas kept his anger at Klaus to himself and reported it only in his diary: "My inward sympathy with the mother's heart and with E. He should not have done this to them. . . . The hurtful, ugly, cruel inconsideration and irresponsibility." Thomas Mann's great sympathy for his wife and daughter, suffering so terribly, was rivaled by his lack of sympathy for Klaus, regardless of whatever suffering in his last days drove him to such a momentous decision. While it was saddest of all for Erika, Klaus had not thought of her, only of himself. His insistence on death was "stronger than compassion, stronger than love, faithfulness, gratitude" . . . stronger than anything.

Klaus's parents and sister debated for hours whether or not to continue the lecture tour. They simply couldn't decide what their next step should be. They went to sleep after two in the morning, completely exhausted and still undecided.

The next day, after more discussion, Thomas, Katia, and Erika reached a compromise—Erika had disagreed with her parents over what should be done. Thomas wished to continue his lecture tour, but agreed to decline invitations for social receptions. Katia, suffering in silence, would remain by his side. Erika decided that after their next stop, Copenhagen, she would go off alone to Amsterdam to be with Fritz Landshoff, and reunite with her parents a few days later in Switzerland. This had a practical advantage as well—witnessing "Eri's pain" was what disturbed Thomas most of all about the terrible ordeal, and he had a lot of lecture obligations to fulfill. It was agreed that none of them would attend the funeral. Of the Mann family, only the youngest brother, Michael, who happened to be touring Europe at the time with the San Francisco Symphony Orchestra, made it to Cannes for the burial. He played a largo on his viola while the coffin was lowered into the ground.

Katia broke the news to Thomas's brother. Heinrich Mann was living at the time in Southern California on the largesse of his younger brother; he was also in mourning, following the recent suicide of his second wife. Katia indicated that although Klaus's death was unexpected at the very moment it happened, it was inevitable. She had long realized that "it was necessary to be prepared for it constantly, and I was." As terrible as a mother's grief must be in such a situation, she too found it "worst of all for poor Erika."

Two days later Thomas wrote to Heinrich directly, his closest friend despite all their estrangement over the years. He poured out his heart to his brother but still didn't reveal his own pain:

> Dear Heinrich, these are sad days. Katia sighs heavily, and it pains me to see Erika always in tears. She is abandoned, has lost her companion, whom she always tried to keep clutched to her side. It is hard to understand how he could do this to her. How deranged he must have been in that moment! But it probably had long been his deepest longing. . . . His case is so very strange and painful, such skill, charm, cosmopolitanism, and in his heart a deathwish.

On June 2, Klaus's suitcase, typewriter, and overcoat caught up with Erika and her parents in Zurich. It was too much for Erika to bear; she collapsed at the sight of them. Thomas tried to console her, insisting that there was nothing she could have done, and lamented Klaus's "contradictory mental state, which enforced his deathwish above all else." He reminded Erika of the letter Klaus had received from Georg Jacobi, refusing to publish *Mephisto* in Germany, and of a letter Thomas received in Sweden from Klaus's friend Doris, informing them that in death Klaus had a childlike look of deep fulfillment on his face. This cliché seemed to comfort Thomas as well; he repeated it again in his diary and in his letter to Heinrich.

Why, ultimately, did Klaus Mann commit suicide? Was it his inability to win his father's love and respect? His chronic homelessness? The continued publishing problems he faced? Thomas Mann felt that Klaus's recent disappointment at learning *Mephisto* still could not be published in Germany, owing to Gustaf Gründgens's continued popularity, was largely responsible. Golo Mann was sure that Erika's shift in allegiance from brother to father was a key factor, of which Erika was painfully aware. Elisabeth Mann mentioned that the poor quality of the drugs he bought when he arrived in Cannes made him exceptionally depressed. Sybille Bedford speculated that when he was asked, at a party in Cannes a day or two before, whether he too was a writer, "it was said to him once too often." Surely the state of the world should be considered, as it fell so short of his high ideals and moral standards; even the relentless rain in Cannes that season may have influenced him. With so many reasons favoring suicide, it would have been more surprising had he chosen to live.

In Klaus's diary, he states a reason as clearly as if he had left a suicide note. He gives none of the above explanations, although of course they each played a part. He believed he simply could not write anymore. He found he could no longer write without drugs, and then, not long afterward, it became clear to him that he couldn't write with them either.

Erika alone understood how Klaus's writer's block had taken its toll on him. She described the compulsion to write as being "in his blood. He really had to write, the way other people have to breathe. Without writing, Klaus wasn't capable of living." Yet without Klaus, she wasn't sure *she* was capable of living. "We were a part of each other, so much so that my existence is unthinkable without him," she wrote to a mutual friend.

If Klaus felt betrayed by Erika in the years preceding his death, Erika felt bitterly betrayed by Klaus now. But she had the stronger instincts for survival; she knew she'd somehow find a way to endure. To their old friend Pamela Wedekind, with whom Erika had had no contact in almost two decades, she wrote: "How I shall live, I don't yet know, I only know that I have to."

Little by little Erika took on practical tasks to keep her going: answering condolence letters, gathering Klaus's effects, ordering his tombstone. By June 9 she felt capable of flying to Cannes to arrange for an engraving on his headstone. It was the same biblical citation, in English, that Klaus had chosen to open his unfinished final novel, *The Last Day:*

FOR WHOSOEVER WILL SAVE HIS LIFE SHALL LOSE IT;
BUT WHOSOEVER WILL LOSE HIS LIFE . . . THE SAME SHALL
FIND IT.

Two weeks later Erika left her parents' side once more. She had argued strenuously, to no avail, against her father visiting Germany as part of his European tour. Not only did she refuse to set foot herself on German soil; she wanted to be off the continent altogether if he insisted on going. As the argument escalated, Thomas accused her of being unreasonable— Klaus would never have been so inflexible. "That's why he killed himself," Erika retorted, "which is what I now *won't* do. That's some consolation, but not much." She sailed for New York while Thomas and Katia paid their first visit to Germany in more than fifteen years. Thomas was widely criticized for visiting East as well as West Germany—"I know no zones. My visit is for Germany itself," was his reply—yet everywhere he went he was treated as visiting royalty. For a people recently defeated in a world war, the resources for a steady stream of banquets, flowers, and police escorts could not have been easy to manage, but Thomas Mann's stature in his former homeland was such that "godlike honors" were bestowed upon him by both the East and the West.

Small injustices seemed to plague Klaus even in death. For his profession, the death registry in Cannes had listed "Unknown." Ludwig Marcuse published a "tribute" to Klaus that Erika claimed made her "very ill. . . . If you could bring yourself to say so little on his behalf, *why* did you have to write anything?" His own father wrote a letter about Klaus that started off by expressing considerable remorse, but soon moved on to criticizing Klaus's work ("He worked too quickly. That explains some of the rough spots and sloppiness in his books") and bemoaning his lack of appreciation ("Despite all support and love . . . he made himself incapable of any feelings of faithfulness, consideration or gratitude").

It is a telling document, in which Thomas Mann, six weeks after Klaus's death, admits to his friend, fellow author Hermann Hesse, that he was not entirely blameless when it came to the torment afflicting his son:

> This interrupted life lies heavily on my mind and grieves me. My relationship to him was difficult and not free of guilt. My life put his in a shadow right from the beginning.

A year later, however, in a memorial book for Klaus, Thomas wrote for posterity the praise that Klaus had always longed to hear from his father, but never did: "I truly believe that he belonged to the most talented of his generation; possibly he was the best of them all."

In the autumn of 1949 Erika took on the task of compiling and editing this book, *Klaus Mann zum Gedächtnis* (Klaus Mann in Memoriam), and arranged to have it published the following year by Querido in Amsterdam. She solicited contributions from thirty-three noted literary figures who had been his friends and colleagues, among them the novelists Upton Sinclair and Christopher Isherwood, the poet Muriel Rukeyser, and the historian William Shirer. The name Thomas Mann was prominently placed on the cover, as his piece served as the book's introduction, thereby eclipsing Klaus even while commemorating him. Erika, the impetus behind the book, its editor and translator, wanted her own role to be anonymous.

Erika lived a full twenty years without Klaus, but she was never the same again: her spirit was broken. She became embittered and her health deteriorated. She was physically and emotionally depleted by the loss of Klaus, to the point where Thomas and Katia worried that she too might commit suicide. The lines of her husband's famous poem—"The stars are not wanted now: put out every one; / Pack up the moon and dismantle the sun"—could well have been her personal mantra. Their sister Elisabeth recalled that "when Klaus died, [Erika] was totally, totally heartbroken—I mean that was unbearable for her, that loss. That hit her harder than anything else in her life."

As if Klaus's death weren't enough, one year later Erika was forced to withdraw her application for U.S. citizenship. For many years she had hoped to become officially American, but despite receiving two citations from the Treasury Department and one from the War Department, commending her for her "patriotic services," the decision on her citizenship was inexplicably held up. She wrote to the director of Immigration and Naturalization, explaining why she felt she was deserving of naturalization:

Immeasurable are the times I endangered my life while . . . covering the war as a correspondent accredited to the U.S. Forces. . . . Had I been an American citizen [during the war] I could not possibly have tried harder to be helpful. In fact, I felt like an American, lived like an American, and to all practical purposes was an American. . . . I lived and worked in the United States, and since I wished to go on doing so I deemed it only fair to add myself legally to the good people of this country. My application was made almost four years ago.

Having taken out her "First Papers" (naturalization application) in 1938, she was technically eligible for citizenship in 1942. But by that time she was too busy taking part in the war effort to fulfill the six-month residency requirement, so her citizenship application was left pending. Now that the war was long over and she was permanently settled in California, she imagined that the citizenship process would be easily completed, resulting in her prompt naturalization. She hadn't counted on the arch-conservative and xenophobic policies of the McCarthy era.

Erika and Klaus had already been under suspicion over a decade earlier because of their "premature anti-Fascism," their homosexuality, and their participation (as commentators, not even as soldiers) in the Spanish Civil War. The investigation of Erika was suspended during World War II, but in the anti-Communist climate that developed by war's end, the FBI renewed its investigation like a dog digging up a favorite bone.

In Erika's case, she had actually offered information to the FBI as early as spring 1940. An internal FBI memo noted that Erika approached the FBI office in New York and "indicated a desire to be of assistance." Her motivation: to prevent Nazis from slipping into the United States. One German refugee, she reported to the FBI, was traveling on a German passport with a "J" on it although he was definitely not Jewish (usually it was Nazis who had access to these passports, stolen from Jews, alive or dead). Erika naively assumed that the FBI was interested in tracking Nazis, when in actuality they were far more preoccupied with tracking suspected Communists, Erika included. Because she was so strategically placed in the German exile community, the FBI was eager to make use of her. By way of thanks she became a subject for surveillance for more than a decade. Her aliases, according to the FBI, were Erica Mann, Mrs. Wystan H. Auden, and Erika Julia Hedwig Auden, née Mann.

After the war, the agency's surveillance continued relentlessly for more than four years, despite its inability to tie her to any Communist activities. Erika described the damaging effects on her life:

> Ever since then an investigation has been going on that could not help casting doubts upon my character, gradually ruining my career, robbing me of my livelihood and, in short, changing me from a happy, busy and fairly useful member of society into a humiliated suspect. Friends of mine have been questioned for two and three hours at a stretch until they all but collapsed. When it became obvious that I was neither a Communist, nor a "fellow traveller" . . . the authorities took to digging into my personal life in a way most shocking to those questioned. . . . Small wonder, prospective employers felt ardently disinclined to engage my services. . . .

To understand how her trusted friends and employers could be so unduly influenced by a couple of "spooks," and how the investigation could escalate so quickly without evidence, one must recall that the late 1940s and early 1950s witnessed a witch-hunt of daunting proportions. "Premature anti-Fascists" were among its prime targets (along with card-carrying Communists, subversives of any stripe, homosexuals, and other nonconformists).

During the war, the term "premature anti-Fascist" was used as a code word by the FBI for "Communist" or "Communist sympathizer." After all, why would anyone be against Fascism before 1939, when the onset of the war finally sanctioned ordinary people taking a stand against Fascism, unless he or she was a Communist? Why else would someone speak out before that date against Hitler's brutal police state? Or fight to defend the legitimate Spanish Republic against military overthrow by Franco's forces? The American and British leaders themselves barely objected to the escalation of Fascism in Europe; why should their citizens? Surely the person must be a Communist or Communist sympathizer, otherwise what was there to balk at?

Soon after the war the code word "premature anti-Fascist" jumped out of the classified FBI dossiers and into the lingo of the House and Senate subcommittees that were hunting for Communists and their cronies in every corner of American society. The Red Scare that emerged virtually overnight after the war trampled on civil rights and liberties and justified its illegalities by the air of moral inviolability it assumed. Pejorative claims could be made with scant substantiation and the damage would already be done. People inclined to disbelieve these unfounded claims would still be frightened to associate with the suspected individual, lest they come under scrutiny as well.

And this, according to declassified FBI files, is how Erika herself came under scrutiny, although she never had any inkling of it herself. The FBI discovered that she had socialized with the wrong person, someone with whom she was barely acquainted, and the investigation spread like a virus from him to her. The carrier was the upper-class Englishman Guy Burgess, a graduate of Trinity College, Cambridge, who worked for the BBC. He had developed pro-Communist sympathies during his college days, became a Soviet spy after the war, and eventually defected to the Soviet Union in May 1951. Erika met the man through W. H. Auden, during a wild gay party in England during the war, and he was too drunk to carry on a conversation. She saw him again on one or two occasions, always as part of a group. Asked directly about Guy Burgess by the two surly FBI agents who dropped in on her in October 1951, she could hardly remember him and, when pressed, recalled only that she didn't like the man, and hadn't even bothered to learn his last name. She never discovered that this remote acquaintance was the key to her current misery.

To the INS director she went on to report her bafflement at her current predicament, "ruined—through no fault of my own":

> Personally, I am at a complete loss as to what may have prompted the investigation to take on such disastrous proportions. I have never been granted a hearing. . . . Yet I—and only I—could have supplied whatever information was required. . . .
>
> I [have] had to witness the gradual destruction of all I had built up in more than a decade. This spectacle was all the more painful since it involved the third existence I had made for myself. Nazism drove me from my native Germany where I had been quite a success; Hitler's growing influence in Europe caused me to leave the continent which I had been touring with my own show for more than a thousand performances; and now I find myself ruined— through no fault of my own—in a country I love and whose citizen I had hoped to become.

Erika assumed it was her bisexuality, her leftist leanings, and her strident outspokenness which disturbed the FBI most of all. The FBI agents she encountered certainly disliked her, which is one reason they didn't relent despite a lack of evidence: they vilified her for being a "very vicious person" who was a negative influence on Thomas and Heinrich Mann, responsible for pushing them to their left-wing positions. They exerted enormous effort just trying to track down Erika's movements, although her "mysterious disappearances" inevitably turned out to be hospital visits or travels with her father.

In 1950, the INS asked the FBI for assistance in building a case to deport Erika from the United States. According to FBI documents, "INS has . . . expressed an interest in the subject and has not as yet obtained sufficient evidence upon which to base the issuance of a warrant of arrest in deportation proceedings." The FBI tried to comply with the request for evidence, harassing Erika to the point that she caved in. Even without the official deportation order, she was forced into exile yet again. Her parents, getting on in years, were not all that keen to uproot themselves, but she was unwilling to separate from them. They, too, were seriously disillusioned with the United States, especially after Thomas Mann was denounced in Congress as "one of the world's foremost apologists for Stalin and company."

This epithet was bestowed on Thomas Mann by a California congressman after the author had lent his name to a number of peace organizations—the Committee for Peaceful Alternatives and the American Peace Crusade—and made it known that he was against the rearmament of Germany (as was fellow émigré Albert Einstein), against the Korean War, and against the exclusion of the People's Republic of China from the United Nations. He agreed with Erika that there would be no end to the Cold War stalemate without negotiating with the Soviet Union and China. *Time* magazine accused him of using "his famous name for causes that have nothing to do with literature."

Thomas and Katia's desire to stay put in California was due to their advancing age and their love for the Pacific Palisades villa that had been their home for the past ten years, not to a lingering American patriotism. For Erika's sake they agreed to resettle with her in Switzerland, "not to live there, but to die there," her father wrote in his diary. He and Erika sat down and figured out their finances: emigrating to Switzerland without too much discomfort would require a whopping $140,000, which they didn't have. This sum was eventually raised through the sale of their house ($50,000) and their additional land ($10,000), an outstanding royalty for his book *The Holy Sinner,* chosen for the Book-of-the-Month Club in September 1951 ($50,000), and the sale of all his manuscripts ($30,000). His only condition was that they settle in the German-speaking part of Switzerland—even though Katia had wanted to get a house near

Locarno. They bought a beautiful house four miles from Zurich, high above their town of Kilchberg with a view of the lake, and it was here they settled in for the rest of their days.

Erika was still in her forties when she unpacked her belongings in the new house, but between Klaus's death, the final rejection from Bruno Walter, and the FBI ordeal, she had aged visibly in just a few years. She announced that the move did not signal an attempt to "start over": she wasn't strong enough, nor did she have the will, to undergo the tremendous efforts of building a new life in a new place all over again. She resumed her friendship with Therese Giehse, who lived in Zurich, but made few if any new friends and alienated most of her old ones.

Yet despite her resignation Erika kept working. For a short while she resumed writing children's books, as she had done before her emigration from Germany. *Christoph fliegt nach Amerika* (Christoph Flies to America) was published in Munich in 1953, and a series called *Zugvögel* (Migratory Birds) appeared in print between 1953 and 1955. She also continued to speak out occasionally on political issues that concerned her: nuclear testing; the slaughter of seals in Canada; the war in Vietnam. Her children's books and her political proclamations were intermittent and relegated to the sideline; her primary work remained that of secretary and editor to her father. She continued to accompany him on lecture tours and, when several of his novels were filmed in the 1950s, she insisted upon supervising the screenplays (despite having little experience since the early 1930s with the world of cinema). She even acted a minor role in one of them, *Royal Highness*.

In 1953, the Magician gave Erika a copy of his collection of essays, *Altes und Neues*, inscribed with the dedication: "Eri, the helper, so cautious, loyal and dedicated, affectionate—grateful." Erika had been many things in her life but cautious was not one of them. Neither was she much of a helper to anyone but her father; she was enough of a prima donna that she expected others to play that role for her. Considered by many to be intolerant and judgmental, and increasingly so as she aged, Erika had unlimited tolerance only for her father. When, wracked with depression, he wanted to abandon writing his novel *Felix Krull*, Erika sensitively and patiently encouraged him to keep going, and supported him in countless ways so that he could.

Her brother Golo viewed Erika not only as their father's assistant and editor but also his "court jester." The Magician had been very amused by Erika when she was a child, but this older, considerably changed Erika in the role of court jester could not have been very amusing. Increasingly

Erika and the Magician, Thomas Mann

moody and irritable, she provoked heated arguments with her father and usually won them through sheer stubbornness. She quarreled regularly with Katia, and with her siblings Golo, Michael, and Elisabeth as well. Elisabeth and Erika didn't speak to each other for over a decade because, according to Elisabeth, Erika was jealous of her relationship with their father.

For the remainder of her days, Erika lived a relatively private life, plagued by chronic insomnia, headaches, backaches, bone problems, and other various illnesses that kept her bedridden much of the time. Years of unforgiving judgments, heartbreaking disappointment, extreme hate, and recreational drug abuse seem to have eaten away at her body. She checked into a sanatorium outside Lucerne in June 1953 for mysterious gastric and intestinal problems and chronic insomnia, but none of them were curable. While she was resident at the clinic, a powerful hypnotic drug the doctors gave her failed to induce sleep, and instead she halluci-nated fantastic details of her father's death in an extremely vivid waking dream. Doctors and nurses could not calm her down, and she woke up the entire sanatorium with her hysterical behavior.

The photographer Marianne Breslauer was invited to Thomas Mann's eightieth birthday party in 1955. Upon arrival she was shocked to find his daughter in far worse shape than he was. She recalled that "Erika was in a bad state and . . . I was told that she couldn't walk anymore properly. I don't know what she had, but she was not her own self anymore." The author Sybille Bedford also went to visit Erika in Switzerland, and was surprised to find that

> she couldn't even get up for supper. She had some terrible thing, she had been sent to one of the specialist places near Oxford and they couldn't do anything for her. Of course, Klaus's death must have been appalling for her. . . . Appalling for everyone, but especially for her. I remember sitting by her bedside after going to dinner with Erika and Mielein [Katia], and all on very small glasses of hock, when what one would need would be a large scotch! And Erika was very sweet, we reminisced, and we talked about Kläuschen and I was fond of her.

Thomas Mann died on August 12, 1955. Erika became his full-time literary executor, shoring up his reputation for posterity. She oversaw the screen adaptation of his remaining novels, and even mustered the stamina to act again in one of them, *Felix Krull*. She read the newspaper avidly and would write heated letters to the editor of any paper that mentioned him unflatteringly or reviewed his work harshly. She wrote a moving chronicle of the last year of his life, *The Last Year,* published in both German and English editions.

This book is astounding on two counts. First, it reveals Erika's relationship with her father to have been almost that of a devoted younger lover. Her doting descriptions of him hint at an obsessive passion. She begins the book by describing how "his life was illumined and warmed by grace." He possessed a "rare emotional force." Anyone looking at him could perceive "the radiance that issued from him and illumined all his endeavors." At one point, shortly before his death, she describes the octogenarian lying in his hospital bed as being "so youthfully supple, so mobile, so agile. His clear spirit was so active, so inexhaustibly fruitful, so many-sided in its interests, so energetic, and so tireless." His three salient features, she insists, were modesty, kindness, and humor.

Did Erika sincerely believe this or was she simply trying to present a glowing account of the man for posterity? It seems she genuinely had become blind to his failings. Her former self, assessing her father twenty years early, would have only conceded his ironic humor; after all it was a signature trait of his. Kindness and modesty were in short supply, especially when it came to fatherhood.

For part of the memoir, she quotes directly from a diary she kept at the time. One would expect a book about one's father to be concerned with his life at the expense of one's own, but, bizarrely, her private diary also embraces such an agenda. It records his actions and feelings instead of hers; the only emotional tone we hear from her is one of adoration. On May 8, "Z. [the Magician] happy, in good form and clearly unfatigued," but on May 10, "Z. needs a rest." On May 13, "Z. as patient as ever," and the next day he is "tired at last." In the first half of May 1955, Thomas Mann traveled throughout West Germany giving sold-out lectures on Schiller, receiving an honorary doctorate, and meeting with the president, but her diary reports on his breathing, as if he were merely lying in a sickbed. We have no idea from her diary if Erika is ever patient or tired herself—indeed the pronoun "I" rarely occurs.

Curiously, Erika commented on this feature of her writing herself, a good twelve years previously. In her unfinished autobiography, she mentions the difficulty she found in writing about herself, despite her lifelong love for public attention and for standing in the limelight on a stage. "In fact I rather lack interest in myself. Auto-analysis has never played any part in my writings, where even the word 'I' appears but rarely." This may have something to do with why she abandoned the project. By 1968, when two different publishers implored her to resume and publish her memoirs, she was clearly uninterested.

The other outstanding feature of the book about her father is that Erika assumed a completely different literary persona than she had used previously. In *The Lights Go Down* (1936), Erika had described heartbreaking domestic dramas with understated emotion, rendering the insidious effects of Fascism on individual families all the more devastating. In *School for Barbarians* (1938), she wrote passionately and polemically, bolstering her argument with impeccably researched statistics. Her children's book *A Gang of Ten* (1942), an anti-Fascist adventure story for adolescents, takes a slightly preachy, condescending tone (ascribable to the central character, who closely resembles the author). In *The Last Year*, her final book, she becomes philosophical and at times allegorical.

Reflecting on her waking dream envisioning a gruesome death for her father, she writes, "The nightmare dreamer is delivered up to the horror he himself has created, and derives not the slightest relief from the neutral world. . . . The dreamer knows and perceives nothing but the horror of his dream." She is able to slide gracefully from inner dreams and nightmares to describing the flowers outside her window to commenting on major world events and back again. It is almost as if finally, with her father's death, she allowed herself to take risks as a writer, to try and find her own literary voice.

Only at the end of the memoir, with Thomas's death, does Erika succumb to sentimentality, her former strength and clarity obscured by the intensity of her loss: "Dear, beloved Magician, grace walked with you to the end, and you went forth in tranquility from this green earth about whose fate you have so long and lovingly distressed yourself. For three days, your shell, your slender body, with its stern, brave, unfamiliarly waxen features, lay in the farewell chamber of the clinic. Your lovely ring [one she had given him for his birthday] was on your finger. The stone shone darkly. We buried it with you."

Erika and Katia continued to live together uneasily in the house in Kilchberg without the shared object of their affections to unite them. It was not the domestic arrangement Katia would have wished for herself; she wanted her children to be self-sufficient and independent. Still in mourning for her husband, she wrote to a close friend, "All the children say they need me, but grown-up children can and must live without their mother. The one who really needed me is no longer and I cannot see much sense in my further life."

Katia was a formidable presence in her own right, and the two domineering women often clashed head-on. Erika claimed that Katia was "not only running the house but dominating it (she is truly its mistress)." But Katia's impression was that she was actually dominated by Erika, perhaps not directly but by the demands of Erika's various illnesses. Instead of Erika taking care of her mother in her mother's old age, her mother took care of the daughter in *hers*. When Katia wanted to visit her close friend Molly in Princeton, New Jersey, she felt compelled to put it off. In her imperfect English she wrote, "If Erika's conditions were a little bit more satisfactory. . . . But she is more helpless than ever, cannot walk one single step, the doctors don't know what to do, and yet I feel she cannot spend the whole life in hospitals."

Katia was indeed stuck. She couldn't send Erika to live with one of her other children. Being a daughter, Elisabeth was the most likely choice (sons were rarely thought capable of such a burden)—but Elisabeth still wasn't speaking to Erika. Katia complained to her twin brother, Klaus Pringsheim, "What is ruining . . . my old age, is the more than unfriendly relationship of all my children toward the good, fat eldest." Katia is being facetious here; Erika was extremely thin and frail. The strife was such that it impeded the remaining children's visits with their mother, and made it impossible for them to share responsibility for Erika's care. Katia told her twin that her ornery, quarrelsome daughter was unfairly dependent on her, keeping her tied to the house. Most likely she would be heading to Tokyo, where Klaus Pringsheim lived, if she had not that responsibility to bear alone.

But Erika was her child, her firstborn. Katia admired Erika for all that she managed to do despite her physical (and no doubt emotional) pain. In the early sixties, disabled by a knee injury and plagued by a painful bone illness, Erika set out to compile and edit a three-volume set of her father's letters, a project which brought her back into correspondence with many friends of the family, old acquaintances who also happened to be among the great thinkers and writers of the century. It was a demanding task, but one that required no engagement with the contemporary world from which she had resolutely withdrawn: the work was conflict-free and backward-looking. She did most of it while lying flat on her back.

The feisty, energetic spirit of Erika's former self did return on those occasions when Klaus still seemed to need her. Even before Thomas Mann's death, she found time to pursue getting Klaus's books into print in their native Germany—no easy feat. His autobiography, *The Turning Point*, presented a huge hurdle that brought her face-to-face with her despicable first husband. Unless sections about him were deleted from the book, Gustaf Gründgens, the foremost theater director in Germany, threatened to boycott S. Fischer, the publisher which now owned Querido, and his threat included the entire S. Fischer theater series. Erika was never good at compromise, and capitulating to blackmail was almost impossible for her. But such was her desire for Klaus's work to be in print that finally, after three years of resisting, she deleted the offending sections.

The first posthumous publication of Klaus's many works was the German edition of *The Turning Point*, translated as *Der Wendepunkt* in 1952. It was more than a direct translation of the English; Klaus, when rewriting it himself in German after the war, had added considerable discussion of his homosexuality and his drug addiction, which he had been persuaded to withhold from his more puritanical American readership, especially at a time when he was trying to gain entry into the U.S. Army. The resulting book is Klaus's most truthful, and also his most devastating. The

After Klaus's death, Erika "was not her own self anymore" (according to friend Marianne Breslauer)—but she still loved cigarettes
and fast cars.

critic Friedrich Sieburg reviewed *Der Wendepunkt* for *Die Zeit* and found
Klaus to be a "man who never ceased to confess, who strained painfully
at the chain binding him to Germany." Sieburg's is an astute assessment,
to which one easily could add: and at the chain binding him to his father.
But Sieburg ultimately misunderstood Klaus Mann. His review insists
that Klaus's radical sense of morality, his insistence on forging sexuality,
politics, and art into a coherent ethos, was essentially a contradictory
enterprise: homosexuality isolated Klaus from the very community he

sought. In the end Klaus was no doubt isolated; his lifelong, paralyzing fear became his reality. His radical morality, however, is not what killed him; it is what enabled him to hold on for as long as he did.

After the publication of *Der Wendepunkt* came the reissue of Klaus's novel about Tchaikovsky, *Symphonie Pathetique*, in 1952, and in 1956 *Mephisto*, too, was finally published in Germany—but only in the German Democratic Republic (i.e., East Germany). West German publishers would not touch it—even after 1963, when Gründgens himself committed suicide, just as Klaus had, by way of a sleeping pill overdose. Gustaf Gründgens's popularity was such that, despite his Nazi past, the publication of *Mephisto* remained *verboten* long after both author and subject had died. Again Erika fought back. Earlier that year, she had taken the case of *Mephisto* all the way to the German Supreme Court, where it took three years for the court to come to a specious judgment: it upheld the ban on publication. Gründgens's younger lover Peter Gorski, whom he legally adopted as his son for legacy purposes, had continued the litigation to protect Gründgens's reputation following his death.

As if there were a dearth of current world events to report on, the old insinuation of incest that long plagued the Mann family now resurfaced in the mainstream press. In the midst of the publicity around the court decision on *Mephisto, Die Kölner Rundschau* made a reference to "the failed marriage of Gustaf with Erika Mann, in which Klaus in reality was the wife." *Die Zeit* posed the question, "Did Gründgens destroy the relationship between Klaus and Erika, which was more than that of mere siblings?" Erika, worn out as she was, still decided to pursue a libel case against both newspapers, arguing that their statements implied sexual perversion. The journalists denied her interpretation, and claimed they were only stressing the extraordinary closeness between the siblings. Erika emerged victorious, and was awarded 10,000 deutsche marks from each newspaper.

Despite the Supreme Court ruling in Gründgens's favor, the East German edition of *Mephisto* slipped across the Berlin Wall and into the hands of avid West German readers, who sent it on into the Western world. The Théâtre du Soleil in Paris presented an avant-garde production of the book in 1979, with no unpleasant legal consequences, which led others to take similar risks. Two years later, despite the standing injunction, a paperback version appeared in West Germany. Within a few weeks of publication it became a best seller and started climbing the ranks; today it is considered a classic of exile literature. Debates and trials over the book dragged on indefinitely, while foreign publishers cranked it out in over twenty languages, and the Hungarian director István Szabó adapted it to the screen (winning an Academy Award for Best Foreign Film in 1981). The book's instant success led to the publication of his other works, to the point where Klaus's considerable oeuvre is now entirely in print.

Erika did not survive to see *Mephisto* become a best seller or her brother Klaus acquire the celebrated cult status he has today in Germany. Dissertations are now written about him in German universities, and the recent centennial of his birth was commemorated with radio broadcasts and photography exhibitions. In August 1969, after having been ill for some time with a brain tumor, sixty-three-year-old Erika Mann died in Zurich, in the same hospital her father passed away in fourteen years earlier. She died the one way she never managed to live—peacefully.

It was really only a matter of her body catching up with her soul: the Erika she had used to be—the one who loved adventure and absurdity, who overflowed with wit and charm, who attracted people to her as effortlessly as moths to a light—had already died twenty years earlier. In her will she left some of her assets to W. H. Auden, to whom she hadn't spoken in decades, in gratitude for what he had done for her. Her indomitable mother survived her by more than a decade. Although some of Erika's work too has now started to gain recognition in Germany decades after her death, today she is mostly remembered, if remembered at all, as the daughter of Thomas Mann, the wife of W. H. Auden, and the sister of Klaus Mann.

NOTES

CHAPTER ONE

Page 1 "We were six children . . .": Elisabeth Mann, interview by author, May 13, 1999.

Page 2 "Why was that stupid old lady . . .": Klaus Mann, *The Turning Point: Thirty-five Years in This Century* (London: Oswald Wolff, 1984), 10–11.

Page 2 "acted twin-like . . .": Klaus Mann, *Turning Point*, 54.

Pages 2–3 "Hand in hand . . .": Klaus Mann, *Turning Point*, xv.

Page 5 "grow with the years . . .": Katia Mann, *Unwritten Memories*, trans. Hunter Hannum and Hildegarde Hannum (London: André Deutsch, 1974), 66.

Page 5 "Thomas Mann, recipient . . .": Cited in Marianne Krüll, *Im Netz der Zauberer: Eine andere Geschichte der Familie Mann* (Frankfurt: Fischer, 1993), 341.

Page 6 "I just wanted to say . . .": Katia Mann, *Unwritten Memories*, 154.

Page 6 "I have lived and loved . . .": Cited in Ronald Hayman, *Thomas Mann* (London: Bloomsbury, 1997), 69.

Page 6 "A punishment he imposed . . .": Hayman, *Thomas Mann*, 193.

Page 7 "in marrying her . . .": Hayman, *Thomas Mann*, 70.

Page 7 "A writer isn't quite the thing . . .": Katia Mann, *Unwritten Memories*, 9.

Page 7 "It was always my secret . . .": Cited in Hayman, *Thomas Mann*, 68.

Page 8 "Well, it is a girl . . .": Thomas Mann and Heinrich Mann, *Briefwechsel, 1900–1949* (Frankfurt: S. Fischer, 1968), 39–40.

Page 8 "It turned out to be a girl . . .": Katia Mann, *Unwritten Memories*, 22.

Page 8 "Klaus was a dreamer . . .": Erika Mann, "Der engagierte Schriftsteller in der Emigration: Ein Porträt Klaus Manns," radio interview, Hessische Rundfunk, November 17, 1966.

Page 8 "A girl is not . . .": Katia Mann, *Unwritten Memories*, 22.

Page 9 "When a man has six children . . .": Cited in Anthony Heilbut, *Thomas Mann: Eros and Literature* (New York: Alfred A. Knopf, 1996), 457.

Page 11 "of course, was the captain . . .": Klaus Mann, *Turning Point*, 15.

Page 11 "had enough imagination . . .": Erika and Klaus Mann,"Escape to Life," English draft manuscript, p. 7, housed in the Erika und Klaus Mann Archive, Literaturarchiv Monacensia, Munich (hereafter Monacensia).

Page 14 "but no one came down . . .": Golo Mann, *Reminiscences and Reflections: A Youth in Germany* (New York: W. W. Norton, 1990), 16.

Page 15 "Where is your Eissi?": Erika Mann to Frau Gamst, February 8, 1960, in Erika Mann, *Briefe und Antworten*, 2 vols., ed. Anna Zanco Prestel (Munich: Edition Spangenberg, 1985), 2:91.

Page 15 "to be sure, was not Klaus": Erika Mann, "I, of All People," draft notes toward an autobiography, 14, Monacensia.

Page 16 "I always wanted to go on the stage . . .": Erika and Klaus Mann, *Escape to Life* (Boston: Houghton Mifflin, 1939), 3–4.

Page 17 "I was of the mistaken opinion . . .": Erika Mann, in Erika and Klaus Mann, *Escape to Life*, 4.

Page 17 "The governess looked pale with malice . . .": Klaus Mann, *Turning Point*, 27.

Page 17 "The report of the governess . . .": Klaus Mann, *Turning Point*, 28.

Page 19 "presently became the chieftain . . .": Klaus Mann, *Turning Point*, 31.

Page 19 "degenerate, stupid and criminal . . . we were invincible": Erika Mann, *Writers in Freedom: A Symposium Based on the XVII International Congress of the P.E.N. Club Held in London in September, 1941* (Port Washington, NY: Kennikat Press, 1941), 85.

Page 19 "breezy and dangerous . . . the tough, unbound life . . .": Klaus Mann, *Turning Point*, 31.

Page 19 "as unpredictable as valiant . . .": Klaus Mann, *Turning Point*, 31.

Page 19 "the Kaiser was not next to God . . .": Erika Mann, *Writers in Freedom*, 85.

Page 19 "was no match . . .": Golo Mann, *Reminiscences and Reflections*, 22.

Page 20 "Don't you know that Germany . . .": Golo Mann, *Reminiscences and Reflections*, 24.

Page 20 "You have underestimated . . .": Cited in Nigel Hamilton, *The Brothers Mann* (New Haven: Yale University Press, 1979), 127.

Page 21 "Are we supposed to give . . .": Golo Mann, *Reminiscences and Reflections*, 24.

Page 21 "We had once loved our father . . .": Golo Mann, *Reminiscences and Reflections*, 25.

Page 21 "I can remember all too well . . .": Golo Mann, *Reminiscences and Reflections*, 25.

Page 21 "This wartime father seems . . .": Klaus Mann, *Turning Point*, 38.

Page 21 "It is easier to understand . . .": Klaus Mann, *Turning Point*, 39.

Page 22 "political blunder . . .": Klaus Mann, *Turning Point*, 40.

Page 22 "We were already mourning . . .": Thomas Mann, *Briefe*, 3 vols., ed. Erika Mann (Frankfurt: S. Fischer Verlag, 1961–1965), 3:464.

Page 22 "which I cannot remember today . . .": Klaus Mann, "A Family against a Dictatorship," unpublished draft of a lecture, p. 7, Monacensia.

Page 22 "He used the nom de plume . . .": Cited in Katia Mann, *Unwritten Memories*, 46–47.

Page 23 "Klaus was—it's strange . . .": Elisabeth Mann, interview by author, May 13, 1999.

Page 23 "contrasts astonishingly": Thomas Mann to Hermann Hesse, July 6, 1949, in Thomas Mann, *Letters of Thomas Mann*, sel. and trans. by Richard and Clara Winston (New York: Alfred A. Knopf, 1971), 580.

Page 23 "Its shadow had evidently . . .": Klaus Mann, *Kind dieser Zeit* (Reinbek bei Hamburg: Rowohlt, 1982), 35.

Page 23 "still child's play . . .": Golo Mann, afterword to Klaus Mann, *Briefe und Antworten, 1922–1949*, ed. Martin Gregor-Dellin, 2 vols. (Reinbek bei Hamburg: Rowohlt, 1991), 2:332.

Page 23 "I must, I must . . .": Klaus Mann, *Der Wendepunkt* (Reinbek bei Hamburg: Rowohlt, 1999),113.

Page 23 "She had a very lively . . .": Elisabeth Mann, interview by author, May 13, 1999.

Page 23 "witty and self-possessed": Golo Mann, *Reminiscences and Reflections*, 26.

Page 23 "my spirited, funny sister . . .": Golo Mann, *Reminiscences and Reflections*, 128.

Page 23 "Erika was quite . . .": Thomas Mann, *Diaries, 1918–1939*, trans. Richard and Clara Winston (New York: Harry N. Abrams, 1982), 109. Diary entry dated January 2, 1921.

Page 23 "Am enraptured with Eissi . . .": Thomas Mann, *Diaries, 1918–1939*, 101. Diary entry dated July 25, 1920.

Page 23 "germ of a father-son . . .": Thomas Mann, *Diaries, 1918–1939*, 100. Diary entry dated July 5, 1920.

Page 24 "the thoughtful face of the father . . .": Erika and Klaus Mann, "Portrait of Our Father: Thomas Mann," *Atlantic Monthly* 163, no. 4 (April 1939): 448.

Page 24 "Her soft, metallic voice, so coquettish . . .": Klaus Mann, "Der Vater lacht," in *Maskenscherz: Die frühen Erzählungen* (Hamburg: Rowohlt, 1981), 71.

Page 24 "forbidden and subversive . . .": James Robert Keller, *The Role of Political and Sexual Identity in the Works of Klaus Mann* (New York: Peter Lang, 2001), 44.

Page 25 "Who knows what actually . . .": Klaus Mann, *Turning Point*, 23.

Page 25 "Don't attempt to unveil . . .": Klaus Mann, *Turning Point*, 23.

Page 26 "'You'll feel very sorry . . .": Klaus Mann, *Turning Point*, 48–49.

Page 26 "Jennie triumphed . . .": Klaus Mann, *Turning Point*, 50.

Pages 26–27 "It was this freezing, pathetic . . .": Klaus Mann, *Turning Point*, 52.

Page 27 "such an unhealthy coldness . . .": Thomas Mann, *Diaries, 1918–1939*, 96. Diary entry dated May 5, 1920.

Page 27 "a folly from which . . .": Thomas Mann, *Diaries, 1918–1939*, 100. Diary entry dated July 11, 1920.

Page 27 "We seldom saw our father . . .": Erika and Klaus Mann, "Portrait of Our Father," 441.

Page 28 "imposing proof of Father's . . .": Klaus Mann, *Turning Point*, 5.

Page 29 "totally nude and up to some nonsense . . .": Thomas Mann, *Diaries, 1918–1939*, 103. Entry dated October 17, 1920.

Page 29 "remained a stranger . . .": Klaus Mann, *Der Wendepunkt*, 26.

Page 29 "Fame and authority . . .": Klaus Mann, *Turning Point*, 196.

Page 29 "it is no easy job to be the child . . .": Klaus Mann, *Turning Point*, 248.

Page 29 "It was a tragedy . . .": Klaus Mann, *Turning Point*, 248.

Page 30 "were the founders, executive committee, and . . .": Erika Mann, "Kindertheater," *Tempo*, September 28, 1928.

Page 30 "'Accept my tears . . .'": Katia Mann, *Unwritten Memories*, 45.

Page 31 "After a very short time indeed . . .": Erika Mann, *Writers in Freedom*, 85.

Page 31 "After the War . . .": Erika Mann, "Don't Make the Same Mistakes," in *Zero Hour: A Summons to the Free*, ed. Stephen Vincent Benét, Erika Mann, et. al. (New York: Farrar and Rinehart, 1940), 25.

Page 31 "The 'Youth Movement' rejected . . .": Erika Mann, "Don't Make the Same Mistakes," 30.

Pages 31–32 "I gathered around me . . .": Klaus Mann, *Kind dieser Zeit*, 129.

Page 32 "out of pure love for Mother": Cited in Ursula Hummel and Eva Chrambach, *Klaus und Erika Mann, Bilder und Dokumente* (Munich: Edition Spangenberg, 1990), 15.

Page 32 "I can't imagine . . .": Klaus Mann, *Briefe und Antworten*, 69.

Page 32 "There was one lad . . .": Klaus Mann, *Turning Point*, 83.

Pages 32–33 "I couldn't bear it . . .": Klaus Mann, *Turning Point*, 84.

Page 33 "those bad, unbridled children!": *Letters of Heinrich and Thomas Mann*,

1900–1949, ed. Hans Wysling, trans. Don Reneau (Berkeley: University of California Press, 1998), 130. Letter dated October 17, 1923.

Page 33 "Sodom and Gomorrah . . .": Klaus Mann, *Turning Point*, 86–87.

CHAPTER TWO

Page 35 Comment by French journalist Victor Tissot is cited in Thomas Friedrich, *Berlin between the Wars* (New York: The Vendome Press, 1991), 61.

Page 36 "gorgeously corrupt": Klaus Mann, *Turning Point*, 88.

Page 37 "Perversion's really swell": Klaus Mann, *Kind dieser Zeit*, 133.

Page 37 "The Tü-Tü crowd . . .": Klaus Mann, *Der Wendepunkt* (Reinbek bei Hamburg: Rowohlt, 1999), 129–30.

Page 37 "meshugener idea": Klaus Mann, *Der Wendepunkt*, 129–30.

Page 37 "great balm and narcotic": Klaus Mann, *Turning Point*, 85–86.

Page 38 "I had the time of my life": Klaus Mann, *Turning Point*, 87.

Page 38 "violent pleasures and excesses": Erika Mann, "Don't Make the Same Mistakes," 25.

Page 39 "It wasn't a bad idea . . .": Thomas Mann: *Briefe*, 1:216.

Page 39 "ten times, fifty times, and a hundred times . . .": Friedrich Lorenz, "Gespräche mit Erika Mann," *Neues Wiener Journal*, March 1962, cited in Irmela von der Lühe, *Erika Mann: Eine Biographie* (Frankfurt: Campus Verlag, 1993), 29.

Page 39 "Unfortunately, the editor soon found out . . .": Klaus Mann, *Turning Point*, 104.

Page 39 "he suffered from the feeling . . .": Golo Mann, afterword to Klaus Mann, *Briefe und Antworten*, 2:323.

Page 40 "too vain and immature to reject . . .": Klaus Mann, *Turning Point*, 124.

Page 41 "another trick to bamboozle the grown folks": Klaus Mann, *Turning Point*, 105.

Page 41 "There was nothing Mr. von Bonn . . .": Klaus Mann, *Turning Point*, 105.

Page 41 "he was an orderly boy": Klaus Mann, *Turning Point*, 111.

Pages 41–42 "He had traveled widely and continuously . . .": Christopher Isherwood, in Erika Mann, ed., *Klaus Mann zum Gedächtnis* (Amsterdam: Querido, 1950), 66.

Page 42 "He who is too deeply associated . . .": Klaus Mann, *The Pious Dance* (New York: PAJ Publications, 1987), 138.

Page 43 "had no prejudices against . . .": Klaus Mann, *Turning Point*, 96.

Page 43 "but a softened and rejuvenated . . .": Klaus Mann, *Turning Point*, 94.

Page 44 "I know that you don't like it . . .": Klaus Mann, *Briefe und Antworten*, 1:13. Letter dated November 5, 1922.

Page 44 "But you don't know how unhappy . . .": Erika Mann to Pamela Wedekind, unpublished letter dated August 1925, Monacensia.

Page 44 "a play about young people of course . . .": Klaus Mann, *Turning Point*, 107.

Page 45 "At first you'll feel rather hard done by . . .": Klaus Mann, "Anja and Esther," trans. Laurence Senelick, in Laurence Senelick, *Lovesick: Modernist Plays of Same-Sex Love, 1894–1925* (London: Routledge, 1999), 169–96 (quotation from p. 190).

Page 45 "as a token of Klaus's inward . . .": Senelick, *Lovesick*, 166.

Page 46 "Dear Children! . . .": Thomas Mann, letter dated October 19, 1927, in Erika Mann, *Briefe und Antworten*, vol. 1, 1922–1950, ed. Anna Zanco Prestel (Munich: Deutscher Taschenbuch Verlag, 1988), 17.

Page 46 "the K.H. experience was more mature . . .": Cited in Hayman, *Thomas Mann*, 75.

Page 47 "a sentimental friendship . . .": Klaus Mann, *Turning Point*, 108.

Page 47 "I read Kläuschen's book . . .": Thomas Mann, *Briefe*, 1:239. Letter dated May 7, 1925.

Page 48 "everything was based on reality . . .": Katia Mann, *Unwritten Memories*, 63.

Page 48 "the depiction in *Disorder* . . .": Klaus Mann, *Tagebücher, 1936–1937* (Munich: Spangenberg, 1990), 110. Diary entry dated February 25, 1937.

Page 48 "strategic literary response . . .": Keller, *Political and Sexual Identity*, 33.

Page 48 "the eyes of an archangel": Erika and Klaus Mann, *Escape to Life*, 158.

Page 48 "wouldn't bother reading . . .": Klaus Mann, *Briefe und Antworten*, 1:30. Letter dated January 15, 1926.

Pages 48–49 "there could be no question . . .": Marcel Reich-Ranicki, *Thomas Mann and His Family* (London: Collins, 1989), 167.

Page 49 "experienced next to nothing . . .": Reich-Ranicki, *Thomas Mann and His Family*, 11.

Page 49 "a neurotic Hermes": Klaus Mann, *Turning Point*, 116.

Page 49 "The younger generation has found its poet . . ." Gustaf Gründgens, "About Klaus Mann," *Der Freihafen* (Hamburg), vol. 2 (1925/6): 16; cited in Senelick, *Lovesick*, 198.

Page 50 "didn't suit him at all": Katia Mann, *Unwritten Memories*, 97.

Page 50 "All their own attachments . . .": Sybille Bedford, interview by author, July 31, 1999.

Page 51 "Klaus could never sleep . . .": Sybille Bedford, July 31, 1999.

Page 51 "deine Freundin": Thomas Mann, *Briefe*, 1:257. Letter dated June 28, 1926.

Page 51 "Many many greetings . . .": Erika Mann, *Briefe und Antworten*, 1:13. Letter dated July 1926.

Page 53 "was all talent, no substance . . .": Klaus Mann, *Turning Point*, 115.

Page 53 "More bitchy, Klaus!...": Klaus Mann, *Turning Point*, 116.

Pages 53–54 "Should I, can I forbid it?...": Thomas Mann to Ernst Bertram, unpublished letter dated February 4, 1925, cited in Hamilton, *Brothers Mann*.

Page 54 "chilly curiosity.": Klaus Mann, *Turning Point*, 116.

Page 54 "beautiful performance of dignity and grief": Klaus Mann, *Turning Point*, 117.

Page 54 "a felon against the German people": Senelick, *Lovesick*, 167.

Page 55 "I am no boarding-school mistress": Thomas Mann, *Neues Wiener Journal*, February 19, 1926.

Page 55 "We sneered at the critics...": Klaus Mann, *Turning Point*, 124.

Page 56 "flippant aggressiveness...": Klaus Mann, *Turning Point*, 130.

Page 56 "'I don't know what's wrong...'": Klaus Mann, *Turning Point*, 130.

Pages 56–57 "land of stunning mixtures...": Klaus Mann, *Turning Point*, 132.

Page 57 "savage and delicate...": Klaus Mann, *Turning Point*, 73.

Page 57 "True, in his particular case...": Klaus Mann, *Turning Point*, 135.

Page 59 "Not one cent was left...": Klaus Mann, *Turning Point*, 146.

Page 59 "the taxi driver can pay...": Klaus Mann, *Turning Point*, 150.

Page 60 "kept in that luxurious prison...": Klaus Mann, *Turning Point*, 153.

Page 60 "be a writer all right...": Klaus Mann, *Turning Point*, 143.

Page 60 "After Moscow, Warsaw was...": Erika and Klaus Mann, *Rundherum: Abenteuer einer Weltreise* (Reinbek bei Hamburg: Rowohlt, 1982), 154.

Page 61 "the whole trip seemed like...": Erika and Klaus Mann, *Rundherum*, 154.

Page 61 "a most unusual gesture...": Klaus Mann, *Turning Point*, 158.

Page 61 "Not like a couple of grown-up...": Klaus Mann, *Turning Point*, 158.

Page 62 "new kind of female writer...": Erika Mann, "Frau und Buch," *Tempo*, March 21, 1931.

Page 63 "zigzagged Europe together...": Klaus Mann, *Turning Point*, 191.

Page 63 "burst literally asunder": Klaus Mann, *Turning Point*, 193.

Page 64 "journey without sleep": Erika Mann, "Fahrt ohne Schlaf," *Tempo*, May 27, 1931.

Page 65 "rather a flop...": Klaus Mann, *Turning Point*, 247.

Page 65 "If [Klaus] were not the son...": *Der Völkische Beobachter*, no. 272, November 15, 1930.

Page 66 "something very wonderful and very pure...": Marianne Breslauer, interview by author, August 3, 1999.

Page 67 "Everything is lost!...": Klaus Mann, *Turning Point*, 250.

Page 68 "Many people think life dreary...": Klaus Mann, *Turning Point*, 249.

Page 69 "He must have hit... his heart": Klaus Mann, *Turning Point*, 257.

Page 72 "longing for death . . .": Klaus Mann, "Ricki Hallgarten—Radikalismus des Herzens," in *Die neuen Eltern: Aufsätze, Reden, Kritiken, 1924–1933* (Reinbek bei Hamburg: Rowohlt, 1992), 390.

Page 72 "his deadly impertinence . . .": Erika Mann, *Briefe und Antworten*, 1:24. Letter dated May 28, 1932.

Page 72 "Eucodal. Cocaine . . . the physical shock from the morphine . . .": Klaus Mann, *Tagebücher, 1934–1935* (Munich: Spangenberg, 1989): 143–44. Diary entry dated September 9, 1935.

Page 73 "Don't do it, Hulda, don't do it . . .": Unpublished, undated [1933] letter from Erika to Klaus, Monacensia.

Page 74 "She was a fabulous person . . .": Marianne Breslauer, interview by author, August 3, 1999.

Page 75 "I rather like Frau Giehse": Klaus Mann, *Turning Point*, 237.

Page 76 "Was there no bloody aura . . .": Klaus Mann, *Turning Point*, 236–37.

Page 76 We must not fall into . . .": Klaus Mann, "Heute und Morgen: Zur Situation des jungen geistigen Europas," in *Die neuen Eltern*, 152.

Page 76 "short-sighted egotism . . .": Erika Mann, "Don't Make the Same Mistakes," 53.

Page 77 "The ingenious son publicly accused . . .": Klaus Mann, *Turning Point*, 245.

Page 78 "people should mind their own business": Erika Mann, in Erika and Klaus Mann, *Escape to Life*, 2.

Page 78 "none of our business": Erika Mann, "Don't Make the Same Mistakes," 30.

Page 78 "pet enemy": Klaus Mann, *Turning Point*, 242.

Page 78 "Of course, I was a 'pacifist' . . .": Erika Mann, "Don't Make the Same Mistakes," 30.

Page 79 "'intellectuals' with horn-rimmed glasses . . .": Erika Mann, "Don't Make the Same Mistakes," 31.

Page 79 "uplifted by her message . . .": Erika Mann, "Don't Make the Same Mistakes," 32.

Page 79 "Thirty or forty young men . . .": Erika Mann, "Don't Make the Same Mistakes," 33

Page 79 "Do you hear that? . . .": Erika Mann, "Don't Make the Same Mistakes," 33.

Pages 79–80 "In the hall, everything became . . .": Erika Mann, "Don't Make the Same Mistakes," 34.

Page 80 "was literally almost murdered": Klaus Mann, "A Family against a Dictatorship," 8.

Page 80 "sick at the pit of my stomach": Erika Mann, "Don't Make the Same Mistakes," 35.

Page 80 "You are an actress . . .": Erika Mann, "I, of All People," 23.

Page 80 "declared war against the Mann family": Klaus Mann, *Turning Point*, 242.

Page 80 "realized that my experience . . .": Erika Mann, "Don't Make the Same Mistakes," 36.

Page 81 "despite different arguments . . .": Erika Mann, "Don't Make the Same Mistakes," 49.

Pages 81–82 "The would-be dictator . . .": Klaus Mann, *Turning Point*, 245–46.

Page 82 "gay and harmless, it sounded": Erika Mann, "I, of All People," 22.

Page 84 "Those among our spectators . . .": Erika Mann, "I, of All People," 25.

Page 85 "This life, which actually should only be shared . . .": Klaus Mann, *Tagebücher, 1931–1933* (Munich: Spangenberg, 1989), 111–12. Diary entry dated January 23, 1933.

Page 85 "in that estranged country of mine": Klaus Mann, *Turning Point*, 246.

Page 85 "thought about suicide": Klaus Mann, *Tagebücher, 1931–1933*, 57. Diary entry dated June 13, 1932.

Pages 85–86 "In the mornings . . .": Klaus Mann, *Tagebücher, 1931–1933*, 118. Diary entry dated February 19, 1933.

Page 86 "Concerning this . . .": Annemarie Schwarzenbach, in Uta Fleischmann, ed., *Wir werden es schon zuwege bringen, das Leben: Annemarie Schwarzenbach an Erika und Klaus Mann, Briefe, 1930–1942* (Pfaffenweiler: Centaurus Verlag, 1993), 83. Letter dated January 6, 1933.

Page 86 "the slightest enjoyment . . .": Thomas Mann, *Diaries, 1918–1939*, 249. Diary entry dated November 22, 1935.

Page 86 "I hear he takes morphine . . .": Thomas Mann, *Diaries, 1918–1939*, 240. Diary entry dated May 16, 1935.

Page 86 "Klaus unwell . . .": Thomas Mann, *Diaries, 1918–1939*, 249. Diary entry dated November 22, 1935.

Page 86 "my fault, my failure": Klaus Mann, *Tagebücher, 1931–1933*, 153. Diary entry dated July 5, 1933.

Page 87 "had only had sex for cash . . .": Klaus Mann, *Tagebücher, 1931–1933*, 152. Diary entry dated July 2, 1933.

Page 87 "Worse is the shadow . . .": Klaus Mann, *Tagebücher, 1931–1933*, 152. Diary entry dated July 2, 1933.

Page 87 "I seldom have a response . . .": *Tagebücher, 1931–1933*, 153. Diary entry dated July 5, 1933.

Page 87 "their faces seemed so innocent . . .": Klaus Mann, *Turning Point*, 239.

Page 87 "certainly not a derelict youth . . .": Klaus Mann, *Turning Point*, 239.

Page 90 "all of the stories, tragedies, persons . . .": Erika Mann, *The Lights Go Down*, trans. Maurice Samuel (London: Secker and Warburg, 1940), 277.

Page 90 "had been a Nazi spy . . .": Klaus Mann, *Turning Point*, 263.

Page 91 "We are having spring cleaning . . .": Klaus Mann, "A Family against a Dictatorship," 9.

Page 91 "My luggage consisted of . . .": Klaus Mann, *Turning Point,* 265.

Page 91 "We could not breathe . . .": Klaus Mann, *Turning Point,* 268.

Page 91 "according to the fantastic . . .": Klaus Mann, *Turning Point,* 267.

Page 92 "there is nothing in my life . . .": Klaus Mann, "A Family against a Dictatorship," 5.

Page 92 "I was neither Jew nor Communist": Erika Mann, "I, of All People," 13.

Page 93 "to spare him . . .": Klaus Mann, *Tagebücher, 1934–1935,* 35. Diary entry dated May 26, 1934.

Page 93 "no mere accident . . .": Thomas Mann, *Diaries, 1918–1939,* 127. Diary entry dated March 15, 1933.

Page 93 "annoyed with Klaus": Thomas Mann, *Tagebücher, 1933–1934* (Frankfurt: S. Fischer, 1977), 25. Diary entry dated March 29, 1933.

Page 93 "Feeling of loneliness always . . .": Klaus Mann, *Tagebücher, 1931–1933,* 124. Diary entry dated March 14, 1933.

Page 94 "My fears now revolve . . .": Thomas Mann, *Diaries, 1918–1939,* 154. Diary entry dated April 30, 1933.

Page 94 "I count on your discretion . . .": Thomas Mann to Golo Mann, cited in Donald Prater, *Thomas Mann: A Life* (New York: Oxford University Press, 1995), 206.

Pages 94–95 "they'll publish extracts . . .": Thomas Mann, cited in Prater, *Thomas Mann,* 209

Page 95 "a very risky undertaking": Erika Mann, television interview by Fritz J. Raddatz, first broadcast over WDR, Germany, January 10, 1968.

CHAPTER FOUR

Page 97 "1,200th hotel room, I greet you": Klaus Mann, "Gruß an das zwölfhundertste Hotelzimmer," cited in *"Ruhe gibt es nicht, bis zum Schluss": Klaus Mann (1906–1949): Bilder und Dokumente,* ed. Uwe Naumann (Reinbek bei Hamburg: Rowohlt, 1999), 131.

Page 98 "Come back! . . .": Klaus Mann, *Turning Point,* 267.

Page 98 "All the suitcases . . .": Klaus Mann, *Tagebücher, 1934–1935,* 36. Diary entry dated June 2, 1934.

Page 98 "Thought about how sad . . .": Klaus Mann, *Tagebücher, 1931–1933,* 153. Diary entry dated July 5, 1933.

Page 98 "an uprooted vagabond . . .": Klaus Mann, *Turning Point,* 351.

Page 99 "Hope to receive November money . . .": Klaus Mann, *Briefe und Antworten,* 1:150. Letter dated October 24, 1933.

Page 99 "Neither [personal] pleasure nor pain . . .": Klaus Mann, in Erika and Klaus Mann, *Escape to Life,* 14.

Page 100 "There is the possibility for me . . .": Klaus Mann, *Briefe und Antworten,* 1:90. Letter dated May 12, 1933.

Page 101 "brotherly friendship": Klaus Mann, *Der Wendepunkt*, 427.

Page 102 "the fuss over the Jews": Thomas Mann, *Diaries, 1918–1939*, 145. Diary entry dated April 5, 1933.

Page 102 "the Jewish banks": Thomas Mann, *Diaries, 1918–1939*, 141. Diary entry dated March 31, 1933.

Page 103 "the little Jew Tennenbaum": Thomas Mann *Diaries, 1918–1939*, 153. Diary entry dated April 30, 1933.

Page 103 "they are beginning to clamp down . . .": Thomas Mann, *Diaries, 1918–1939*, 147. Diary entry dated April 7, 1933.

Page 103 "I could have a certain understanding . . .": Thomas Mann, *Diaries, 1918–1939*, 153. Diary entry dated April 20, 1933.

Pages 103–4 "Basically I am much too good . . .": Thomas Mann, *Briefe*, 1:331–32. Letter dated May 15, 1933.

Page 104 "be exceptionally cautious . . .": Thomas Mann, *Diaries, 1918–1939*, 175. Diary entry dated October 4, 1933.

Page 105 "the matter of *Die Sammlung* . . .": Thomas Mann, *Diaries, 1918–1939*, 170. Diary entry dated September 7, 1933.

Page 105 "the character of the first issue . . .": Klaus Mann, *Briefe und Antworten*, 1:132. Letter dated September 13, 1933.

Page 105 "aware that my books are not . . .": Thomas Mann, *Letters*, 202. Letter dated December 23, 1933.

Page 106 "Long letter from the Magician . . .": Klaus Mann, *Tagebücher, 1931–1933*, 168. Diary entry dated September 15, 1933.

Page 107 "a fantastic woman": Igor Pahlen, interview by author, August 4, 1999.

Page 107 "I have to say that Erika Mann and Therese Giehse . . .": Pahlen, interview.

Page 107 "Erika Mann never asked anyone . . .": Pahlen, interview.

Page 108 "Motorized police formed a ring . . .": Erika Mann, Swiss television interview, 1969.

Pages 108–9 "I know, that such a cabaret stage . . .": Erika Mann, *Briefe und Antworten*, 1:58–59. Letter to the editor, dated November 22, 1934.

Page 109 "Some towns have banned . . .": Letter from Annemarie Schwarzenbach to the *Züricher Post*, undated [December 1934], clipping in Monacensia.

Page 110 "I can't stand this separation from Erika . . .": Annemarie Schwarzenbach, in Fleischmann, *Annemarie Schwarzenbach an Erika und Klaus Mann*, 121–22. Letter dated December 21, 1934.

Page 110 "Constantly under a slight heroin influence . . .": Klaus Mann, *Tagebücher, 1934–1935*, 82–83. Diary entry dated December 28, 1934.

Page 110 "stop a little—also to oblige E . . .": Klaus Mann, *Tagebücher, 1934–1935*, 89. Diary entry dated January 2, 1935.

Page 110 "I THANK GOD, for her . . .": Klaus Mann, *Tagebücher, 1934–1935*, 92. Diary entry dated January 14, 1934.

Page 110 "everything that everybody wanted": Marianne Breslauer, interview by author, August 3, 1999.

Page 111 "Eri told me that you're deep in trouble . . .": Annemarie Schwarzenbach, in Fleischmann, *Annemarie Schwarzenbach an Erika und Klaus Mann*, 123. Letter dated December 21 [1934].

Page 111 "nobody was ever interested in Annemarie's problems . . .": Breslauer, interview.

Page 113 "intimate friends who seldom saw each other . . .": Christopher Isherwood, *Christopher and His Kind* (New York: Farrar, Straus, Giroux, 1976), 85.

Page 113 "laughed, made a little grimace . . .": Christopher Isherwood, in *Klaus Mann zum Gedächtnis*, 66.

Page 113 "beautiful poise and courage . . .": Isherwood, *Christopher and His Kind*, 206.

Page 113 "I have something rather personal . . .": Isherwood, *Christopher and His Kind*, 206.

Page 114 "He would have married me to the poker": Cited in Humphrey Carpenter, *W. H. Auden: A Biography* (Boston: Houghton Mifflin, 1981), 177.

Page 115 "nine-tenths a man": Carpenter, *W. H. Auden*, 177.

Page 116 "What else are buggers for?": W. H. Auden, cited in Carpenter, *W. H. Auden*, 196.

Page 116 "I didn't see her till the ceremony . . .": W. H. Auden to Stephen Spender, dated Friday [late June 1935], cited in Brian Finney, *Christopher Isherwood: A Critical Biography* (New York: Oxford University Press, 1979), 120.

Page 116 "serious friendship": Golo Mann to Humphrey Carpenter, May 10, 1979, cited in Carpenter, *W. H. Auden*, 296.

Page 116 "I can't say we're friends . . .": Orlon Fox, "Friday Nights," in Stephen Spender, ed., *W. H. Auden, A Tribute* (London: Weidenfeld and Nicolson, 1974), 175.

Page 116 "the slightest idea how to begin to write . . .": W. H. Auden, *Letters from Iceland* (New York: Random House, 1969), 106.

Page 116 "how much I like and admire . . .": Unpublished, undated letter from W. H. Auden to Erika Mann, Monacensia.

Page 117 "consoling to think I can still go . . .": Cited in Jennie B. Gardner, "Use Boycott against Fascism, Manns Advise Memphians," Memphis, Tennessee, undated newspaper clipping in Monacensia.

Page 117 "who has the youth has the future": "Erika Mann Defines Youth's Significance in World Destinies," *AAUW Convention Daily* (Cincinnati, OH), vol. xii, no. 3 (May 7, 1941): 1. Clipping in Monacensia.

Page 117 "a German who wanted to be a European . . .": Klaus Mann, *Turning Point*, 347.

Page 117 "striving for a true community . . .": Klaus Mann, *Turning Point*, 347.

Page 117 "cult of official heroes . . .": Klaus Mann, *Turning Point*, 287.

Page 118 "I could never embrace a gospel . . .": Klaus Mann, *Turning Point*, 286–87.

Pages 118–19 "But all the time he was writing . . .": Erika and Klaus Mann, *Escape to Life*, 159.

Page 119 "seemed entirely normal . . .": Klaus Mann, *Turning Point*, 288.

Page 119 "temperamentally drawn to other wanderers . . .": Christopher Isherwood, in *Klaus Mann zum Gedächtnis*, 67.

Page 119 "suicide was a thread . . .": Hans Mayer, *Outsiders: A Study in Life and Letters* (Cambridge, MA: MIT Press, 1982), 244.

Page 119 "far beneath Klaus's brightness . . .": Christopher Isherwood, in *Klaus Mann zum Gedächtnis*, 69.

Page 120 "Regarding the boys . . .": Klaus Mann, *Tagebücher, 1934–1935*, 155. Diary entry dated December 12, 1935.

Page 120 "for all his genius and intelligence . . .": Klaus Mann, *Pathetic Symphony: A Novel about Tchaikovsky* (New York: Allen, Towne and Heath, 1948), 6.

Page 120 "it's silly to love women . . .": Klaus Mann, *Pathetic Symphony*, 29.

Page 120 "I know all about him . . .": Klaus Mann, *Turning Point*, 283.

Page 120 "I could describe all of it . . .": Klaus Mann, *Der Wendepunkt*, 355.

Page 121 "E stands between me . . .": Klaus Mann, *Tagebücher, 1934–1935*, 140. Diary entry dated October 27, 1935.

Page 121 "the tuna [heroin] problem . . .": Klaus Mann, *Tagebücher, 1934–1935*, 155. Diary entry dated December 31, 1935.

Page 121 "it is dreadful, that I must . . .": Klaus Mann, *Tagebücher, 1934–1935*, 146. Diary entry dated November 25, 1935.

Page 121 "I am not granted . . .": Klaus Mann, *Tagebücher, 1936–1937*, 69. Diary entry dated August 16, 1936.

Page 121 "disapproved of the 'lifestyle' . . .": Golo Mann, afterword to Klaus Mann, *Briefe und Antworten*, 2:322.

Page 121 "inartistic and immoral": Golo Mann, *Memories of My Father* (Bonn: Inter Nationes, 1965), 19.

Page 121 "the craving for drugs is hardly distinguishable . . .": Klaus Mann, *Tagebücher, 1934–1935*, 139. Diary entry dated October 22, 1935.

Page 122 "That your 'protest' in the newspaper made me sad . . .": Erika Mann, *Briefe und Antworten*, 1:72. Letter dated January 19, 1936.

Page 122 "difficult for me to look . . .": Erika Mann, *Briefe und Antworten*, 1:72. Letter dated January 19, 1936.

Page 123 "You are stabbing in the back . . .": Erika Mann, *Briefe und Antworten*, 1:73–74. Letter dated January 19, 1936.

Page 123 "unconditionality": Klaus Mann, *Tagebücher, 1936–1937*, 149. Diary entry dated August 4, 1937.

Page 123 "[Erika] threatened never to want to see him again . . .": Elisabeth Mann, interview by author, May 13, 1999.

Page 124 "You are, aside from me and Medi . . ": Katia Mann to Erika Mann, January 21, 1936, cited in Inge Jens and Walter Jens, *Frau Thomas Mann: Das Leben der Katharina Pringsheim* (Reinbek bei Hamburg: Rowohlt, 2003), 192.

Page 125 "the day may come, *might* come . . ": Erika Mann, *Briefe und Antworten*, 1:84. Letter dated January 23, 1936.

Page 125 "*I am finally saving my soul . . .*": Thomas Mann to Annette Kolb, February 2, 1936, cited in Hayman, *Thomas Mann*, 424.

Page 126 "sparkling charm and saucy wickedness": Klaus Mann, *Turning Point*, 281.

Page 126 "his utterly cynical ambition . . .": Erika and Klaus Mann, *Escape to Life*, 111.

Page 127 "Why do I think so much . . .": Klaus Mann, *Tagebücher, 1931–1933*, 22. Diary entry dated December 24, 1931.

Pages 128–29 "Finally it came to this point . . .": Erika Mann, *Versuch einer Outline für eine geplante Fernsehsendung*, 1966 typescript, Monacensia.

Page 129 "just continue the show . . .": Erika Mann, *Versuch einer Outline*.

Page 129 "we could not stay in Europe any longer": Erika Mann, *Versuch einer Outline*.

Page 129 "it was a heartfelt blow . . .": Erika Mann, "Don't Make the Same Mistakes," 61–62.

Page 129 "the air in Europe . . .": Klaus Mann, *Turning Point*, 292.

Page 129 "Would I find conditions . . .": Klaus Mann, *Turning Point*, 292.

Page 130 "this soiree was really the beginning . . .": Erika Mann, cited in Helga Keiser-Hayne, *Erika Mann und ihr politisches Kabarett* (Reinbek bei Hamburg: Rowohlt, 1995), 182.

Page 130 "The guests, all rich Americans . . .": Therese Giehse, cited in Kaiser-Heyne, *Erika Mann und ihr politisches Kabarett*, 183.

Page 130 "What comes next? . . .": Klaus Mann, *Tagebücher, 1936–1937*, 74. Diary entry dated September 18, 1936.

Page 131 "wise and weary": Klaus Mann, *Turning Point*, 291.

CHAPTER FIVE

Page 133 "*Michael reste la nuit . . .*": Klaus Mann *Tagebücher, 1936–1937*, 77. Diary entry dated September 27, 1936.

Page 134 "A tremendous flirt . . .": Klaus Mann, *Tagebücher, 1936–1937*, 84. Diary entry dated November 9, 1936.

Page 134 "great annoyance throughout the height . . .": Erika Mann, *Briefe und Antworten*, 1:100. Letter dated October 24, 1936.

Page 134 "turned toward men . . .": Sybille Bedford, interview by author, May 11, 1999.

Page 135 "The troupe, I think, sails on the 4th . . .": Erika Mann, *Briefe und Antworten*, 1:99. Letter dated October 24, 1936.

Page 135 "All the little jokes, emphases, and foolishness . . .": Erika Mann, *Briefe und Antworten,* 1:99. Letter dated October 24, 1936.

Page 136 "would have raised the sum . . .": Erika Mann, *Briefe und Antworten,* 1:102. Letter dated November 27, 1936.

Page 137 "somewhat fierce quarrel": Klaus Mann, *Tagebücher, 1936–1937,* 92. Diary entry dated December 27, 1936.

Page 137 "did the same thing to our contract . . .": Erika Mann to Klaus Mann, unpublished letter dated February 1, 1937, Monacensia.

Page 137 "a winning hostess . . .": Review by *New York Times* theater critic Brooks Atkinson, cited in "Erika Mann, Actress and Writer Who Denounced Hitler, Is Dead," *New York Times* (September 3, 1969), 44.

Page 137 "I suppose that 'failure' is an unduly harsh word . . .": Klaus Mann, *Turning Point,* 299–300.

Page 139 "didn't want to be what I call Hitler-conscious . . .": Erika Mann, television interview by Fritz J. Raddatz, January 10, 1968.

Page 139 "Before I left the Bedford . . .": Erika Mann to Klaus Mann, unpublished letter dated February 1, 1937.

Page 139 "actually left the friendly . . .": Erika Mann to Klaus Mann, unpublished letter dated February 1, 1937.

Page 140 "personal chances here are good": Erika Mann, *Briefe und Antworten,* 1:110. Letter dated February 1, 1937.

Page 141 "The medium there . . .": Erika Mann, television interview by Fritz J. Raddatz, January 10, 1968.

Pages 142–43 "We must do all in our power . . .": Erika Mann, in *Hitler: A Menace to World Peace* (New York: American Jewish Congress, 1937), 30.

Page 143 "It was a terrible time to slip away . . .": Erika Mann to Klaus Mann, unpublished letter dated February 1, 1937.

Page 143 "Erika's tears . . .": Klaus Mann, *Tagebücher, 1936–1937,* 98. Diary entry dated January 10, 1937.

Page 143 "It must, however, be said that large sections . . .": Erika and Klaus Mann, *Escape to Life,* 201.

Pages 143–44 "I perceive, again, very strongly . . .": Klaus Mann, *Tagebücher, 1936–1937,* 110. Diary entry dated February 25, 1937.

Page 144 "I don't think I ever heard . . .": Christopher Isherwood, in *Klaus Mann zum Gedächtnis,* 65–66.

Page 144 "complex situation: E[rika], New York . . .": Klaus Mann, *Tagebücher, 1936–1937,* 122. Diary entry dated April 9, 1937.

Page 144 "Don't eat too much H[eroin] . . .": Erika Mann to Klaus Mann, unpublished letter dated February 1, 1937, Monacensia.

Page 144 "Don't take any more 'tuna' . . .": Erika Mann to Klaus Mann, unpublished letter dated March 22, 1937, Monacensia.

Page 144 "belongs to my most cherished memories": Klaus Mann, *Turning Point,* 303.

Page 145 "Not quite openly, and seriously, so": Klaus Mann, *Turning Point*, 304.

Page 145 "In the evening, picked up the little Curtiss . . .": Klaus Mann, *Tagebücher, 1936–1937*, 133. Diary entry dated May 15, 1937.

Page 145 "Stayed with him. Happiness and mystery . . .": Klaus Mann, *Tagebücher, 1936–1937*, 134. Diary entry dated May 19, 1937.

Page 146 "we have to invent new curse words . . .": Erika Mann to Klaus Mann, unpublished letter dated June 5, 1937, Monacensia.

Page 146 "How will I be able to survive . . .": Klaus Mann, *Tagebücher, 1936–1937*, 136. Diary entry dated May 28, 1937.

Page 147 "has his and our name . . .": *Letters of Heinrich and Thomas Mann*, 212. Letter dated July 30, 1937.

Page 147 You know how highly . . .": *Letters of Heinrich and Thomas Mann*, 210. Letter dated July 30, 1937.

Pages 147–48 "the charmed fairy-tale prince . . .": Klaus Mann, *Der Wendepunkt*, 395.

Page 148 "I like the sad story . . .": Klaus Mann, *Tagebücher, 1936–1937*, 147. Diary entry dated July 30, 1937.

Page 148 "only a slim tale": Klaus Mann, *Turning Point*, 306.

Page 148 "to forget all about the inspired melancholia . . .": Klaus Mann, *Turning Point*, 307.

Page 149 "Erika always was of the opinion . . .": Elisabeth Mann, interview by author, May 13, 1999.

Page 149 "new, interesting tablets": Klaus Mann, *Tagebücher, 1936–1937*, 160. Diary entry dated September 24, 1937.

Page 149 "is quite strange and decent . . .": Erika Mann to Klaus Mann, unpublished letter dated March 22, 1937.

Page 151 "succeeded in charming his large audience . . .": Jennie B. Gardner, "Use Boycott against Fascism, Manns Advise Memphians," Memphis, Tennessee, undated newspaper clipping in Monacensia.

Page 151 "Whenever she spoke to the public . . .": Unpublished letter from Igor Pahlen to the author [1999].

Page 151 "patience is exhausted . . .": Erika Mann, *Writers in Freedom*, 84.

Page 152 "one gets used to everything": Erika and Klaus Mann, *Escape to Life*, 342.

Page 152 "by means of sundry tricks . . .": Erika and Klaus Mann, *The Other Germany*, 13.

Page 152 "conservative club women and radical politicians . . .": Erika and Klaus Mann, *The Other Germany* (New York: Modern Age books, 1940), 13–14.

Page 153 "A case of collective insanity . . .": Erika and Klaus Mann, *The Other Germany*, 21.

Page 153 "the 'bad boy' among the nations": Erika and Klaus Mann, *The Other Germany*, 31.

Page 153 "It was a ticklish, not to say painful job . . .": Klaus Mann, *Turning Point,* 325.

Page 153 "'I don't understand very much about baseball . . .'": Erika Mann, "Thomas Mann and His Family," *Vogue,* March 15, 1939.

Page 155 "Life, with all its struggles, its enchantments . . .": Erika and Klaus Mann, *Escape to Life,* 14.

Page 155 "as if it were a solution or a narcotic": Klaus Mann, *Turning Point,* 309.

Page 155 "Neither effort, however, was adequate . . .": Klaus Mann, *Turning Point,* 309–10.

Page 156 "Daringly progressive, even revolutionary . . .": Klaus Mann, *André Gide and the Crisis of Modern Thought* (New York: Creative Age Press, 1943), 172.

Page 156 "The texture of the novel . . .": Klaus Mann, *André Gide,* 184.

Page 156 "Is it any wonder . . .": Reich-Ranicki, *Thomas Mann and His Family,* 170.

Page 157 "secretly had the wicked intention": Klaus Mann, *Briefe und Antworten,* 2:78. Letter dated July 22, 1939.

Page 157 "Thommy is not permitted . . .": Annette Kolb to René Schickele, September 3, 1934, cited in Jens and Jens, *Frau Thomas Mann,* 204.

Page 157 "it would do him good . . .": *Letters of Heinrich and Thomas Mann,* 228. Letter dated July 20, 1939.

Page 157 "Well, then: fully and thoroughly read it . . .": Klaus Mann, *Briefe und Antworten,* 2:79. Letter dated July 22, 1939.

Page 158 "August is his son . . .": Thomas Mann, *The Beloved Returns (Lotte in Weimar)* (New York: Alfred A. Knopf, 1969), 65.

Page 158 "To be the son of a great man . . .": Thomas Mann, *The Beloved Returns,* 154.

Page 158 "Pleasant utterances, almost incidental . . .": Klaus Mann, *Tagebücher, 1936–1937,* 110. Diary entry dated February 25, 1937.

Page 159 "Dear Magician . . .": Klaus Mann, *Briefe und Antworten,* 2:81. Letter dated August 3, 1939.

Page 159 "what was happening in Spain . . .": Klaus Mann, *Turning Point,* 312.

Page 159 "is hardly a master of the language . . .": Erika Mann, *School for Barbarians* (London: Lindsay Drummond, 1939), 63.

Page 160 "even its pain and anger . . .": Thomas Mann, foreword to Erika Mann, *School for Barbarians,* vii–viii.

Page 160 "sensational but thoroughly documented": "Germany's Children," *Time,* October 10, 1938.

Page 161 "the southern accent that I love": Erika Mann, *School for Barbarians,* 2.

Page 162 "Things have gone too far already . . .": Erika Mann, "Don't Make the Same Mistakes," 72.

Page 162 "make all Americans listen . . .": Paul Jordan-Smith," "What I Liked Last Week," *Los Angeles Times,* November 10, 1940, C6.

Page 162 "I am really at home . . .": Erika Mann, "My Fatherland, the Pullman," *Vogue* (no date). Clipping in Monacensia.

Pages 162–63 "'I suppose they're okay . . .'": Christopher Isherwood, *Diaries,*vol. 1, *1939–1969* (New York: HarperCollins, 1997), 6.

Page 163 "full of gaiety and gossip": Christopher Isherwood, *Diaries,* 1:8.

Page 163 "couldn't possibly kill anyone . . .": Christopher Isherwood, *Diaries,* 1:99–100.

Page 163 "no war is always better . . .": Christopher Isherwood, *Diaries,* 1:100.

Page 163 "Gustaf's cold charms": Klaus Mann, *Tagebücher, 1938–1939* (Munich: Spangenberg, 1990), 114. Diary entry dated June 17, 1939.

Page 164 "the chemical life": Cited in Carpenter, *W. H. Auden,* 265.

Page 164 "For an author, sons are an embarrassment . . .": Quoted by Golo Mann, afterword to Klaus Mann, *Briefe und Antworten,* 2:322.

Page 164 "supposed that it couldn't be easy . . .": Isherwood, *Christopher and His Kind,* 85.

Pages 164–65 "This strange house in Brooklyn . . .": Klaus Mann, *Tagebücher, 1940–1943* (Munich: Spangenberg, 1991), 67. Diary entry dated October 8, 1940.

Page 165 "Undecided?" . . . "Not my magazine! . . .": Klaus Mann, unpublished diary dated November 9, 1940, cited in Klaus Mann, *Turning Point,* 337.

Pages 165–66 "looks exactly the way a real secretary . . .": Klaus Mann, *Turning Point,* 338.

Page 166 "that tragic twerp": Glenway Wescott, *Continual Lessons: The Journals of Glenway Wescott, 1937–1955,* ed. Robert Phelps (New York: Farrar, Straus, Giroux, 1990), 73. Entry dated July 21, 1940.

Page 167 "What will you call it? . . .": Charles H. Miller, *Auden: An American Friendship* (New York: Charles Scribner's Sons, 1983), 76

Page 167 "without vanity or self-consciousness . . .": Christopher Isherwood, in *Klaus Mann zum Gedächtnis,* 65.

Page 168 "After the fall of France I felt compelled . . .": Erika Mann, interview by Roswitha Schmalenbach, on "Musik für einen Gast," Sendung des Radio-Studios Basel, 1963.

Page 168 "made for goats and smugglers . . .": Klaus Mann, *Turning Point,* 335.

Page 168 "urbane as ever . . .": Christopher Isherwood, *Diaries,* 1:100.

Page 168 "But, as always, there is something very attractive . . .": Christopher Isherwood, *Diaries,* 1:100.

Page 169 "much envy and anxiety": Klaus Mann, *Tagebücher, 1940–1943,* 51. Diary entry dated August 23, 1940.

CHAPTER SIX

Page 172 "I realised that the whole thing . . .": Erika Mann, BBC broadcast, October 25, 1941, London.

Page 172 "out of the Calais air, the Messerschmitts . . .": Erika Mann, BBC broadcast.

Page 172 "'You are not to open fire.' . . .": Erika Mann, BBC broadcast.

Page 172 "safe so far": Diary entry dated September 20, 1940, quoted in Klaus Mann, *Turning Point*, 334.

Pages 172–73 "You were always very strict . . .": Klaus Mann to Erika Mann, unpublished, undated letter, Monacensia.

Page 173 "Mr. Hitler was very much mistaken . . .": Erika Mann, radio interview by John Steele on WMCA (New York) about her broadcasts from London. [Autumn 1940.]

Page 173 "it is my profession to accept this trip . . .": Erika Mann, *Briefe und Antworten*, 1:170. Letter dated May 1, 1941.

Page 174 "has asked me himself . . .": Erika Mann, *Briefe und Antworten*, 1:171. Letter dated May 1, 1941.

Page 174 "The most terrible thing is the understanding . . .": Erika Mann, *Briefe und Antworten*, 1:172. Letter dated June 8, 1941.

Page 174 "It seems certain that [Erika] is going . . .": Klaus Mann, *Briefe und Antworten*, 2:154. Letter from Thomas Mann dated June 11, 1941.

Page 174 "How cruel and capricious . . .": Diary entry dated June 2, 1941, quoted in Klaus Mann, *Turning Point*, 344.

Page 175 "The other drop of bitterness . . .": Klaus Mann, *Briefe und Antworten*, 2:147. Letter dated May 25, 1941.

Page 175 "I suppose this is the most lonely summer . . .": Diary entry dated August 10, 1941, quoted in Klaus Mann, *Turning Point*, 346.

Page 175 "like two mother lions" . . . "That nut Klaus . . .": Erika Mann to Annemarie Schwarzenbach, unpublished letter dated May 1, 1942, Monacensia.

Page 176 "sweet Jesus why?": Erika Mann, *Briefe und Antworten*, 1:186. Letter dated November 13, 1942.

Page 176 "Death, which used to seem so . . .": Klaus Mann, "Ricki Hallgarten—Radikalismus des Herzens," in *Die neue Eltern*, 411.

Page 176 "was saved by 'sheer accident'": Erika Mann to Muriel Rukeyser, unpublished letter dated September 18, 1967, Monacensia.

Page 177 "Tomski called and asked . . .": Klaus Mann, *Tagebücher, 1940–1943*, 116. Diary entry dated October 24, 1942.

Page 177 "Son of famous novelist . . .": Klaus Mann, "The Last Decision," *Zweimal Deutschland: Aufsätze, Reden, Kritiken, 1938–1942* (Reinbek bei Hamburg: Rowohlt, 1994), 380.

Pages 177–78 "I am going to tell you the inside story . . .": Klaus Mann, "The Last Decision," 380.

Page 178 "whose youth and birth tore at him . . .": Muriel Rukeyser, in *Klaus Mann zum Gedächtnis*, 132–33.

Page 178 "Thinking back on Klaus's life . . .": Erika Mann to Muriel Rukeyser, unpublished letter dated June 28, 1967, Monacensia.

Page 178 "some gossip or misconception . . .": Klaus Mann to Muriel Rukeyser, unpublished letter dated January 11, 1942, Berg Collection, New York Public Library.

Page 178 "Every testimony counts . . .": Diary entry dated August 11, 1941, quoted in Klaus Mann, *Turning Point,* 347.

Page 178 "And he would write . . .": Muriel Rukeyser, in *Klaus Mann zum Gedächtnis,* 132.

Page 178 "Dear T. . . .": Unpublished, unsent letter, Monacensia.

Page 179 "Am I not already half estranged . . .": Klaus Mann, *Der Wendepunkt,* 457–58.

Page 179 "Hitler has polluted": Diary entry dated July 5, 1940, quoted in Klaus Mann, *Turning Point,* 331.

Page 179 "When we talked of the traps . . .": Muriel Rukeyser, in *Klaus Mann zum Gedächtnis,* 132.

Page 179 "he never seemed to remember . . .": *Turning Point,* 126.

Page 180 "Good luck, my son! . . .": *Turning Point,* 128.

Page 180 "thousand mistakes I have made . . .": Klaus Mann, *Briefe und Antworten,* 2:175. Undated letter [August 1942].

Page 180 "the most essential things are the unspeakable ones . . .": Klaus Mann, *Briefe und Antworten,* 2:175. Undated letter, written in August 1942.

Page 180 "Whole family reading frantically . . .": Klaus Mann, *Briefe und Antworten,* 2:176. Telegram dated September 1942.

Page 180 "the stony heat and the despair . . .": Muriel Rukeyser, in *Klaus Mann zum Gedächtnis,* 131.

Page 180 "in a moving, suspended moment . . .": Muriel Rukeyser, in *Klaus Mann zum Gedächtnis,* 133.

Page 181 "I can only repeat, what I said at the window": Klaus Mann, *Briefe und Antworten,* 2:179. Letter from Thomas Mann dated September 2, 1942.

Page 181 "very active agents . . .": This and all subsequent quotations from Klaus Mann's FBI file were obtained under the Freedom of Information Act and are in the possession of the author.

Page 184 "rien à faire . . .": Klaus Mann to Muriel Rukeyser, unpublished letter dated December 29 [1942?], Berg Collection, New York Public Library.

Page 184 "very gratifying young proletarian types . . .": Klaus Mann, *Tagebücher, 1938–1939,* 139. Diary entry dated October 20, 1939.

Page 184 "what attracted Klaus . . .": Sybille Bedford, interview by author, July 31, 1999.

Page 186 "Homosexuality, which he never perceived as deviance . . .": Friedrich Landshoff, interview by Fredric Kroll, in *Klaus-Mann-Schriftenreihe,* vol. 6, ed. Fredric Kroll (Hannover: Edition Klaus Blahak, 1996), 421.

Page 186 "heaven in bed": Klaus Mann, cited in Jerry Rosco, *Glenway Wescott Personally: A Biography* (Madison: Univ. of Wisconsin Press, 2002), 121.

Page 186 "it was like going to bed . . .": Glenway Wescott, cited in Rosco, *Glenway Wescott Personally*, 121.

Page 186 "he only really liked rough trade . . .": Sybille Bedford, interview by author, May 11, 1999.

Page 186 "Sadness, without end . . .": Klaus Mann, *Tagebücher, 1940–1943*, 21–22. Diary entry dated February 18, 1940.

Page 187 "stirred up riots and arguments . . .": Erika Mann, "I, of All People," 3.

Page 189 "I *want* to go into the Army . . .": Klaus Mann, *Wendepunkt*, 461.

Page 190 "The obsession that haunted me . . .": Klaus Mann, *Turning Point*, 362–63.

Page 191 "life weariness and poverty": Klaus Mann to Erika Mann, unpublished letter dated April 18, 1942, Monacensia.

Page 192 "Klaus, who never in his whole life . . .": Curt Riess, *Meine berühmten Freunde* (Freiburg: Herder, 1987), 92.

Page 193 "Obviously, neither writing nor loving . . .": Klaus Mann, *Briefe und Antworten*, 2:198. Letter dated April 27, 1943.

Page 193 "For a mother it is a hard fate.": Katia Mann to Klaus Mann, unpublished letter dated April 24, 1943, cited in Jens and Jens, *Frau Thomas Mann*, 235.

Page 193 "So far removed from everything . . .": Klaus Mann, *Tagebücher, 1940–1943*, 134. Diary entry dated June 13, 1943.

Page 193 "I am sending you my portrait . . .": Klaus Mann, *Briefe und Antworten*, 2:192. Letter dated February 28, 1943.

Page 196 "to send urgent cables . . .": Klaus Mann to Muriel Rukeyser, unpublished letter dated October 4, 1943, Berg Collection, New York Public Library.

Page 196 "as to whether my desire . . .": Klaus Mann, *Briefe und Antworten*, 2:209. Letter dated October 16, 1943.

Page 197 "At our farewell, Z. [the Magician] embraced me . . .": Klaus Mann, *Tagebücher, 1940–1943*, 182. Diary entry dated December 3, 1943.

Page 197 "almost happy": Erika Mann, "Die Schrift an der Wand," radio interview, Bayerische Rundfunk, October 20, 1952.

Page 197 "We German refugees, the first victims . . .": Klaus Mann, radio broadcast of "An American Soldier Revisiting His Former Homeland," in *Turning Point*, 368.

Page 199 "perfectly preposterous! . . .": Erika Mann to Klaus Mann, unpublished letter dated January 15, 1945, Monacensia.

Page 199 "brooding, wondering and pondering . . .": Erika Mann to Klaus Mann, unpublished letter dated September 4, 1944, Monacensia.

Page 201 "mental illness": Erika Mann to Klaus Mann, unpublished letter dated March 27, 1941, Monacensia.

Page 201 "unsuitable object . . .": Katia Mann to Klaus Mann, unpublished letter dated October 20, 1948, Monacensia.

Page 201 "to be just as big a mistake . . .": Katia Mann to Klaus Mann, unpublished letter dated August 29, 1944, Monacensia.

Page 202 "gentille comme tout, if exceedingly crazy . . .": Erika Mann, *Briefe und Antworten*, 1:199. Letter dated September 4, 1944. Monacensia.

Page 202 "One night sitting with Frank Owen . . .": Marcel Wallenstein, "Salinas Kansas Predicted No Good End for Betty Peden, but See What She Is Doing in London," *Kansas City Star,* March 19, 1944. I am grateful to Ken Cuthbertson of Albuquerque, New Mexico, for calling my attention to this article.

Page 203 "But for all this activity . . .": Erika Mann, "Back from Battle," *Toronto Star,* July 8, 1944, 12.

Page 204 "my Tomski has come along . . .": Erika Mann to Klaus Mann, unpublished letter dated January 15, 1945, Monacensia.

Page 205 "a strange acquisition . . .": Erika Mann to Klaus Mann, unpublished letter dated January 15, 1945, Monacensia.

Page 205 "Tomorrow I'll fly all the way . . .": Erika Mann to Katia Mann, unpublished letter dated September 20, 1945, Monacensia.

Page 205 "Looking forward to witnessing together . . .": Telegram from Erika, Thomas, and Katia Mann to Klaus Mann, cited in Klaus Mann, *Turning Point,* 326.

CHAPTER SEVEN

Page 207 "an outsider or an exception . . .": Klaus Mann, *Der Wendepunkt*, 461.

Page 207 "stultify and brutalize": Golo Mann, afterword to Klaus Mann, *Briefe und Antworten*, 2:340.

Page 207 "belief, not only in the desirability . . .": Editorial, *Decision* (October 1941): 3.

Pages 207–8 "Yes, and the atomic bomb . . .": Klaus Mann, *Briefe und Antworten*, 2:234. Letter dated August 11, 1945.

Page 208 "political conversations as in the 1930s . . .": Golo Mann, afterword to Klaus Mann, *Briefe und Antworten*, 2:343.

Page 208 "endowed with material wealth . . .": Klaus Mann, *The Ordeal of the European Intellectuals* (Berlin: Transit, 1993), 24. (Originally published in *Tomorrow* magazine in June 1949 under the title "Europe's Search for a New Credo," p. 5.)

Page 208 "does not leave any . . .": Klaus Mann, *Ordeal of the European Intellectuals,* 56.

Page 208 "better Germany": Klaus Mann, "A Family against a Dictatorship," 14.

Page 208 "when the Dictator has vanished . . .": Klaus Mann, "A Family against a Dictatorship," 17.

Page 209 "it will take years or decades . . .": Klaus Mann, *Briefe und Antworten*, 2:230. Letter dated May 16, 1945.

Page 209 "deplorable, terrible nation . . .": Klaus Mann, *Briefe und Antworten,* 2:230. Letter dated May 16, 1945.

Page 209 "indulged in illusions": Klaus Mann, "An American Soldier Revisiting His Former Homeland," reprinted in Klaus Mann, *Turning Point,* 367.

Page 209 "It would be a very grave mistake . . .": Klaus Mann, *Briefe und Antworten,* 2:230. Letter dated May 16, 1945.

Pages 210–11 "Standing there in the garden . . .": Klaus Mann, "An American Soldier," 368–69.

Page 211 "I suppose it belonged to some writer . . .": Klaus Mann, "An American Soldier," 369.

Page 211 "A *Lebensborn* was a place . . .": Klaus Mann, "An American Soldier," 369.

Page 211 "somehow touching to see . . .": Klaus Mann, "An American Soldier," 370.

Page 212 "I decided to be more careful . . .": Klaus Mann, "An American Soldier," 371.

Page 212 "His musical tastes were deplorably one-sided . . .": Klaus Mann, "An American Soldier," 372.

Page 212 "which is worse, your daughter": Klaus Mann, *Briefe und Antworten,* 2:231. Letter written May 24, 1945.

Page 213 "What a strange country this was . . .": Klaus Mann, "An American Soldier," 372.

Page 213 "You only need to read aloud . . .": Erika Mann, *Briefe und Antworten,* 1:201–2. Letter written June 8, 1945.

Page 213 "The Germans, as you know, are hopeless . . .": Erika Mann to Klaus Mann, unpublished letter dated January 15, 1945, Monacensia.

Page 213 "Erika could hate . . .": Sybille Bedford, interview by author, July 31, 1999.

Page 213 "lost to us long before . . .": Erika Mann, *Briefe und Antworten,* 1:203. Letter written June 8, 1945.

Page 214 "an adventure for which I'd been prepared . . .": Erika Mann, "They Who Live by the Sword," *Liberty* (October 27, 1945), 20.

Page 214 "No spookier adventure . . .": Erika Mann, *Briefe und Antworten,* 1:206. Letter written August 22, 1945.

Page 214 "had turned into a veritable insane asylum": Erika Mann, *Briefe und Antworten* , 1:206–7. Letter written August 22, 1945.

Page 214 "They'll be needed to answer questions . . .": Erika Mann, "They Who Live by the Sword," 21.

Page 215 "only one, in which the best qualities . . .": Thomas Mann, cited in Hayman, *Thomas Mann,* 511.

Page 216 "As for my own lyre . . .": Klaus Mann, *Briefe und Antworten,* 2:219. Letter written October 13, 1944.

Page 216 "Dismissal. Uncertainty. Uprootedness. Nausea.": Klaus Mann, *Tage-*

bücher, 1944–1949 (Munich: Spangenberg, 1991), 95. Diary entry dated August 29, 1945.

Page 216 "Am I making a mistake?": Klaus Mann, *Tagebücher, 1944–1949*, 95. Diary entry dated August 30, 1945.

Page 216 "If only I could get out of the Army . . .": Klaus Mann, *Briefe und Antworten*, 2:236. Letter written August 11, 1945.

Page 217 "an entertaining, young non-Aryan": Klaus Mann, *Briefe und Antworten*, 2:240. Letter written February 23, 1946.

Page 217 "a *bit* being a civilian again . . .": Klaus Mann, *Briefe und Antworten*, 2:236–37. Letter written October 9, 1945.

Page 218 "quarrelsome and megalomaniac lunatic . . .": Klaus Mann, *Briefe und Antworten*, 2:241. Letter written February 23, 1946.

Page 218 "I just sat there like a kid . . .": Robert Lawrence, interview by author, New York, December 8, 2003.

Page 219 "farewell letter": Klaus Mann, *Tagebücher, 1944–1949*, 101. Diary entry dated November 15, 1945.

Page 219 "cool reconciliation": Klaus Mann, *Tagebücher, 1944–1949*, 102. Diary entry dated November 29, 1945.

Page 219 "new tension . . . new reconciliation": Klaus Mann, *Tagebücher, 1944–1949*, 102. Diary entry dated November 30, 1945.

Page 219 "a brilliant manipulator of the facts . . .": Lawrence, interview.

Page 219 "Klaus was very professional . . .": Lawrence, interview.

Page 219 "his old brain-child": Klaus Mann to Erika Mann, unpublished letter dated October 3, 1947, Monacensia.

Page 220 "these uncles are going to regret . . .": Klaus Mann to Erika Mann, unpublished letter dated October 3, 1947, Monacensia.

Page 220 "It's a good film idea, too . . .": Klaus Mann, *Briefe und Antworten*, 2:231. Letter dated May 16, 1945.

Page 220 "Klaus and I were going to do some films together . . .": Lawrence, interview.

Page 221 "Not that I have anything against Gründgens . . .": Klaus Mann, "Kunst und Politik," in *Auf Verlorenem Posten: Aufsätze, Reden, Kritiken, 1942–1949* (Reinbek bei Hamburg: Rowohlt, 1994), 327.

Page 223 "confinement psychosis . . .": Klaus Mann, *Briefe und Antworten*, 2:245. Letter dated May 10, 1946.

Page 223 "pick up an old Ford and a young driver . . .": Klaus Mann, *Briefe und Antworten*, 2:245. Letter dated May 10, 1946.

Page 223 "A house to rent and a car and driver . . .": Katia Mann to Klaus Mann, in Klaus Mann, *Briefe und Antworten*, 2:248. Letter dated May 21, 1946.

Page 224 "Neither Paris nor turn-of-the-century Munich . . .": Thomas Mann, *Die Entstehung des "Doktor Faustus": Roman eines Romans* (Frankfurt: Fischer, 1967), cited in Alexander Stephan, *Communazis* (New Haven: Yale University Press, 2000), 49.

Page 224 "Erika was a very powerful personality . . .": Elisabeth Mann, interview by author, May 13, 1999.

Page 224 "secretary, biographer, nurse, daughter-adjutant": Thomas Mann, *Tage-bücher, 1946–1948* (Frankfurt: S. Fischer, 1989), 219. Diary entry dated February 1, 1948.

Page 224 "concentrated all her attention on her father": Golo Mann, afterword to Klaus Mann, *Briefe und Antworten*, 2:345–46.

Page 224 "Klaus would never have had a jealous thought . . .": Sybille Bedford, interview by author, July 31, 1999.

Page 224 "It is only the parts of my life . . .": Klaus Mann, quoted in Reich-Ranicki, *Thomas Mann and His Family*, 173.

Page 225 "Good news from the 'Queen Elizabeth' . . .": Klaus Mann, *Tagebücher, 1944–1949*, 121. Diary entry dated May 16, 1947.

Page 225 "She returned home . . .": Elisabeth Mann, interview by author, May 13, 1999.

Page 225 "the best horse in his stable": Erika Mann, "Account of FBI Inquisition," unpublished handwritten document, Monacensia.

Pages 225–26 "under the secretarial name of Homer Smith . . .": Thomas Mann, *Letters*, 555. Letter dated May 11, 1948.

Page 226 "He wrote his lectures in German . . .": Erika Mann, television interview by Fritz J. Raddatz, January 10, 1968.

Page 226 "he could hardly understand the questions . . .": Erika Mann, television interview by Fritz J. Raddatz, January 10, 1968.

Page 227 "Either leave Berlin and risk that we, the Americans . . .": Erika Mann, "Town Hall on the Air," national radio broadcast, October 8, 1948.

Page 227 "nothing other than a Stalinist agent": *Echo der Woche*, October 22, 1948.

Page 228 "the son of Thomas Mann is forty-one years old . . .": Cited in Kroll, *Klaus-Mann-Schriftenreihe*, 6:387.

Page 228 "a droll pursuit": Klaus Mann, *Briefe und Antworten*, 2:255. Letter dated December 23, 1946.

Page 228 "he simply needed the money . . .": Sybille Bedford, interview by author, July 31, 1999.

Pages 228–29 "I find it increasingly difficult to work and to live . . .": Letter from Klaus Mann quoted by Peter Viereck in *Klaus Mann zum Gedächtnis*, 168.

Page 229 "an allegory of the post-war world in crisis": Peter T. Hoffer, *Klaus Mann* (Boston: G. K. Hall, 1978), 122.

Page 229 "I improvise. Besides, overall . . .": Klaus Mann to the editor and critic Peter de Mendelsohn (later to be the first biographer of Thomas Mann and the editor of his diaries), unpublished letter dated September 17, 1948, Monacensia.

Page 229 "in the darkest pessimism . . .": Klaus Mann to Erika Mann, unpublished letter dated October 3, 1947, Monacensia.

Page 231 "in difficulties": Klaus Mann, *Tagebücher, 1944–1949*, 167. Diary entry dated June 7, 1948.

Page 231 "good natured and silent": Thomas Mann, cited in Hayman, *Thomas Mann*, 552.

Page 231 "suspicion of burglary": Klaus Mann, *Tagebücher, 1944–1949*, 168. Diary entry dated June 11, 1948.

Page 232 "began reading *The Magic Mountain* anew . . .": Klaus Mann, *Tagebücher, 1944–1949*, 170. Diary entry dated June 22, 1948.

Page 232 "Why can't I write anymore? . . .": Klaus Mann, *Tagebücher, 1944–1949*, 172. Diary entry dated June 30, 1948.

Page 232 "nearly overfilled with children and nephews": Thomas Mann, *Tagebücher, 1946–1948*, 278. Diary entry dated June 26, 1948.

Page 232 "unpleasant invasion": Thomas Mann, *Tagebücher, 1946–1948*, 279. Diary entry dated June 28, 1948.

Page 232 "not entirely satisfactory . . .": Klaus Mann, *Tagebücher, 1944–1949*, 173. Diary entry dated July 4, 1948.

Page 232 "rather dramatic—in a disagreeable kind of way": Klaus Mann, *Tagebücher, 1944–1949*, 173. Diary entry dated July 5, 1948.

Page 232 "tried it again . . .": Klaus Mann, *Tagebücher, 1944–1949*, 174. Diary entry dated July 11, 1948.

Page 233 "Don't do it! . . .": Klaus Mann, *Briefe und Antworten*, 2:274. Letter dated July 12, 1948.

Page 233 "ashamed of my weakness . . .": Klaus Mann, *Briefe und Antworten*, 2:275. Letter dated July 14, 1948.

Page 233 "spoiled him": Thomas Mann, *Letters*, 556. Letter dated July 12, 1948.

Page 233 "My two sisters committed suicide . . .": Thomas Mann, *Letters*, 556. Letter dated July 12, 1948.

Page 233 "If he wanted to kill himself . . .": Elisabeth Mann, interview by Ronald Hayman, February 28, 1994, cited in Hayman, *Thomas Mann*, 551.

Page 233 "As you may have read . . .": Erika Mann, *Briefe und Antworten*, 1:247. Letter written August 27, 1948.

Page 234 "He no longer invited Klaus . . .": Golo Mann, afterword to Klaus Mann, *Briefe und Antworten*, 2:345.

Page 234 "natural, that is, fatherly, basis": Katia Mann to Klaus Mann, unpublished letter dated November 22, 1948, Monacensia.

Page 235 "My God, how can one be so hell-bent . . .": Katia Mann to Klaus Mann, unpublished letter dated November 6, 1948, Monacensia.

Page 235 "I am not going to continue . . .": Klaus Mann, *Tagebücher, 1944–1949*, 174. Diary entry dated January 1, 1949.

Page 235 "A suicide wave of the most outstanding . . .": Klaus Mann, *Ordeal of the European Intellectuals*, 60.

Page 236 "because Mr. Gründgens plays . . .": Klaus Mann, *Briefe und Antworten*, 2:304. Letter dated May 12, 1949.

Page 236 "more tedious and more painful . . .": Peter Viereck, *Klaus Mann zum Gedächtnis*, 168.

Page 237 "decidedly better": Klaus Mann, *Tagebücher, 1944–1949*, 216. Diary entry dated May 12, 1949.

Page 238 "what remains of 'the stuff' . . .": Klaus Mann, *Tagebücher, 1944–1949*, 217. Diary entry dated May 17, 1949.

Page 238 "a sickly [female] hermit and neurotic mouse . . .": Klaus Mann, *Briefe und Antworten*, 2:314. Letter dated May 20, 1949.

Page 238 "I have been lucky with my family . . .": Klaus Mann, *Briefe und Antworten*, 2:81. Letter written August 3, 1939.

Pages 239–40 "I don't want to say much . . .": Erika Mann, *Briefe und Antworten*, 1:256–57. Letter dated May 15, 1949.

CHAPTER EIGHT

Page 243 "Upon arrival at the hotel, the worst shock": Thomas Mann, *Tagebücher, 1949–1950*, 57. Diary entry dated May 22, 1949.

Page 243 "the long hand of [Klaus's] irresistible, impelling death-impulse": Thomas Mann, *Tagebücher, 1949–1950*, 57. Diary entry dated May 22, 1949.

Page 243 "My inward sympathy with the mother's heart . . .": Thomas Mann, *Tagebücher, 1949–1950*, 57. Diary entry dated May 22, 1949.

Page 243 "stronger than compassion . . .": Thomas Mann, *Die Briefe Thomas Manns, Regesten und Register*, ed. Hans Bürgen and Hans-Otto Mayer, 3 vols. (Frankfurt am Main: S. Fischer, 1976–), 3:639. Letter dated June 28, 1949.

Page 244 "Eri's pain": Thomas Mann, *Tagebücher, 1949–1950*, 58. Diary entry dated May 22, 1949.

Page 244 "it was necessary to be prepared for it constantly . . .": *Letters of Heinrich and Thomas Mann*, 260. Letter (written by Katia Mann) dated May 24, 1949.

Page 244 "Dear Heinrich, these are sad days . . .": *Letters of Heinrich and Thomas Mann*, 260–61. Letter dated May 26, 1949.

Page 245 "contradictory mental state . . .": Thomas Mann, *Briefe*, 3:89. Letter dated June 2, 1949.

Page 245 "it was said to him once too often": Sybille Bedford, interview by author, May 11, 1999.

Page 245 "in his blood. He really had to write . . .": Erika Mann, "Der engagierte Schriftsteller in der Emigration: Ein Porträt Klaus Mann," Hessische Rundfunk, broadcast November 17, 1966.

Page 245 "We were a part of each other, so much so . . .": Erika Mann, *Briefe und Antworten*, 1:261. Letter dated June 17, 1949.

Page 246 "How I shall live, I don't yet know . . .": Erika Mann, *Briefe und Antworten*, 1:260. Letter dated June 16, 1949.

Page 246 "That's why he killed himself . . .": Thomas Mann, letter to Hans Reisiger, June 28, 1949, cited in Hayman, *Thomas Mann*, 562.

Page 246 "I know no zones . . .": Thomas Mann, speech given in Frankfurt and Weimar, cited in Hayman, *Thomas Mann*, 563.

Page 246 "Unknown": Shelley L. Frisch, introduction to Klaus Mann, *Turning Point*, [6].

Page 246 "very ill. If you could bring yourself to say so little . . .": Erika Mann, *Briefe und Antworten*, 1:262. Letter dated June 19, 1949.

Page 247 "This interrupted life lies heavily . . .": Thomas Mann, *Briefe*, 3:91–92. Letter dated July 6, 1949.

Page 247 "I truly believe that he . . .": Thomas Mann, foreword to *Klaus Mann zum Gedächtnis*.

Page 247 "when Klaus died . . .": Elisabeth Mann, interview by author, May 13, 1999.

Page 248 "Immeasurable are the times . . .": Erika Mann to Mr. Edward J. Shaughnessy, Director of Immigration and Naturalization, New York District Office, dated December 11, 1950, Monacensia.

Page 249 "Ever since then an investigation . . .": Erika Mann to Mr. Edward J. Shaughnessy, Monacensia.

Page 251 "one of the world's foremost apologists . . .": *U.S. Congressional Record*, June 18, 1951, cited in Hayman, *Thomas Mann*, 585.

Page 251 "his famous name for causes . . .": *Time*, June 15, 1951, cited in Hayman, *Thomas Mann*, 585.

Page 251 "not to live there, but to die there": Thomas Mann, *Tagebücher, 1951–1952*, 149. Diary entry dated December 15, 1951.

Page 252 "court jester": Golo Mann, afterword to Klaus Mann, *Briefe und Antworten*, 2:346.

Page 254 "Erika was in a bad state . . .": Marianne Breslauer, interview by author, August 3, 1999.

Page 254 "she couldn't even get up . . .": Sybille Bedford, interview by author, July 31, 1999.

Page 254 "so youthfully supple, so mobile, so agile . . .": Erika Mann, *The Last Year of Thomas Mann* (New York: Farrar, Straus and Cudahy, 1958),117.

Page 255 "In fact I rather lack interest in myself . . .": Erika Mann, "I, of All People," 4.

Page 256 "All the children say . . .": Katia Mann to Molly Shenstone, October 2, 1955, cited in Jens and Jens, *Frau Thomas Mann*, 267–68.

Page 256 "not only running the house but dominating it . . .": Erika Mann, "Interjections from Outside" in Katia Mann, *Unwritten Memories*, 153–54.

Page 256 "If Erika's conditions were a little bit . . .": Katia Mann to Molly Shenstone, October 19, 1964, cited in Jens and Jens, *Frau Thomas Mann*, 283.

Page 257 "What is ruining . . . my old age . . .": Katia Mann to Klaus Pringsheim, August 5, 1961, cited in Jens and Jens, *Frau Thomas Mann*, 282–83.

Page 258 "man who never ceased to confess . . .": Friedrich Sieburg, quoted in Reich-Ranicki, *Thomas Mann and His Family*, 159.

Page 259 "the failed marriage of Gustaf with Erika Mann": Papers pertaining to the libel lawsuit against *Die Kölner Rundschau* and *Die Zeit* are held in Monacensia.

INDEX

Auden, W. H.: "Dictator's Song,"
140–41; exile in the U.S. of, 162–64;
FBI investigation of, 182–83;
marriage to Erika of, 114–17, 130–31,
250, 260; relationship with Klaus of,
163–65, 174; translation of *Die
Pfeffermühle* by, 135; tribute to
Thomas Mann by, 213; writing for
Decision journal, 166
Aufbau weekly, 213
Auschwitz, 212–13, 214–15, 221
autobiographies: of Erika, 15, 187–89,
255; of Klaus, 15–16, 178–80, 192,
228, 232, 238, 257–59. *See also*
writing of Erika; writing of Klaus

Bad Tölz summer home, 2, 11, 18
Baldwin, James, 235
"The Barred Window" (K. Mann), ix,
147–48
BBC, 168–69, 171–75
Beach, Sylvia, 93
Bedford, Sybille, x; on Erika, 134, 201,
254; on Klaus, 99, 184, 186, 245; on
the lost generation of the 1930s, 119;
on sibling relationship of Erika and
Klaus, 50–51, 224
Before Life Begins (K. Mann), 47
Beneš, Edvard, 144
Benét, Stephen Vincent, 166
Bergner, Elisabeth, 39
Bergschule Hochwaldhausen, 30–31
Berlin, 35–41, 61; during the Cold War,
226–27; Erika and Klaus's departure
from, 82; homosexual scene in, 38;
modern culture in, 35–36; postwar
visit by Klaus to, 227–28
Die Berliner Illustrierte Zeitung, 54
Bermann Fischer, Gottfried, 104–6,
122–23, 158, 222, 238
Biddle, Francis, 195
Blood of the Walsungs (T. Mann), 3, 65
The Blue Angel (film), 7, 211–12
Bonn, Ferdinand von, 41
books. *See* writing of Erika; writing of
Klaus; *names of specific works*

Borgese, Elisabeth. *See* Mann, Elisabeth
Borgese, G. A., 201
the *Börsenblatt*, 105–6
Bowles, Jane, 164
Bowles, Paul, 164
Brecht, Bertolt, 40, 74, 77, 101
Brereton, Lewis Hyde, 187–88
Breslauer, Marianne, x, 66, 74,
110–11, 254
Britten, Benjamin, 164
Bronnen, Arnolt, 77
Büchner, Georg, 1
Buddenbrooks (T. Mann), 5–6, 27
Burgess, Guy, 250
The Burglars (K. Mann), 17

Cabell, Ury, 186
California, 224. *See also* postwar years:
Erika; U.S. years
Camp Crowder Message, 195
Capy, Marcel, 78–79
Chaplin, Charlie, 56, 61
childhood years, 1–2, 10–15; acting pur-
suits during, 1–2, 16–17, 23, 29–30,
37; Klaus's writing during, 16,
22–23, 27, 29–30; sibling relation-
ship during, 10–13, 15, 16, 18–19, 24
The Children's Story (K. Mann), 48–
49, 56
Christoph fliegt nach Amerika
(E. Mann), 252
"The City" (E. Mann), 89
Cocteau, Jean: *Decision* contribu-
tion, 166; *Les enfants terribles*, 3, 65;
impact on Klaus of, 49, 93, 218, 230;
Die Sammlung contribution, 101;
view of *The Siblings* (K. Mann), 65
Cold War, 208, 226–28, 235, 251
Committee for Peaceful Alternatives,
251
Communism, 117–19
Cooper, Duff, 168, 173
The Counterfeiters (Gide), 156
Crevel, René, 93, 101, 118–19, 121, 145
Curtiss, Thomas Quinn: FBI interview
of, 191; National Guard service of,

175, 179; relationship with Klaus of, ix, 145–49, 176–77, 234

Davis, George, 164–65
Death in Venice (T. Mann), 46
Decision literary journal, 165–68, 174–76, 183–84
Deutsch für Deutsche anthology, 221
"Dictator's Song" (Auden), 140–41
Dietrich, Marlene, 7, 128–29
Disorder and Early Sorrow (T. Mann), 3, 47–48
Doctor Faustus (T. Mann), 222, 226
Dohm, Hedwig, 3–4, 17
Don Carlos (Schiller), 56
"Don't Make the Same Mistakes" (E. Mann), 161–62
Dracula play, 58
drug use. *See* narcotics

The Earth Spirit (Wedekind), 42
Ehrenberg, Paul, 6–7, 46
Einstein, Albert, 101, 103–4, 163
Eisenhower, Dwight D., 203
Les enfants terribles (Cocteau), 3, 65
Escape to Life: The Erika and Klaus Mann Story documentary, viii, x
Escape to Life, German edition (Weiss), x
Escape to Life (E. and K. Mann), 11–12, 112, 153–55
exile years, 15, 59, 76, 97–131, 119; *Decision* literary journal, 165–68, 174–76; denaturalization, 111–14, 116; departure from Germany, 90–95, 116; Erika's BBC work, 168–69, 171–75; Erika's marriage to W. H. Auden, 114–17; Erika's time in Switzerland, 93; financial challenges of, 99, 175–76; friends' responses to, 98; Klaus's drifting during, 93, 97–99, 101, 111, 117, 119, 143–48; *Die Sammlung* project, 99–102, 105–6, 111, 125; Spanish Civil War reporting, 158, 249. *See also* U.S. years; World War II

fascism. *See* anti-fascism; Nazism
"The Father Laughs" (K. Mann), 24
Faust (Goethe), 125, 126
FBI investigations, 181–84, 190–92, 194–96, 248–52
Feakins, William B., 149
Felix Krull (T. Mann), 252, 254
First Congress of Intellectuals, 118–19
First Congress of Soviet Writers, 118
Fischel, Bert, 18
Fischer, Samuel, 104, 123
Fischer publishing. *See* S. Fischer publishing
Fitzgerald, F. Scott, 119
Flanner, Janet, 166, 214, 218
Flucht in den Norden (K. Mann), 158
Foreign Films, Inc., 217–20
Frank, Hans, 212, 214–15
free school movement, 30–32
Freud, Sigmund, 104–5
Freunde um Bernhard (Schwarzenbach), 66
Friede, Mr., 58

A Gang of Ten (E. Mann), 189, 255
Garbo, Greta, 58–59
Gasser, Manuel, 219
Geheeb, Paulus, 32, 45
Geiger, Rod, 217–21
Genêt (Janet Flanner), 166, 214, 218
German Expressionism, 36
German Youth Movement, 31–33, 79
Gide, André: Klaus's admiration of, 49, 93, 156; Klaus's lecture on, 227–28; political views of, 117; *Die Sammlung* contributions, 101
Giehse, Therese: marriage to John Simpson of, 116–17; New York visit of, 135–41; in *Die Pfeffermühle*, 82–84, 106–10, 113, 129; relationship with Erika of, 74–75, 85–86, 93, 95, 131, 134, 144, 219, 252; in *The Siblings* (K. Mann), 65
Goebbels, Joseph, 80, 111–12, 122–23
Goethe, Johann Wolfgang von, 125, 126, 158

Mies van der Rohe, Ludwig, 36
Moes, Wladyslaw, 46
"The Monk" (K. Mann), 193–94
Monnier, Adrienne, 93
Moore, Marianne, 166
"Moral Education through German Uplifting" (H. Mann), 101–2
"The Morale Singer" (E. Mann), 83–84
La mort difficile (Crevel), 119
Mother Courage (Brecht), 74
Muck, the Magic Uncle (E. Mann), 14
"My Fatherland, the Pullman" (E. Mann), 162

narcotics: Erika's experimentation with, 63, 73–74, 144, 149; Klaus's death from, 240, 243; Klaus's use of, 37–38, 63, 72–74, 86, 99, 110, 119–21, 137, 144, 149, 228, 231, 235
Nazism: arrival in Bavaria of, 88–90; book burnings, 104–5; concentration camps, 128, 212–13, 214–15, 221; denaturalization lists, 111–12, 125; as described in *The Other Germany*, 152–53; education programs of, 159–61; election of 1932, 81–82; homosexual purge of, 117–18, 126; impact on Erika's career of, 80–81; the Manns' early responses to, 76–81; Nuremburg war trials, 214–15; origins and growth of, 71–72, 76–77, 78, 88–90, 128–29; in postwar Germany, 212–15; propagation goals of, 211; Reichstag fire of 1933, 88; response to *Die Sammlung*, 105–6, 111. *See also* anti-fascism; Hitler, Adolf; World War II
Neddermeyer, Hans, 112–13
Die Neue Rundschau journal, 3, 213
New School for Social Research, 140–41
Niddens country house, 215
"The Night of the Long Knives" purge, 117–18, 126
Nobel Prize for Literature, 5, 164

"Notes from Moscow" (K. Mann), 118
Nuremberg "Race" Laws, 142–43

Odenwaldschule, 32, 45
"Open Letter to Emmy Sonnemann" (K. Mann), 221
"The Ordeal of the European Intellectuals" (K. Mann), 235
Oscar Wilde (Sternheim), 39
The Other Germany (K. and E. Mann), 152–53, 220

Pagliero, Marcello, 217–18
Pahlen, Igor, x, 106–8, 151
Paisà screenplay (K. Mann), 216–20
Palmer, Lilli, 62
Pandora's Box (Wedekind), 42
Pasternak, Boris, 101
Pathetic Symphony: A Novel about Tchaikovsky (K. Mann), 120, 146–47, 259
Pears, Peter, 164
The Peppermill (E. Mann). See *Die Pfeffermühle* (E. Mann)
The Permanent Goethe (ed. T. Mann), 225–26
Peter Voss, 62
Die Pfeffermühle (E. Mann), 82–84, 87–88; American performances of, 130–31, 134–41; attacks on, 108–10, 125, 128–29; banning of, 128; English translations of, 135–36; Erika as Pierrot in, 84, 114; European tour of, 108–10, 111–13; final performance of, 128–29; Zurich performances of, ix, 95, 106–8
pictures: of childhood, 9, 10, 11, 12, 13, 16; of early adulthood, ii, 40, 52, 54, 63, 64, 73, 83, 86, 92; of *Decision* literary journal cover, 167; of *Escape to Life* publicity, 112; of exile years, 102, 115, 124, 148, 150, 198, 200, 204; of FBI investigation of Klaus, 185; of General Brereton, 188; of Herzog Park house, Munich, 210; of *Die Pfeffermühle/The Peppermill*, 84, 138; of postwar years, 230, 253,

Shaw, George Bernard, 38
Sheean, Vincent, 183, 201
Shirer, William, 247
sibling relationship of Erika and
Klaus: during childhood, 10–13,
15, 16, 18–19, 24; Erika's response
to Klaus's death, 243–47; FBI
investigation of, 182–83; gradual
estrangement in, 59, 98–99, 146,
172–73, 176, 186–87, 199–200, 205,
218–19, 222, 224, 231–32, 245; impact
of Thomas on, 186–87, 222–24;
intimations of incest in, 3, 50–51,
182–83, 259; Klaus's dependency
on, 110, 169; during Klaus's suicide
attempts, 233–35, 239–40; primacy
of, 59, 65, 111–12, 120–21; twinlike
behavior in, vii, 2, 205; writing
collaborations, 59–61, 62, 152–55,
231–32
The Siblings (K. Mann), 3, 65, 74
Sieburg, Friedrich, 258
Simpson, John, 116–17
Sinclair, Upton, 104–5, 233, 247
Six Actors in Search of an Author
(Pirandello), 39
Sklenka, Hans, 87
Sonnemann, Emmy, 221
Soviet Union, 117–19, 226–27, 250
Spanish Civil War, 158, 249
Speck, Wieland, viii
Speed (K. Mann), 184
Spender, Stephen, 116
Stars and Stripes, 197–99, 209–13
Sternheim, Carl, 39, 55–56, 221
Sternheim, Thea (Mopsa), 55–56, 72, 86
Stoffel fliegt übers Meer (E. Mann and
Hallgarten), 62
Strauss, Richard, 212
Streicher, Julius, 215
suicide, 176; Annemarie Schwarzen-
bach's attempts at, 110–11, 121, 176;
of Gustaf Gründgens, 259; Klaus's
attempts at, 232–33, 238–40;
Klaus's death by, 240, 243; Klaus's
interest in, 22–23, 29, 67, 85–86,

119–22, 147–48, 176–78, 235–37;
Mann family history of, 25, 233;
of René Crevel, 118–19; of Ricki
Hallgarten, 67–69
Süskind, W. E., 37, 41, 98
Symphonie Pathetique (K. Mann), 120,
146–47, 259
Synthesis journal, 220
Szabó, István, 260

The Tales of Jacob (T. Mann), 104–5
Tchaikovsky, Pyotr Ilich, 120,
146–47, 259
Terezín concentration camp, 212–13
"Thoughts in Wartime" (T. Mann), 20
Tissot, Victor, 35
"Today and Tomorrow: On the Situa-
tion of Young European Intellectu-
als" (K. Mann), 75
Tomski. *See* Curtiss, Thomas Quinn
travels of Erika and Klaus, 41; to the
Alps, 88; in Erika's Ford, 62–64;
Klaus's first tour of Europe, 41–42;
Klaus's trip to the Soviet Union,
118–19; to Morocco, 63; planned
trip to Persia, 67–68, 72, 121;
round-the-world trip, 56–61; to
Venice, 72–74. *See also* exile years
Treffpunkt im Unendlichen (K. Mann),
66–67
The Turning Point (K. Mann), 178–81,
192, 228, 232, 238, 257–59
Tü-Tü cabaret, 37

University in Exile, 140–41
U.S. years, 133–69; *Decision* literary
journal, 165–68, 174–76, 183–84;
departure from the U.S., 251; Erika
as California resident, 223–24;
Erika's application for citizenship,
247–48, 250–52; Erika's lecture
career, 141–43, 173, 176, 204–5;
Erika's political activism, 226–28;
Erika's war correspondent work,
187, 199, 201, 203–4, 213–15; Erika's
work with Thomas, 222–26; FBI

writing of Klaus (*continued*)
English, 184, 229; German translations of, 257–58; on Gustav Gründgens, 125–28, 147, 236, 245, 259–60;
on homosexuality, 44–46, 54–55,
117–18; obsessive nature of, 119–20;
postmortem publications, 257–60;
postwar setbacks in, 220–21,
228–30, 232, 235–37, 245; predictive
content of, 75, 128; *Die Sammlung*
project, 99–102, 105–6, 111, 125;
screenplays, 216–20; on suicide and
death, 22–23, 29, 67, 85–86, 147–48,
235–37; theater criticism of, 41; on
Thomas Mann, 24; Thomas's views
of and impact on, 27, 47, 49, 53–54,
157–59, 180–81, 247. *See also names of
specific works*

You Can't Go Home Again (Wolfe), 209
young adulthood. *See* acting pursuits
of Erika; sibling relationship of
Erika and Klaus; travels of Erika
and Klaus; writing of Erika; writing
of Klaus

Zehn Millionen Kinder (E. Mann), 159–61
Zero Hour: A Summons to the Free essays,
161–62
Zugvögel (E. Mann), 252
Zweig, Stefan, 166
"Zwölf Uhr Mittagsblatt," 41